With a flexible financial solution, life can be fun with a daredevil scamp.

Insurance, banking or investment: no matter which it is, every Fortis company believes in flexible solutions. Not just for the short term, but also for the distant future.

Because no two people want the same thing, because children always do the unexpected and because no one can look ten years into the future.

The Fortis group includes AMEV, Fortis Bank and MeesPierson. They can provide additional information.

If you would like to know more about the Fortis group, please call us on 31 (0)30 257 65 48.

FORTIS

Solid partners, flexible solutions

regulated by the Securities and Futures Authority in the conduct of investment business in the UK.

LabMorgan

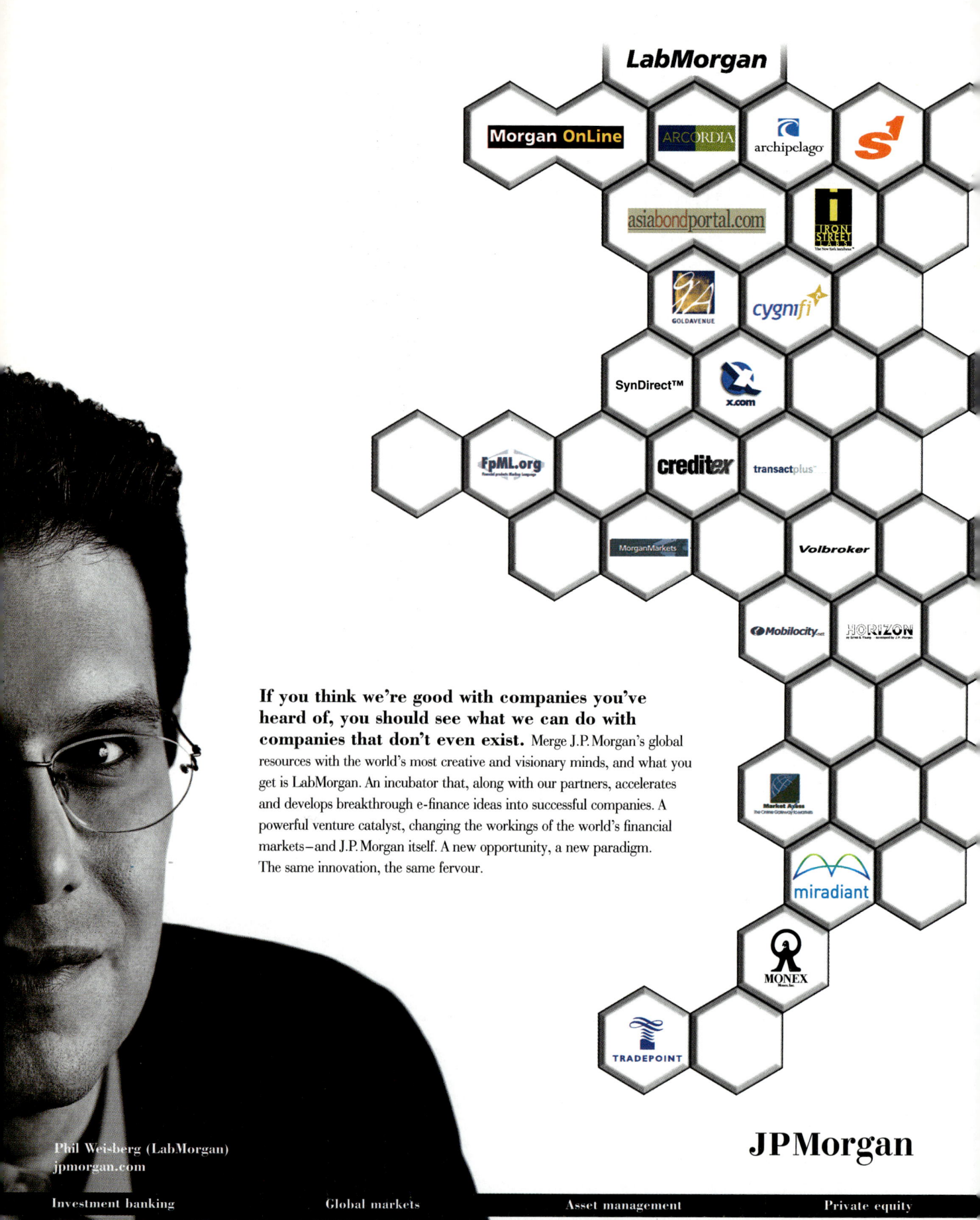

Morgan OnLine · ARCORDIA · archipelago · s1
asiabondportal.com · IRON STREET
GOLDAVENUE · cygnifi
SynDirect™ · x.com
FpML.org · creditex · transactplus
MorganMarkets · Volbroker
Mobilocity · HORIZON
Market Axess
miradiant
MONEX
TRADEPOINT

If you think we're good with companies you've heard of, you should see what we can do with companies that don't even exist. Merge J.P. Morgan's global resources with the world's most creative and visionary minds, and what you get is LabMorgan. An incubator that, along with our partners, accelerates and develops breakthrough e-finance ideas into successful companies. A powerful venture catalyst, changing the workings of the world's financial markets—and J.P. Morgan itself. A new opportunity, a new paradigm. The same innovation, the same fervour.

Phil Weisberg (LabMorgan)
jpmorgan.com

JPMorgan

Investment banking · Global markets · Asset management · Private equity

©2000 J.P. Morgan & Co. Incorporated. J.P. Morgan Securities Inc., member SIPC. J.P. Morgan Securities Ltd., member London Stock Exchange, regulated by FSA. Morgan Guaranty Trust Company of New York, member FDIC. J.P. Morgan Securities Asia Pte Ltd. regulated by SFC Hong Kong, MAS of Singapore, and FSA of Japan. J.P. Morgan is the marketing name for J.P. Morgan & Co. Incorporated and its subsidiaries worldwide. J.P. Morgan, LabMorgan, MorganMarkets, Morgan OnLine, and the honeycomb design are trademarks of J.P. Morgan & Co. Incorporated. Other brands, products, or services are trademarks or registered trademarks of their respective holders.

THE WORLD IN 2001

EDITOR: Dudley Fishburn
MANAGING EDITOR: Harriet Ziegler
DEPUTY EDITOR: Stephen Green
EDITORIAL ASSISTANT: Alice Fishburn
RESEARCHER: Nimit Jani
DESIGN AND ART DIRECTION: Bailey and Kenny
DESIGN ASSISTANCE: Anita Wright
CHARTS AND MAPS: Michael Robinson, Edgar Gonzalez, Russ Street, Nicola Bailey
ILLUSTRATIONS: Derek Cousins, Geraldine Spence
PICTURE EDITOR: Juliet Brightmore
ADVERTISING DIRECTOR: John Dunn
CIRCULATION DIRECTOR: Des McSweeney
PRODUCTION: Katy Greenway, Carrie Goldsworthy, Andrew Rollings
FOREIGN RIGHTS: Hutton-Williams Agency
ASSOCIATE PUBLISHER: David Gill
PUBLISHER: David Hanger

© 2000 The Economist Newspaper Limited. All rights reserved. Neither this publication nor any part of it may be reproduced, stored in a retrieval system, or transmitted in any form or by any means, electronic, mechanical, photocopying, recording or otherwise, without the prior permission of The Economist Newspaper Limited. Published by The Economist Newspaper Limited.

ISBN 0 86218 166 6

Where opinion is expressed it is that of the authors and does not necessarily coincide with the editorial views of the publisher or The Economist.

All information in this magazine is verified to the best of the authors' and the publisher's ability. However, The Economist Newspaper Limited does not accept responsibility for any loss arising from reliance on it.

PHOTOGRAPHIC SOURCES: AFP; Allsport UK; Art Archive; Associated Press; Aviation Images/Mark Wagner; Collections/Image Ireland/Alain Le Garsmeur; Corbis/Roger Ressmeyer, Karen Su; Corbis Sygma/Brooks Kraft; Mary Evans Picture Library; Foster and Partners/Richard Davies; Ronald Grant Archive; Impact Photos/Philip Gordon, Robin Laurance, Alex Macnaughton, Caroline Penn; Katz Pictures/Serge Attel, A. Casasoli, Andrea Künzig, Daniel Laine; Network Photographers/Fritz Hoffmann; Reuters New Media Inc/Corbis; Rex Features; Science Photo Library/Michael W. Davidson; Frank Spooner Pictures; StillPictures/J.C. Vincent; Stone; Colin Thomas; TimePix/Sergei Guneyev/Katz Pictures; Time Magazine/Steve Liss/Katz Pictures.

Printed by TPL Printers (UK) Ltd (Kidderminster, England)
Reprographics by Mullis Morgan Group Ltd

The Economist
THE ECONOMIST GROUP

25 St James's Street, London, SW1A 1HG
Telephone: 020 7830 7000
E-mail: theworldin@economist.com
Internet: http://www.theworldin.com

---

7 Digest
9 Editor's introduction

2001
13 The first 100 days
14 You've never had it so good
18 The Italian exception
21 The new economy goes global
22 Oh happy island
25 Diary for 2001

BRITAIN
27 Rule Blairtannia
28 The economy: All set fair
29 Still Victorian
32 Northern Ireland turns the page
34 Better buildings, at last
35 Reform! Reform!
36 The coming of e-government
38 Chris Patten: Success is not always loveable

EUROPE
41 Europe's busy year
42 The euro in your pocket
42 The triumph of nations
43 Germany surprises itself
46 Open sesame
47 Brian Beedham: It really is a new world now
48 French magic
48 Benelux *Forecast*
49 Modern Italy's old-fashioned ways
50 The Nordic countries *Forecast*
50 Spain: Unceasing violence
51 Ireland *Forecast*
52 Eastern Europe: A dappled continent
55 Russian gloom or boom?
56 Russian racketeers
56 Turkey *Forecast*

NORTH AMERICA
59 What augurs after the inauguration?
60 The economy: Time for the party to wind down
62 Two million behind bars
63 Richard Daley: A tale for all cities
66 The eagle and the fox
66 A cornucopia of trouble
69 When did you last see your father?
70 Football in your face
70 When defence looks like attack
71 Nature strikes back
72 Canadian-ness

INTERNATIONAL
73 NGOs: New Gods Overseas
74 The Middle East's misery
75 Peacekeeping: Tough love
76 Peter Singer: How are your morals?
79 The Gulf *Forecast*
79 Latin America gets a taste for wealth
80 Has Brazil's moment come?
81 Africa's darker shades of black
81 Egypt *Forecast*
82 Where's the world's worst?
84 Letter from 2050

ASIA PACIFIC
87 China learns the world's rules
88 Out of the red
89 Here comes a new Japan
90 Indonesia *Forecast*
90 Golf: Many players, one champ
93 Two-speed Asia, one big problem
94 Robert Rubin: Wise to be wary
95 All work, more play
95 The choice is yours, Jong Il
96 Impossible India's improbable chance

THE WORLD IN FIGURES
97 Forecasts for 60 countries
109 Forecasts for 20 industries

BUSINESS AND MANAGEMENT
115 Global warriors strike back
116 The next measure of national machismo
119 The half-life of nuclear power
122 How should the bosses be paid?
123 John Chambers: You ain't seen nothing yet
124 Which way to the hydrogen economy?
124 Your new mobile
127 Dead trees go digital
130 Gadgets for all
132 Bad air days
134 Home on the Net

FINANCE AND ECONOMICS
141 First the valley, then the uplands
142 Banks that bulge
143 Tax Europa
146 Get global or get lost
149 Accountancy: Let's all tell the same lies
150 The virtue of wealth
152 Frank Zarb: When investors vote

SCIENCE
155 The mathematics of mayhem
156 Speaking in fewer tongues
157 Send in the clones
158 Faster than fast
158 Pill paupers
161 Bill Gates: Now for an intelligent Internet
162 2001: a space odyssey updated

Imagine a 142,000 ton ship that can turn like this.

We did. Our new modular propulsion system places the propeller and the rudder together to make ships so maneuverable, they can turn 30% tighter. This speeds up docking, makes navigating safer and saves fuel, too. At ABB, we believe the most important thing we build today is knowledge. Because the power that will drive the next hundred years is the power of ideas.

www.abb.com

©2000 ABB LTD.

Brain Power.™   **ABB**

ECONOMICS 2001

The world gets remarkably more prosperous, **Clive Crook**, *The Economist*, page 14
Britain's happy state, **Anatole Kaletsky**, *The Times*, page 28
The economics of euroland, **Robert Cottrell**, *Financial Times*, page 41
America's slower 2001, **Zanny Minton-Beddoes**, *The Economist*, page 60
Will we make the same mistakes again? **Robert Rubin**, *former Secretary of the US Treasury*, page 94
Markets become mature, **Hamish McRae**, *The Independent*, page 141
Why wealth brings happiness, **Madsen Pirie**, *Adam Smith Institute*, page 150

POLITICS 2001

Blair's victory in Britain's next general election, **Anthony King**, *Essex University*, page 27
Europe needs to be more political, **Chris Patten**, *European Commission*, page 38
Why is France so different? **Jean Daniel**, *Nouvel Observateur*, page 48
Italy's election is not just entertainment, **Beppe Severgnini**, *Corriere della Sera*, page 49
Spain's fine, pity about the Basques, **Juan Luis Cebrián**, *El Pais*, page 50
How will Washington's new administration settle in? **Morton Kondracke**, *Roll Call*, page 59
Dismal Africa will improve just a bit, **Patrick Smith**, *Africa Confidential*, page 81
The mathematics of the Internet will change democracy, **Alun Anderson**, *New Scientist*, page 155

HEADACHES 2001

An unreformed Italy will be a pain for Europe, **John Grimond**, *The Economist*, page 18
Life without a father for even more American children, **Jonathan Rauch**, *Brookings Institution*, page 69
How to be ethical in a capitalist world, **Peter Singer**, *Princeton University*, page 76
China finds it a headache dealing with the world, **James Miles**, *International Institute for Strategic Studies*, page 87
Travelling by air will get worse, **Iain Carson**, *The Economist*, page 132
The extinction of languages, **Steve Connor**, *The Independent*, page 156

MANAGEMENT 2001

Who will manage a European union of 20 countries? **Charles Grant**, *Centre for European Reform*, page 42
How to run a city in 2001, **Richard Daley**, *Mayor of Chicago*, page 63
A successful India would manage miracles, **David Gardner**, *Financial Times*, page 96
What is your boss worth? **Edward Carr**, *Financial Times*, page 122
Managing a giant, **John Chambers**, *Cisco Systems*, page 123
Bringing Asia's financial markets together, **Stephen Green**, *Royal Institute for International Affairs*, page 146
When the world has one market, **Frank Zarb**, *Nasdaq*, page 152

IDEAS 2001

Britain's modern architecture is brimming with ideas, **Martin Vander Weyer**, *The Week*, page 34
Newest Labour ideas, **David Lipsey**, *House of Lords*, page 35
A decidedly bad idea. Two million Americans behind bars, **Sebastian Mallaby**, *Washington Post*, page 62
Any idea what Asians will do on their ever longer holidays? **Paul Markillie**, *The Economist*, page 95
A new measure of national machismo, **Daniel Franklin**, *Economist Intelligence Unit*, page 116
Growing cells to help humans, **Shereen El Feki**, *The Economist*, page 157
Improving IT's IQ, **Bill Gates**, *Microsoft*, page 161

Global IP VPN ↗
e-business collaboration phone fax Intranet ERP...
keep it flowing

everytime
everything
everywhere
here

Every day, everywhere, businesses need to communicate externally and internally. Global One helps you to easily manage vital e-business information flow with Global IP VPN, a unique cost-effective end-to-end managed service.

Global IP VPN keeps your information flowing with:
- Any-to-any network connectivity for easy scalability
- Simplified management for business flexibility
- Converged IP/data/voice service classes for high added value
- Protected network bandwidth for security
- Quality and performance backed by service level guarantees

It is no wonder Global One supplies more multinational companies with IP VPNs using Multiprotocol Label Switching (MPLS) technology than any other operator. Global One offers one of the world's most comprehensive portfolios of e-business services with over 1,400 service centers in more than 850 cities and 80 countries.

That's why Global One is the one you can trust.

GlobalOne ℠

A Member of the France Telecom Group

www.globalone.net

Americas
Tel: +1 877 460 4141 (United States and Canada)
Tel: +1 703 689 5138 (Latin America)

Asia / Pacific
Tel: +852 2583 6000

Europe
Tel: +33 1 4079 83 30

2001 will be a year in which the world becomes a richer and sharply more decent place. Europe will expand its wealth at the fastest rate for a decade. As America's president settles into the White House, he will be preoccupied by a concern about which he can do nothing: a gently slowing economy. Scarcely noticed in the West, the 2.3 billion people of China and India will organise their societies so as to double their prosperity every ten years. This will be mankind's most remarkable achievement in 2001: the poor of the world growing speedily richer. Communist China will sign up to that supposed capitalist monster, the World Trade Organisation; as a result it will become, in time, a more democratic place.

It is here that the decency of 2001 will strike home. Globalisation will raise the standards of human rights, law, ethics and corporate governance around the world, even in dismal Africa. The revolution in communications lies behind this imperative. Was there ever a change in human behaviour so rapid or so benevolent? No pollution, no barriers, no dogmas, no sweatshops exist in the freer exchange of information. The arrival of "third generation" mobile phones, of broadband technologies (broadband availability in Europe will double in 2001), of interactive television, of an intelligent Internet (which you make do the thinking) are all certainties in the next 12 months.

Governments, democratic and dictatorial, get much of their influence from rationing or directing flows of information. This power is seeping away. They will, without exception, become smaller and less domineering in 2001. Look at America and Europe: taxes will fall across the board, driven lower by the competition and prosperity of the IT age. (Only in Britain will the tax-take rise, reducing the majority by which the Labour government will win re-election.)

For the dangers of the year, look for those things that are plainly out of balance. In America, that means the trade deficit and the dollar. In Europe, it means the neighbours. The most frightening statistics to be found in *The World in 2001* are these: not one of the seven Arab countries bordering the Mediterranean has a legitimate government; their populations will explode to 163m in the year ahead, 56% of whom will be under 25, creating a multitude of angry, unemployed young men. Add an irascible Israel into this cauldron of testosterone and Europe's southern border will surely be the world's most unsettled place. Lucky America: all its neighbours in the hemisphere (except Cuba) will flourish, having accepted democracy, capitalism and reform. In Japan, a whole society is trying to find its balance again, after ten miserable years. But consider this danger: the new Japan, which is slowly emerging, will account for only 14% of the world's wealth but 40% of its sovereign debt: $3.4 trillion.

These are some of the forecasts in *The World in 2001*. They will certainly not all be right. The publication will appear on the news-stands of 95 countries; it will be translated into 17 languages. I hope that in one of those places and one of those tongues, you will find it an enjoyable read.

Dudley Fishburn
Editor, *The World in 2001*

The most profitable airlines

in the world really

know their numbers.

www.boeing.com

Boeing numbers, that is. It's a fact that the more Boeing

airplanes an airline operates, the higher it ranks in

profitability and passenger satisfaction. Meaning the

better the line up, the better the bottom line for everyone.

BOEING
Forever New Frontiers

We're an investment bank that knows technology. Or is it the other way around?

The answer is "both." Our people are leaders in financing and advising high-tech businesses. And in providing ground-breaking technology research. But our stake in technology is larger than that. For example, through our private equity funds, we're a leading investor in the technology industry. And we're a leading force promoting technology's role in reshaping the financial markets. All in all, you could say that Goldman Sachs is synonymous with technology leadership. Or is it the other way around?

Goldman Sachs

UNRELENTING THINKING

www.gs.com

Issued by Goldman Sachs International, regulated by the Securities and Futures Authority. ©Goldman, Sachs & Co., 2000. All rights reserved.

THE WORLD IN 2001

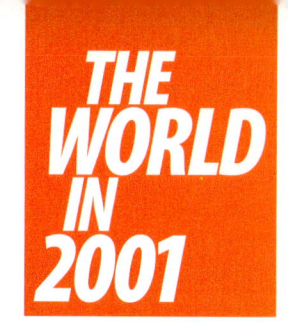

The first 100 days

America's new administration will get off to an unhappy start in 2001, predicts **John Micklethwait**. We will all be the worse for it.

It is the job that every politician in the world craves. It is also a job that was won only after the closest campaign in American history, and after a succession of recounts and legal challenges that have left the office itself, and the man who holds it, sadly tarnished.

Yet, come January 20th, as the president stares down at the inauguration crowds, he could be forgiven for thinking that the easy part is over. It is a time, having promised so much, to set priorities. What the new president does in his first year, perhaps even in those famous "first 100 days", will set the tone—not just for his administration but for the next generation.

Reality dictates that he must concentrate his fire selectively. Congress is balanced on a knife edge between the two parties. In the Senate, the numbers are more or less even; in the House of Representatives, the Republicans hold a wafer-thin majority. The new president will have to restrain any partisan instincts and be prepared, from the very beginning, to work closely with people who may be ideologically opposed to him.

Setting priorities is not just a matter of presidential housekeeping: it is about seizing opportunity. In his valedictory speech at the Democratic Convention in Los Angeles, Bill Clinton recalled the last time America had seemed so blessed with might and money in the mid-1960s. "When I graduated from high school, I assumed, like most Americans, that our economy was on automatic—that our civil-rights problems would be solved in Congress and the courts." The next ten years were dominated by race riots, assassinations, Vietnam, a recession and Watergate. "Thirty years later," argued Mr Clinton, "we have an even better chance this time. Still, I have lived long enough to know that opportunities must be seized or they will be lost."

In delivering this warning to his successor, Mr Clinton was perhaps criticising himself. The most consummate politician of his age delivered peace and prosperity during his eight years in office. He also chalked up some individual successes—such as the passing of NAFTA and welfare reform. But he flunked the main chances for serious structural change. And many of the problems stemmed from his first 100 days. He got side-tracked into minor issues such as gays in the military, and his one serious effort—health-care reform—failed spectacularly. As for foreign policy, he seemed always to be reacting to events overseas until well into his second term.

The new president will have learned from Mr Clinton's errors. He will want to use his first days to lay out his own "vision thing", to set the agenda by which he will govern: but not, if he is wise, in too much detail. It will be a time for using the greatest bully pulpit on earth to inspire and change

John Micklethwait: United States editor, *The Economist*

minds—not to bore them with minutiae. But he will have to be careful. Few presidents have been elected on such a slim margin of support, and at the back of his mind he will know that he does not have the mandate for anything too radical.

What then should he do? The president's main priority abroad should simply be to make abroad a priority. That means not only anticipating the inevitable string of crises. It also means establishing a much clearer agenda. Two particular areas beckon. The first should be China and Russia. Mr Clinton oversaw at least four different China policies, and almost as many Russian ones. Some of the fault lies with Beijing and Moscow. But it also reflects an unclear message from Washington which his successor would do well to tidy up. A second priority should be the multilateral organisations. The United Nations is in a serious mess, not least because of America's sulky neglect. A stronger, leaner UN would not only be a good thing in itself; it would also allow America to subcontract some of its duties as the world's policeman.

At home, it would be unrealistic not to expect the president to spend some of his precious political capital fulfilling promises that were crucial to his election, such as how to spend (or not spend) the huge anticipated budget surpluses. But he should husband most of his resources for three larger issues: education, Social Security and electoral reform.

The kids need you, Mr President

The need for change in America's schools is glaring. The United States already spends more than nearly any other country and achieves worse results: hence the need for structural reform to make schools more accountable. That has traditionally been a Republican message, but it is one that many Democrats—particularly the urban poor—now embrace. The White House will want to reach out to both sides. But even if it does garner bipartisan support, two more obstacles will have to be jumped. First, the federal government accounts for only 8% of all school spending. And second, the teachers' unions will resist change.

Both presidential candidates promised to do something about Social Security, the pay-as-you-go pensions system that is under-funded and falling apart. Using some of the surplus to boost the fund is one option; another is privatising a small part of it, and allowing investment in the stockmarket. Having won, the president will want to consider his options.

Finally, the president should not lose sight of the need for electoral reform. As well as overhauling the procedure for choosing a president, he will still have to tackle the problem of campaign finance. Asking a man to change the system that raised close to $2 billion to deliver him the White House is a tall order. But there are signs that the president knows that something has to be done to restore Americans' faith in their democracy. Supporting a bill sponsored by John McCain, a Republican, that would ban "soft money", regulate sham advertising and expand the public funding of campaigns would be the beginning of an answer, but not the final word.

Education, Social Security and electoral reform—this is an ambitious list: the president would be lucky to succeed in two of them. But together with a more deliberate foreign policy it would show that America's great opportunity is finally being seized. The likelihood is, however, that the president will be so hobbled, even in many eyes discredited, right from the start of his time in office, that all these matters will escape him. He may well come to look on his first 100 days with as much regret as his predecessor probably does. □

You've never had it so good

The global economy is in great shape. The challenge for 2001 will be to encourage growth, not criticise it, argues Clive Crook.

Economies are tougher than people think, and need to be. At the start of 2001 the world economy is even more off-balance than a year ago. That makes it easy to come up with scary scenarios: collapsing currencies, plunging share prices, panic and recession. Only a fool would say that none of these could happen. After all, bad policy has done much to create the risks, and it is safe to assume that governments will get no wiser. Still, despite everything that trade and finance ministers throw at it, the world economy will most likely do well again in 2001, growing at more than 4% (only half a point more slowly than in 2000), with rich-country inflation at an acceptable 3% and unemployment low—unprecedentedly low in many cases—throughout the industrialised world. Nerve-wracking it may be, but this is surely a golden age.

Much depends, as always, on America. This is no longer just a matter of sheer size, though that still counts, obviously. America's position in the business cycle, hence its net demand for the rest of the world's output, drives activity everywhere. But now something even more significant is at stake. In 2001 and beyond, much the most important economic question for the world is this: will the productivity breakthrough that underlies America's record-breaking, low-inflation expansion turn out to be real—and, if it is, can it be exported?

The answer is that the miracle is not quite for real. Global circumstances—sluggish demand in Europe, Japan and in much of the third world—have flattered America's "new economy". Inflation is already rising in the United States, and will rise further in 2001, albeit slowly. It would be rising a lot faster if the rest of the world had not been so happy to supply

Clive Crook: deputy editor, *The Economist*

America's prodigious appetite for imports. The excess of demand over supply in America represents the false side of the miracle. It is also a danger, because its counterparts are a colossal trade deficit and massive borrowing from overseas. If these carried on growing, a bust would be unavoidable. But they won't. In 2001, as American growth moderates to something unmiraculous, just very impressive, the trade and capital gaps will shrink.

Mind you, even ignoring the illusory part of the miracle, a genuine, long-lasting improvement remains. As 2001 is going to confirm, America's sustainable, low-inflation rate of growth has increased, from 2-2.5% to roughly 3%. No more than that, you ask? Admittedly, this news will disappoint the most zealous new-economy visionaries. People who know their economic history will be anything but disappointed: they understand how great an achievement such a rise will be.

And is the breakthrough exportable? Yes, definitely, as 2001 will start to prove. America has great advantages when it comes to embracing new technologies: above all, highly adaptable workers, willing to change jobs and cross the continent in pursuit of opportunity. Europe, Asia and the developing world has nothing to match them—so they lag, and until that changes they always will. But this is only a question of degree. If telecommunications, PCs and the Internet have raised productivity growth in the United States— and they have—the same will happen soon everywhere else, even if to a milder extent. Strong signs of this have yet to appear. They will start to do so in the coming year.

Yet it often seems that in the world economy there is no such thing as good news. Gloom can be found in any success. Sadly, the tendency to bemoan prosperity is becoming more than a mere irritation: it is actually starting to threaten prosperity. As a result, in 2001, second in importance only to whether businesses in Europe, Asia and the developing countries can follow America's productivity lead is whether governments will let them.

The reason to doubt it is the "backlash". To critics of globalisation—in politics, in universities, in the media and in the ever-proliferating legions of "non-governmental organisations"—the fact that America has sprinted ahead is not good news but bad news. As they see it, rather than creating opportunities for faster growth in the rest of the world, it has widened the gap between rich and poor. Yes, even pathological egalitarians are more productive these days. They have a new kind of inequality to worry about: the "digital divide". Their solution is not to work at removing impediments to faster growth outside America, but the opposite: America in particular and the industrialised countries in general are being told to grow more slowly and detach themselves from the rest of the world.

Tempting as it is merely to mock this view of the world, it is no laughing matter. The anti-capitalists have scored notable successes and their influence, with governments and with international institutions such as the World Bank and the International Monetary Fund, is growing. Equally worrying is the influence that they are having with big western companies, which nowadays feel obliged to bow down before bogus nostrums of "corporate responsibility"—which apparently

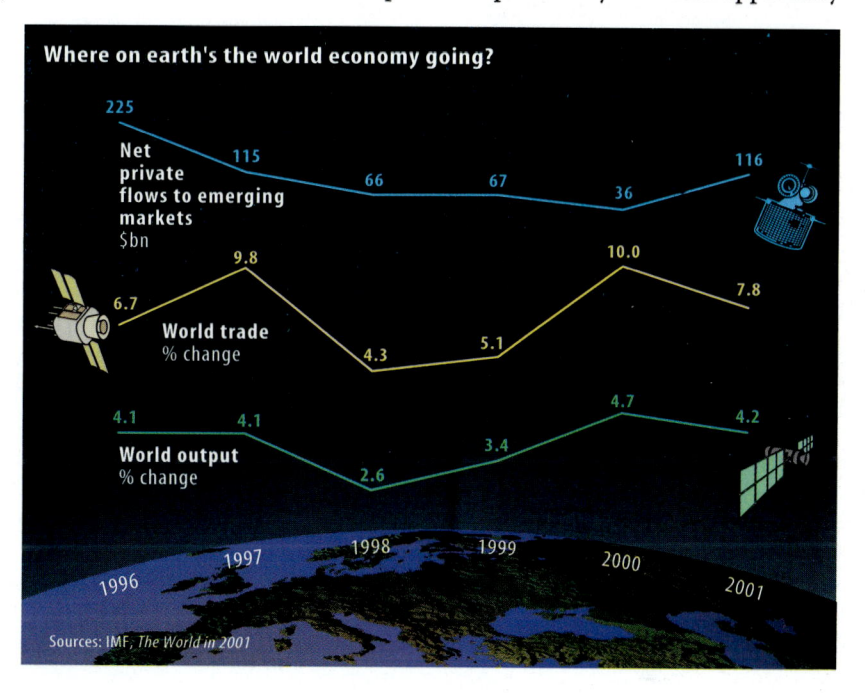

Where on earth's the world economy going?

Net private flows to emerging markets $bn: 225 (1996), 115 (1997), 66 (1998), 67 (1999), 36 (2000), 116 (2001)

World trade % change: 6.7 (1996), 9.8 (1997), 4.3 (1998), 5.1 (1999), 10.0 (2000), 7.8 (2001)

World output % change: 4.1 (1996), 4.1 (1997), 2.6 (1998), 3.4 (1999), 4.7 (2000), 4.2 (2001)

Sources: IMF; The World in 2001

means denying workers in the developing countries their best chance of escaping poverty.

The anti-capitalists have been winning the battle of ideas—despite having no ideas worthy of the name. In 2001, their influence on governments and in boardrooms is going to increase. It will make starting a new round of global trade talks harder: much though one is needed, it is unlikely to happen in 2001. It will render the necessary disciplines imposed by the IMF on bad governments even less effective, the aid and advice given by bodies such as the World Bank even less productive, and the outward investment of rich-country multinationals even more timid.

There is a lot of ruin in a global economy—and in 2001, the world is going to grow handily despite the anti-capitalists' gains. Odd, though, isn't it? Today, the economic opportunities for attacking poverty are truly amazing. Instead of seizing them eagerly, much of the world will do it reluctantly and apologetically. What a shame. □

Crowded marketplace.

Business today means competition from all sides. Information overload. Greater pressure on margins. Technology limitations. Too many short-term fixes. Too few long-term answers. Zurich Financial Services Group. Providing solutions that take the chill off the pressures you face. Utilizing innovative approaches to insurance and asset management. Backed by over a century of experience. And 68,000 employees in 60 countries around the world. Now's the time. Come in from the cold.

ZURICH

Your aspirations. Our passion.

www.zurich.com

Leaders THE WORLD IN 2001

The Italian exception

Italy will defy any attempts to reform itself. Although this trait is often charming, it will make the country an embarrassment in 2001, suggests **John Grimond**.

All nations like to consider themselves singular. The French are stout in their defence of *l'exception française*, the French way. The British, an island-people with a long and unbroken tradition of parliamentary rule, see themselves as uniquely independent. The Americans have their own "exceptionalism", which academics define in terms of individualism, a belief in self-help and a lack of class conflict, but which was once expressed more simply by Ronald Reagan as the consequence of "a divine plan" for people with a special love of freedom. And the Italians? They, too, can claim to be set apart, thanks to their special genius in combining industriousness with an ability to enjoy themselves: they work to live, they do not live to work. In 2001, however, a different sort of Italian exceptionalism will be on show: the peculiar inability of Italy to become what Romano Prodi, a former prime minister, called a "normal democracy".

Crisis and instability are the hallmarks of normality, Italian-style. The government that will be formed after the general election that must be held by April will be Italy's 59th since the second world war, and it will be little short of a miracle if it fares much better than most of its predecessors. The trouble is that the Italian state appears to be almost unreformable.

Most of the other countries of Europe, whether or not they feel themselves to be burdened by an unhappy past, have spent the past decade or two reforming their institutions and bedding down their democracies. The ex-communist countries are obvious examples, but the trend has not been confined to Central and Eastern Europe. France has shortened its presidential term, embarked on a devolution of power to Corsica and started to root out corruption. Germany has absorbed an entire country, moved its capital from Bonn to Berlin and reformed its tax system. Britain has set up parliaments in Scotland and Wales, overhauled the House of Lords and incorporated the European Convention on Human Rights into its law. Spain, in the 25 years since the death of General Francisco Franco, has gone through a profound economic, cultural and political transformation that now makes it look as modern as any state in Europe. Too bad that Italy remains a mess.

Despite all the noble efforts of the 1990s to root out corruption, rewrite the constitution and encourage the evolution of a more stable two-party system by getting rid of proportional representation (PR), little has changed. The anti-corruption effort has run into the sand, amid accusations that the magistrates behind it are politically motivated. The commission to reform the constitution was scuppered by the leader of the opposition, Silvio Berlusconi—largely because he was thwarted in his effort to cut the magistracy down to size. And too few voters turned out last April to give effect to the referendum that would have abolished PR.

The result is a familiar paralysis. Instead of a new, streamlined state, Italy now has more than 40 parties, many of them tiny outfits formed by vain politicians who will sell their services to the highest bidder. They achieve very little: in the first four years of the "reforming" 1996 parliament, only 61 of the 6,096 bills considered by the lower house actually became law. The average life of all those governments has crept up, but the country will nonetheless have had four of them, and three prime ministers, in the lifetime of the current parliament. Administrations still come and go at the whim of politicians, rather than voters. The prime ministership itself is as weak as ever, while pressure-groups and unions are as strong as ever. This means, among other things, that serious issues such as the looming pensions problem remain untackled.

Might this change in 2001? Don't count on it. The next government will inevitably be another coalition. It just might be another centre-left affair, now that Giuliano Amato, the incumbent prime minister, has agreed to step aside and let the more telegenic Francesco Rutelli, mayor of Rome, take the leadership. But if the left hangs on to office, it will almost certainly be hostage to small parties, of which a variety is all-but guaranteed.

More likely, if the opinion polls are to be believed, is a return to office by the right, led by Mr Berlusconi. This would present an even more bizarre spectacle than a government of the centre-left. For a start, Mr Berlusconi's partners are a rum lot. One is Umberto Bossi, the once secessionist, now federalist, always exhibitionist leader of the Northern League. The other is Gianfranco Fini, the leader of the post-fascist National Alliance. Mr Berlusconi's own "party", Forza Italia (Let's go, Italy), is hardly conventional; it is organised less like a representative political organisation than the supporters' club of a football team.

Then there is Mr Berlusconi himself. Whether or not cleared of the various criminal charges on which he has been convicted, he remains in control of virtually half the country's television market. That alone would rule him out for high political office in any normal modern democracy. "There

John Grimond: foreign editor, *The Economist*

LOCKHEED MARTIN

www.lockheedmartin.com

| Satellite Technology | Defense. Navigation. Earth sciences. Telecommunications. Every day, millions of people depend on satellites for services that are essential to national priorities. Developing and integrating satellite technology to help military and commercial customers deliver those services—and accomplish their missions—is the essence of what we do. The world is changing. Lockheed Martin is changing with it.

soldiers' lives depend on them.

travelers steer by them.

whole industries revolve around them.

that's what we think about most

when we build them

Our only limits are the ones we place on ourselves.

Viatel's new vision of communications doesn't begin with fibre or end at today's network edge.

Instead, we see information that flows across integrated pan-European, North American, trans-Atlantic and metropolitan networks, making local, national and regional boundaries invisible.

We see technology that moves at the speed of light today and even faster tomorrow.

We see a world of innovation — in pricing and delivery — that connects every customer and every destination.

From here to as far as the eye can see, one network, one vision.

No borders. No barriers. No limits.

Viatel from anywhere in Europe **00800.0064.4444**
Viatel in the U.S. **1.800.244.1798**
www.viatel.com

VIATEL®

© 2000 Viatel, Inc.

is an attitude among Italians not to trust the ruling class," said the treasury minister Vicenzo Visco recently, "and they are right." Too often, he added, "our politicians, trade unions and entrepreneurs are unable to understand what is going on, or they are so indifferent to the general interest that they destroy everything. Or they are so involved in making money for themselves—stealing, in other words—that they don't care about the economy." If this were a malcontent talking about Russia, or Nigeria, or Pakistan, it might be unremarkable. That it was a senior minister talking about a major European country, prominent in the European Union, NATO and all the other leading clubs, is, in truth, astonishing. Even more astonishing is that it is set to continue, even while throwbacks like Serbia start to clean up their act. Truly, Italy is becoming more of an embarrassment than an anomaly. □

The new economy goes global

America has enjoyed a surge in productivity, thanks largely to information technology. In 2001, Europe and Japan will see similar gains, forecasts **Pam Woodall**.

In 1987 Robert Solow, a Nobel Laureate in economics, famously said "you can see the computer age everywhere but in the productivity statistics." This became known as the productivity paradox: the failure of massive investment in information technology (IT) to lift productivity growth. During the past few years, however, America's productivity growth has speeded up, to an annual average of 2.9% since the end of 1995, twice the rate of the previous two decades. In the year to mid-2000, productivity leapt by 5%. Thus the paradox appears to have been solved—but only in America. In Japan and Europe productivity has failed to pick up.

Sceptics argue that most of the increase in American productivity is purely cyclical and will not last. During economic booms, firms work employees harder, so productivity rises; then it falls in the next downturn. The sceptics believe that IT is simply not in the same league as previous technological revolutions such as electricity or the car. But they are wrong to dismiss computers and the Internet so lightly.

The cost of information technology is falling much faster than for any previous technology. Over the past three decades the real price of computer-processing power has fallen by 99.999%, an average decline of 35% a year. Plunging costs make computers and communications more affordable, allowing them to be adopted more quickly and used more widely throughout the economy than previous technologies. For comparison, the real price of electricity fell by a modest

Pam Woodall: economics editor, *The Economist*

6% a year between 1890 and 1920.

IT has several other valuable characteristics. First, it can boost efficiency in many different parts of a firm and in every sector of the economy. Electricity and steam increased productivity largely in manufacturing, but IT can also boost the efficiency of services. Second, by improving access to information on prices and products, IT helps markets to work better, thereby ensuring a more efficient allocation of resources. And last, but by no means least, by reducing the cost of information and communications, IT helps to globalise markets for products and for capital. In turn, globalisation spurs competition and speeds up the diffusion of technology through foreign trade.

Putting an "e" in productivity
Non-farm productivity in the United States
Annual average % increase

Period	%
1970-75	2.35
1975-80	1.16
1980-85	1.72
1985-90	1.31
1990-95	1.53
1995-2000	2.9

Source: US Department of Labor

These are all reasons why IT will help to raise productivity. At least part of the spurt in America's productivity growth is structural, not cyclical. However, from this fact many people draw two conclusions, both of them flawed. The first is that faster growth justifies the lofty heights of Wall Street. But although America's sustainable rate of productivity growth is probably now around 2.5% a year, well above its previous pace, this is nowhere near enough to justify the level of share prices.

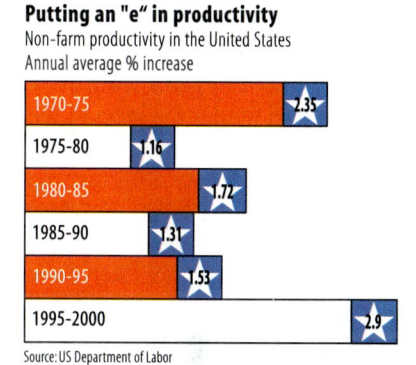

A second conclusion that is popularly drawn from its recent spectacular economic performance is that America will reap the lion's share of the benefits from the IT revolution. There is little sign of faster productivity growth in the other big economies, and many Americans expect it to stay that way because the tired "old" economies of Europe and Japan lack the necessary innovation and entrepreneurial culture. Of the world's 50 biggest IT companies, only four are European, nine are Japanese and 36 are American. American firms' first-mover advantage in computers and the Internet will, it is argued, put Europe and Japan at a big disadvantage.

On the contrary: Japan and Europe are likely to enjoy bigger gains from IT than America. Historically, the biggest economic gains from a new technology come not from its invention and production, but from its use. Europe and Japan do not need to create cutting-edge technology to close the gap with America: they can grow rapidly simply by buying or imitating United States technology and B2B e-commerce. For all the talk about first-mover advantage, there are actually advantages in being second. Not only is IT equipment today much cheaper than a few years ago, but second movers can wait and see what works, cherry-pick the best bits, and then avoid the mistakes of American firms.

Moreover, corporate America, after a decade of so of vigorous restructuring, has already cut out a lot of economic waste. Japan and Europe, by contrast, still have scope for big cost savings, simply because their economies are much less efficient. By increasing transparency, the Internet will attack archaic business practices that keep prices high and productivity low. If consumers can, at a click, discover lower prices on the Net, this will force domestic producers and retailers to cut prices. In Japan, the Internet will introduce more competition into the network of cosy relationships that links manufacturers with preferred suppliers and retailers. As a result, productivity growth over the next decade may well be even faster in Japan and Europe than in America.

There are big obstacles that may prevent Japan and Europe reaping the full gains from IT. In particular, job protection laws could hinder the swift re-allocation of workers from old to new industries. But things are changing. Many European economies are pushing through reforms to cut taxes and make labour markets more flexible. Japan and Europe may have been slower to adopt IT, but as they get round to it, the economic rewards are likely to start showing up in 2001.

Oh happy island

Britain will be a great place to live in 2001. But everyone will still complain like hell, predicts **Dudley Fishburn**.

Here are seven reasons why it will be a good year for the 59m people living in a small island somewhere north of France.

1. There will be almost no unemployment. Indeed, there will be a sharp increase in employment. Britain and America are among the handful of countries of which this will be true.

2. Britain's GDP will grow for the 11th consecutive year and at a good clip of 3%, probably more. This will establish it as the fourth biggest economy. And there is every sign that the prosperity will continue: no landing ahead, soft or hard.

3. It will be a country buoyed up by immigration. In 2001, the number of French people living in Britain will exceed 300,000. The number of EU citizens living and working in the country, free from any kind of immigration control or work-permit bureaucracy, will touch nearly a million. Add in students, asylum-seekers and immigrants from elsewhere and Britain will bubble. Remember also that there are 15m British citizens living outside the country: they too will contribute to its cosmopolitan success.

4. There will be a general election, probably in the spring of 2001, which will last a dizzy three weeks, produce an 80% turnout and change nothing. A strong, middle-of-the-road, modern government under Tony Blair's prime ministership will continue in office for five more years.

Dudley Fishburn: editor, *The World in 2001*

5. An ever-greater number of Brits of all ages will be attending university. Over 30% of 18-year-olds will go on to higher education. Since the future prosperity of Britain's service-driven economy rests solely on brain power, this is an all-important competitive advantage: most European countries have a lower participation rate in university education. British universities lag behind their American counterparts but they are still mostly fine institutions.

6. Britain's Treasury will enjoy a budget surplus in 2001 while holding a tax-take at one of the lowest levels in the rich world. Some 40% of the nation's wealth will be suborned by government in 2001, compared with 49% in France or 42% in Germany. Since a huge fraction of money spent by government is always wasted, waste in Britain will be proportionately less than in other European countries.

7. Britons will add handsomely to their pile of financial assets in 2001. Unusually for Europeans, the British have saved for their pensions in advance. Private pension assets alone will top £900 billion ($1.3 trillion) next year: Germans, by contrast, will have assets of only £87 billion. Indeed, Britain's saved pensions assets will be greater than all the rest of the EU put together. This huge pot of capital, much of it invested productively overseas, will keep the cushion of British prosperity nicely plumped in the years ahead.

Seven reasons for Britons to be happy. Yet the surest prediction for 2001 is that the country will moan and grouse and complain without break throughout the next 12 months, a long whine orchestrated, not least, by the country's "quality" press and broadcasters. Foreigners (and famously the Australians who coined the phrase "whingeing Poms") have often noticed this unappealing habit of the British middle-class. As the country progressively lost confidence over the three generations of the previous century it became trapped by a mentality that everything was wrong with the world. But here is a conundrum. The British usually complain most loudly about any person or institution that dares to be successful. What will they do when the joke is on themselves?

MONT BLANC

The black magic. The seductive combination of state of the art technology and traditional European craftsmanship, make the Montblanc Leather Collection an elegant yet practical accessory.

www.montblanc.com

Montblanc Boutiques. 13 Old Bond Street (opens Christmas 2000). 60/61 Burlington Arcade. 10/11 Royal Exchange. Canada Place, Canary Wharf. Harrods, Knightsbridge. Selfridges, Oxford Street. Call 020 7663 4830 for further details and national stockists.

Top restaurants on the menu.

NOKIA 6210

Find great restaurants, descriptions – even directions including the nearest public transport – using uB-mobile services on the Nokia 6210 phone.

With the Nokia 6210 in your hand, you have access to a world of mobile Internet services, such as banking and email. And to find nearby restaurants (or current exhibitions or cosy hotels) scroll through the menu to the WAP browser and access uB-mobile. • The Nokia 6210 makes WAP access fast – up to 14.4 kbps in high-speed networks. • With the Nokia 6210 in your hand, you have things under control.

Make the most of your Nokia 6210! As a Club Nokia member, you have access to many exclusive WAP features. Register your new Nokia 6210 and get a free *personal badge to make your Nokia phone truly personal. Join today at **www.club.nokia.com**!

NOKIA
CONNECTING PEOPLE

www.nokia.com

THE WORLD IN 2001 Diary

DIARY FOR 2001

January
Sweden takes on the presidency of the EU.

Greece joins Europe's single currency.

Australia is 100. More celebrations in Sydney.

Canada's central bank appoints a new governor.

Mont Blanc tunnel re-opens between France and Italy.

World Economic Forum meets in Davos, Switzerland.

January 20th—the United States inaugurates its 43rd president.

100th anniversary of Queen Victoria's death.

February
Presidential election in Sierra Leone.

Chinese year of the snake—associated with romance and deep thinking.

Russia's Mir space station falls to earth.

America chooses its farming champion. Farmer X will have grown 400-odd bushels of corn per acre. Three times the national average and an omen for future food gluts.

Carnival time in Rio de Janeiro and New Orleans.

March
Regional elections in Baden-Württemberg and Rhineland-Palatinate, Germany—good pointers to the outcome of the federal election in 2002.

Municipal elections in France. The grandson of Charles de Gaulle will stand as the National Front mayoral candidate in Paris.

OPEC meets in Vienna.

Vietnamese Communist Party Congress.

The Eden Project, the world's largest greenhouse, opens in Cornwall, England. Three eco-systems and thousands of species of plant under one roof.

April
Parliamentary elections in Italy and Albania. Presidential election in Peru.

The 2001 Mars Odyssey is launched. It will arrive at the red planet in October to study radiation and look for water.

April 21st—Earth Day

Stakeholder pensions start in Britain.

April 29th—Census day in Britain.

Athens' new Elefetherios Venizelos airport is due to open for international flights. Expect delays.

May
British general election.

Presidential election in Iran. Parliamentary elections in the Philippines and Poland.

British football's FA Cup final. The first to be played away from Wembley since 1923.

June
Parliamentary election in Bulgaria. Presidential elections in Bolivia and Mongolia.

Deadline to secure full implementation of the Good Friday agreement in Northern Ireland.

Total solar eclipse in southern Africa and South America.

EU summit in Gothenburg, Sweden.

The Messehalle, the world's largest glass-fronted building, opens in Frankfurt.

July
Belgium takes on the presidency of the EU.

Parliamentary election in Japan. Presidential election in Uganda.

Juan Antonio Samaranch steps down after 21 years as president of the International Olympic Committee. The host for the 2008 games is chosen.

Investors in Singapore and Australia trade shares on both exchanges.

Iranian gas starts pumping into Turkey.

The Proms, the world's largest music festival, open at the Royal Albert Hall, London. Enjoy a series of music festivals all over Europe.

G8 summit in Genoa, Italy.

August
District elections in Pakistan. General Pervez Musharraf has promised a national election by October 2002.

IAAF Athletics World Championships in Edmonton, Canada.

1.5m people attend Europe's biggest carnival in Notting Hill, London.

40th anniversary of the building of the Berlin Wall.

September
Parliamentary election in France and Norway.

Opening of the Berlin Jewish museum.

Jewish New Year 5762.

September 21st—UN international day of peace.

October
Parliamentary elections in Australia and Argentina. Presidential elections in Bangladesh, Gambia and Zambia.

Over 800m Hindus worldwide celebrate Diwali—the festival of lights.

"Little Women", the musical, opens on Broadway.

Annual meeting of the IMF and the World Bank, in Washington, DC.

APEC summit in Shanghai.

November
Parliamentary election in Jordan. Presidential elections in Nicaragua, Romania and Honduras.

The world salsa championships in Miami.

November 17th—Muslims worldwide begin fasting for Ramadan.

Mayoral election in New York.

Release of Microsoft's X-Box games console. Expect to see your kids even less.

December
Parliamentary election in Chile.

Two Christmas blockbuster movies go head to head: "Harry Potter" and "Lord of the Rings".

December 1st—AIDS awareness day.

EU summit in Brussels, Belgium.

December 31st—Tenth anniversary of the dissolution of the USSR.

January 1st 2002
The euro arrives in your pocket—notes and coins go into circulation in the eurozone. Expect bewilderment.

Spain takes on the presidency of the EU.

freedom to work in a new way

Orange Wirefree™ working is one of the most exciting developments in business today. Colleagues can work as a team even when they are miles apart, and share information as easily when they are out and about, as sitting at a desk. It gives people the flexibility to work wherever, whenever and however they choose. To find out how your business can take-off in ways that have never been possible before, call the Orange Business Team on 0800 731 3330 or visit www.orange.co.uk

orange™

THE WORLD IN 2001
Britain

Economics: All set fair 28 / **Britain in 1901 and 2001: Still Victorian** 29
Ulster: Northern Ireland turns the page 32 / **Architecture: Better buildings, at last** 34
Politics: Reform! reform! 35 / **Internet advances: The coming of e-government** 36
Chris Patten on Europe: Success is not always loveable 38

Rule Blairtannia

Anthony King

Tony Blair will not enjoy the first few months of 2001. He will have to make up his mind whether or not to hold a general election. The life of the parliament elected in May 1997 does not legally expire till the late spring of 2002, but British prime ministers often choose to go to the country a year early. Otherwise they lose their room for manoeuvre and run the risk of, say, a sudden economic downturn.

On the face of it, the decision in Mr Blair's case should be easy. A suitable date is already in the 2001 diary: May 3rd, when local elections are anyway due to be held in England and Wales. The economy booms. Labour has been ahead in the opinion polls almost continuously since 1992. The Blair government is the first since the last war not to suffer a mid-term slump. The Conservatives have yet to recover from their setbacks in the 1990s under John Major. Their shadow cabinet is undistinguished (even Tories say so privately), and except on Europe they lack any sense of direction.

So why wait? Holding off till late 2001 or 2002 only invites trouble. There could be a stockmarket crash. The economy could turn belly-up. There could be another popular uprising like the one staged in 2000 by farmers and road hauliers.

But the prime minister will still hesitate. He will do so partly because he is who he is. His bold front conceals a nervous temperament. Someone likened him to a man carrying a priceless vase across a slippery floor. He is pretty sure he can reach the other side, but he is not taking any chances. He also has an eye on the past. The Labour Party in the 20th century, even under Harold Wilson, never managed to win two full terms in a row. To a nervous fellow like the prime minister, objective circumstances will also counsel caution. Labour's vote in 2001 will remain, from Labour's point of view, disturbingly soft. Far fewer Labour supporters than previously strongly identify with the party. Even most of those who currently intend to vote for Labour hold the Labour government in low esteem.

All the same, after weighing the odds, Mr Blair will probably choose May 3rd 2001. A June election would come too soon after Labour reversals in the May local elections. October was once a favoured month, but nowadays an October election would mean cancelling, at vast expense, that month's party conference. Waiting till 2002 would not only look timid but give the Conservatives further time to recover. The longer the wait, the more heightened the uncertainty.

Whenever Mr Blair goes, he will win. The reasons will be the same reasons that accounted for the Clinton victories in the United States. The United Kingdom's economy is sound. The country is at peace. Most of the Blair government's policies are moderate—or can be made to seem moderate compared with the Tories'. Mr Blair is no longer as popular as he once was; neither is his government. But the opinion polls make it clear that most voters view the prospect of a Tory return to power with—at least for now—something like grim foreboding.

Europe and the euro will be, at most, distractions at the election, even though the Conservatives are committed to delaying British entry into the eurozone and the great majority of voters agree with them. The reasons are simple. Most voters with strong feelings against the euro are Tory supporters already; the Conservatives have little ground to make up in this quarter. Moreover, whereas the Conservatives have taken up a fixed position on the

Go on, give us a smile Tony

2001
Count me in—2001 is a census year. Britain's 59m people will be captured on paper on April 29th.

Anthony King: professor of government at Essex University; election commentator for the BBC and regular contributor to the *Daily Telegraph*

27

Britain THE WORLD IN 2001

issue, Labour will prove in 2001, as it did in 1997, infinitely flexible. If the voters are unenthusiastic about the euro, Mr Blair and his colleagues will be—or sound—unenthusiastic too. In addition, Mr Blair is committed to a national referendum on the euro. Anti-euro Labour voters can thus have their cake (at the 2001 general election) and eat it too (in a referendum at some unspecified time in the future).

Mr Blair will also be helped by the national mood. Whereas the French in 2001 will still be afflicted by morbid national anxiety, the British will remain a relaxed lot. They know who they are. They see nothing much wrong with what they are. Their language happens to be in the ascendant, allowing the vibrant culture of the English-speaking world to be readily assimilated.

The mainland of Great Britain, though not Northern Ireland, will also remain largely free of cultural conflicts. The issues that inflame the radical right and evangelical Christians in the United States—abortion, gays, the flag, school prayers—fail to cause much excitement in the United Kingdom. Most Brits remain easy-going materialists, their philosophy one of live and let live. Cannabis will be decriminalised before the decade is out. To the great astonishment of foreigners, a recent Gallup survey found that more than half of Britons regard gay and straight relationships as being of equal value. Almost all tolerate homosexuality, a large majority believing it is "neither right nor wrong but simply a fact of life"

To be sure, the United Kingdom in 2001 will not be free of worries. Hard-drug use is on the increase. So is crime. Several of Britain's inner cities have become as demoralised and criminalised as inner cities in America; only their murder rates are lower. The larger number of people seeking asylum in the United Kingdom will continue to ruffle British feathers, especially since a large proportion are not in fear of their lives, merely in search of a good life.

But most Britons in 2001 will experience these problems, if at all, only at second-hand. The Conservatives will gain some votes on the strength of genuine worries about drugs, crime and asylum seekers, and because the country will no longer take any real pleasure in New Labour. The Conservatives, as a result, will undoubtedly gain seats in the House of Commons. But on December 31st 2001 Labour will still be in power and Mr Blair will still be prime minister. □

> **2001**
> The new BMW Mini will roll off British production lines in 2001. You can buy yours in the summer.

All set fair

Anatole Kaletsky

Anatole Kaletsky: columnist on the *Times* and director of Kaletsky Economic Consulting

If politics were really a branch of economics, as it is fashionable to believe these days, then Tony Blair would have no worries in facing the electorate in 2001. With the possible exception of Harold Macmillan in 1959, no British prime minister in history has been able to present such an unblemished record of economic achievement at the end of a term in power.

The macro-statistics of Britain's economic miracle are familiar enough to need little elaboration. Unemployment is at its lowest in a generation and by the middle of 2001 will almost certainly be below 4%—arguably lower even than the American level, once proper account is taken of the large proportion of the United States male population who while away their youth in jail. Inflation has all but vanished and so have the inflationary expectations built into wage settlements, business strategies and interest rates. In terms of incomes per head, Britain has far overtaken Italy, is in a statistical dead-heat with France and will probably be within spitting distance of Germany by the end of 2001.

All this is impressive, but what is truly unusual about Labour's economic record is that the glittering statistics do not just reflect a transient pre-election boom or a cyclical recovery from an earlier recession or currency crisis. Uniquely among post-war chancellors of either party, Gordon Brown has seen his stewardship unmarred by economic crises of any kind. Mr Brown promised to steer the British economy out of its long troublesome history of boom and bust. And by the middle of 2001, even the sceptics will be forced to admit that he has been as good as his word.

Neither the jump in oil prices, nor the continuing strength of sterling against the euro, nor the small further increase in interest rates likely to be imposed by the Bank of England will do the economy any serious damage. Indeed, for the eighth year running, the strength of the economy will defy most forecasters' expectations. The IMF, for example, predicted in its autumn *World Economic Outlook* that Britain's growth would slow from 3.1% in 2000 to 2.8% in 2001; but in reality GDP is likely to expand by nearer 3.5% in both 2000 and 2001, buoyed by growing consumer incomes, rising house prices, stronger exports to a recovering Europe and a slight loosening of the public spending purse-strings by Mr Brown. As a result, unemployment should fall, even on the conservative measure used by the Interna-

Give that dog a bone

Government debt
% of GDP
52.3 / 46.2 / 43.6 / 41.1 / 39.1
1999 2000 2001 2002 2003

Brits on holiday abroad
m
32.3 — 1998
20.8 — 1991
13.1 — 1981
4.2 — 1971

Contribution to the national economy
% contribution to UK GDP
WALES 4.1   SCOTLAND 8.3   N. IRELAND 2.3   ENGLAND 85.3

Sources: EIU, Office for National Statistics, International Passenger Survey

tional Labour Organisation, from 5.3% in the autumn of 2000 to around 4%. And all this will be achieved without any serious breach of the government's rigorous 2.5% inflation target.

Better still, the one macro-economic issue on which the government might have been vulnerable in 2001—its promise to try to take Britain into the euro—has providentially been taken off the agenda. Following the Danish "no" vote, the government is likely to take its "five economic tests" for euro membership much more literally than originally intended. The Treasury will, as promised, conduct its assessment of these tests early in the next parliament. But whereas a positive verdict from the Treasury was once considered a foregone conclusion, the Danish referendum has changed all that. When the time for the assessment arrives in 2001, the Treasury will be encouraged to be both rigorous and more honest. Given the very high standard of proof required by the government's requirement of "clear and unambiguous" economic benefits to Britain, the Treasury is almost certain to say "not yet". The euro decision will therefore be put off at least until 2005.

All this will be very convenient for Messrs Blair and Brown from an electoral standpoint. Yet cynical British voters are unlikely to show much gratitude for Labour's economic record. And in several important ways, they will be right to remain dissatisfied.

Not a productive lot

As prosperity is increasingly taken for granted, not only in Britain but around the world, voters will start to assume that non-inflationary growth is a natural condition of any reasonably well-ordered capitalist system and not a divine gift to be bestowed on a grateful nation by miracle-working politicians. They will also pay more attention to the blots on the British micro-economic record which have been overlooked amid the self-satisfaction over the country's macro-economic performance.

The darkest of these blots is Britain's productivity problem. This is reflected not only in the low level of current productivity relative to other G7 countries, which can be partly shrugged off as a historic legacy of poor management and under-investment. More alarming is the low level of productivity growth, even in the favourable macro-economic conditions now prevailing. This surprisingly low productivity growth—which represents the biggest contrast between the United States and British economic "miracles"—means that the British people are doing better by working longer and harder, not by working "smarter". However well the British economy appears to be doing, its underlying inefficiency is actually getting worse in relation to the rest of the world.

What are the causes of Britain's low productivity disease? During the next 12 months, this question will attract more and more attention as the public's gaze shifts from the creation of more jobs to the improvement of living standards and working conditions for a population which increasingly takes full employment for granted. Two micro-economic issues at the root of the productivity problem will rightly become the focus of public debate: taxation and regulation.

High taxes will be singled out by the Tories as the chief cause of Britain's economic problems. But this cam-

Still Victorian

January 22nd 2001 will be the 100th anniversary of Queen Victoria's death: a moment when Britain, at the high point of its power, caught its breath. Expect a rash of articles recounting both that shock—"We all feel a bit motherless," wrote Henry James, an American novelist—and the long century of dwindling British influence that followed it. It will be an occasion for navel gazing, for letting out a sad historical sigh, for deeply held regrets.

Yet while those 100 years have, of course, changed everything, what will be perhaps more remarkable is how little will have changed. Britain in 1901 was the world's third-largest economy. By 2001 it will have slipped just one place. In 1901, the country's trade was concentrated in the docks of London. In 2001 the world's biggest international airport will be Heathrow, its cargo of service-sector workers bringing wealth and influence as surely as pig-iron and textiles once did. In 1901 there was freedom of movement of capital: British investment around the world was second to none. In 2001 it will be second: but only to America.

Other things have not changed: the average speed of traffic in London has remained at 12 miles an hour. And London's population as a proportion of Britain's is unaltered at 12%. It took Queen Victoria no more time to get to her house, Osbourne, on the Isle of Wight, in 1901 than the same journey would take in 2001. Despite 100 years of huffing and puffing by politicians about education, not much has changed: the ratio of secondary-school students to teachers, at 16 to 1, is precisely the same. The British citizen, of course, has changed out of all recognition, and the social structure has been overturned. Funny, though, that crowds still go to Ascot; Eton College remains the country's foremost school; and the Duke of Westminster, then as now, is one of the richest men. Queen Victoria might even have been amused. □

Change? What change?

paign is unlikely to succeed. Everyone would of course like to pay lower taxes—and Britons would probably be wise to extend private financing to the remaining shibboleths of the public sector: health, education and pensions. But there is no evidence that British voters are ready, so soon after Margaret Thatcher, for a second major campaign to roll back the public sector. And there is even less evidence that taxation is a serious impediment to productivity growth. Despite a small rise in taxes to 37.5% of GDP, Britain in 2001 will have the lowest tax burden in Europe and a tax structure causing fewer distortions than the American, German or French systems.

Regulation is another matter. Britain's regulatory bureaucracy has grown like topsy under Labour and promises to become even more asphyxiating to enterprise in the years ahead. Particularly pernicious has been the interaction between the legislative imperialism of the Eu-

At BMW, agility comes in all sizes. This is because we have always built our cars with rear-wheel drive and near perfect weight distribution. It means our large luxury saloon, the BMW 7 Series, can feel as responsive as our Z3 Roadster. So even though the 7 Series offers the refinement and comfort of a limousine, it also drives like a car built for performance. Which, compared to other cars in this class, is something of a luxury.

You don't have to be small to be agile.

BMW 7 Series

www.bmw.co.uk
Tel. 0800 325 600

The Ultimate Driving Machine

Britain THE WORLD IN 2001

> **2001**
> How can this be legal? In 2001's general election the average Scottish MP will represent 23% fewer people than the average English MP. In America, the Supreme Court ruled this sort of thing unconstitutional years ago. One man, one vote still evades the world's oldest parliament.

ropean Commission and the pedantic and over-zealous enforcement of it by Britain's relentless civil service. Ever more intrusive European regulations on working hours, health and safety, and environmental standards are becoming a genuine bugbear for British businesses.

Tax administration, as opposed to the level of taxation, has become an even bigger annoyance than EU regulation, especially for small businesses. The government's inability or unwillingness to control its overbearing regulators and bullying tax collectors was probably the real root of the fuel-tax protests of September 2000. At the same time, the regulators' failure to advance the cause of competition in regulated industries such as telecoms, railways and air transport has brought back memories of the inefficiencies created in the 1970s by the cosy relations between government bureaucrats and state-owned "national champions" such as British Telecom and British Airways.

In short, Tony Blair's first spell in government has confounded the sceptics by showing that a responsible macro-economic management is not an oxymoron. In its second term, working with a much-reduced majority, the Labour leadership will face a much tougher test. Will Labour understand that the key to economic efficiency is to create genuinely open markets and then leave businesses, especially small businesses, to get on with it? □

Northern Ireland turns the page

The next wave will bring development

Expect Ulster to be the fastest growing part of the United Kingdom and perhaps of the European Union in 2001. A full year of peace will give the economy the chance it needs to pick up speed: and the miserable record of the recent past means that there is much ground to be made up. Nonetheless, Ulster's new-found wealth will not just be a statistical quirk.

The province already has one of the highest rates of disposable income in the country: national wage levels are happily matched with low local costs. Peace will bring useful money from inward investment, the EU and, most importantly, from newly rich Ireland: this money will find much more profitable uses than the British government's subsidy cheques of the past. Unemployment will drop to below 6%, well below the European average. Best of all, expect the old political lags to be swept aside in 2001 (as they were a decade ago in Ireland) by a young generation more interested in profit and pop music than politics.

But before that there will be one last upheaval—perhaps a political collapse of the new local government and a temporary outbreak of violence. Something fresh and hopeful is stirring in the province, but those who have flourished on generations of hate will not let go lightly.

Ulster, one of the most beautiful parts of the United Kingdom, will get a swell of tourists in 2001, mostly from the south. But book your holiday soon. The province's weak planning laws (and its propensity for corruption) mean that concrete will soon spread over the land: small properties everywhere will acquire hideous grandiose gates and warehouses will appear in the worst places. Ulster already has the highest land prices in the kingdom, with farmland changing hands at £4,000 ($6,000) an acre.

In 2001, people in Northern Ireland, though they have a GDP per head only 76% that of the United Kingdom, will start to build with a vengeance. House prices are already spiralling. In most Ulster towns the only new buildings have until recently been government offices: in 2001 private office blocks will get built alongside them.

Ulster is being brought closer to the world. The Belfast to Dublin rail service is receiving £50m ($70m) of investment to cut the time of the journey between the cities to 1 hour 50 minutes. The "sea bridge" to Scotland has reduced access to the mainland to less than two hours. Two million people from outside Ireland will visit in the next year.

There is a long way to go before the impoverished province catches up with its once-despised southern neighbour. Ireland will enjoy a higher standard of living than even Britain in 2001. But as prosperity, investment and concrete spread, the gap between the north and the south of the island will close. And with this economic change will emerge the first scandals about corruption in high places. The guardians of Ulster's old folklore will be shown as shams by tomorrow's wealth. □

What do you want the Internet to be?™

"LIKE FLYING VERY CLOSE TO THE GROUND."
ROLF DIETRICH, ENGINEER & RE-INVENTOR OF THE BICYCLE WHEEL

Wireless Internet

Well, Rolf, get ready to fly. You reinvented the wheel to be faster and more powerful. We're doing the same. We're building the new, high-performance Internet - the Wireless Internet. It combines the mobility of our No.1-ranked Wireless Internet architecture* with the speed, capacity and 99.9999% reliability of our industry-leading Optical Internet backbone. All of which creates new economic opportunities for wireless operators. Enabling the bandwidth-hungry applications and services customers demand over advanced, 3G wireless networks with up to a 100% increase in operating margins over the next five years. So come together, right now with Nortel Networks™. And make the Internet whatever you want it to be. **www.nortelnetworks.com**

NORTEL NETWORKS™

Nortel Networks, the Nortel Networks logo, the Globemark and "What do you want the Internet to be?" are trademarks of Nortel Networks.
© 2000 Nortel Networks. All rights reserved. *The Yankee Group and Herschel Shosteck Associates Ltd.

Britain THE WORLD IN 2001

London's sexier skyline

Better buildings, at last

Martin Vander Weyer

Innovation, eclecticism, reinterpretation: 2001 will witness another stage in the renaissance of British architecture. In the private sector, a benign economy will encourage imaginative developments of housing and offices, and architects as a profession will have more work on their drawing-boards than they have had for a decade.

But it will not be easy to characterise the style of their work in 2001. It will vary from the science-fiction originality of the Eden Project, a giant, glass-roofed "showcase for global bio-diversity" in a disused Cornish clay-pit, to a more mundane resurgence of tower-blocks across the London skyline. After the embarrassment of London's Millennium Bridge, which developed a sickening wobble when pedestrians began to walk across it in the summer of 2000, the urge for experimentation may recede, especially in the engineering aspects of design. But there will still be a premium on bringing excitement to everyday structures. Watch out for the best of public architecture at railway stations: a throwback to Victorian times.

The £53m ($74m) Eden Project, expected to open in the spring, will be among the most talked-about buildings of 2001. Its interlinked geodesic domes, of varying sizes to accommodate the irregular topography of the site, will create two huge, climate-controlled "biomes"—the world's largest tropical greenhouses. A visitors' centre will look down into the glass structure from the rim of the quarry above. With its emphasis on sustainability and use of natural materials, Eden—the work of Nicholas Grimshaw, architect of the Waterloo Eurostar rail terminal—is a project of significance for the new century.

A glazed space of a very different kind will attract attention in London at the beginning of the year: the Great Court of the British Museum, laid out in 1824 by Sir Robert Smirke, has been given a delicate, filigreed canopy by Norman Foster, linking the circular reading room in the centre to the museum's outer quadrangle. But sensitive remodellings of much-loved buildings such as the museum and Somerset House (one of the successes of 2000) will give way in 2001 to starker architectural statements across the capital. In response to soaring demand for office space, the skyscraper is set for a comeback and several new landmarks will begin to rise. Among the most controversial will be Lord Foster's 183-metre Baltic Exchange Tower, dubbed "the erotic gherkin" by detractors, which will replace the Edwardian shipbroking exchange bombed by the IRA in 1992. Three new blocks rising to 30 storeys will add extra floor space to the Canary Wharf complex in Docklands, and a 420-metre tower by Renzo Piano will eventually rise above London Bridge Station to become the tallest in Europe.

At Paddington Station, Grimshaw's firm will be embarking on a £200m redevelopment (one of 14 major station schemes around the country commissioned by Railtrack) which will include a 42-storey tower. The Paddington scheme includes improved road links to the nearby M40 motorway and a regeneration of the adjacent canal basin—an example of the integrated development expected to flow from the Labour government's 10-year £120 billion commitment to transport investment.

Though British airports—most recently Bristol and, beginning in 2001, Richard Rogers's scheme for Heathrow Terminal 5—often provide scope for striking architecture, rail and underground have for many decades been too starved of investment to allow imaginative treatment. But enlarged budgets and the stimulus of the new Jubilee Line stations, especially Lord Foster's cathedral-like space at Canary Wharf, have reinvigorated the sector. One smaller-scale example, due to begin in April, is the £72m rebuilding of the Wembley Park underground station complex, under a single, swooping, high-level roof, to serve the dramatic new 90,000-seat Wembley Stadium.

Due to open in February is the £56m National Space Science Centre in Leicester, the only NASA-accredited museum outside the United States. Manchester, Birmingham and Sheffield will unveil redevelopment schemes. And by the end of the year Bath will celebrate the £10m refurbishment of its historic Spa complex, closed since 1978, with the addition of a dramatic cube-shaped building housing new gymnasia and steam-rooms.

And Britain's devolved political landscape will take physical expression, albeit the subject of controversy over cost in every case. Work will commence on Lord Rogers's Welsh National Assembly building in Cardiff, and will continue on both the £195m Scottish parliament building in Edinburgh, designed by a Catalan, the late Enric Miralles, and Lord Foster's £65m egg-shaped structure for the Greater London Assembly, beside the Thames in Southwark.

These will not be the only buildings to provoke argument in 2001, as a reinvigorated profession explores the limits of diversity, and as the cycles of fashion continue to turn. Though much drab concrete of the post-war era has gone, once-reviled modernist survivals such as Birmingham's Rotunda building may now achieve historic, listed status. As to new work, the two British architects of world standing, Lords Foster and Rogers, remain at the height of their powers. The latter's ill-fated Millennium Dome will soon only be remembered as a false start to a stylishly sustainable new era for British buildings. □

2001

The government sells off 46% of Britain's air-traffic control system in April. Expect turbulence from consumer groups concerned about safety.

Martin Vander Weyer: associate editor of *The Week* and contributor to the *Daily Telegraph*

Reform! Reform!

David Lipsey

Most British general elections are fought between a modernising party and a conservative party (though the Conservatives are often not the conservatives). Usually, the modernising party wins: for example, Labour in 1945, 1964 and 1997 and the Conservatives in 1951, 1970, 1979 and 1987. So if Tony Blair wants to fight the next election as he did the last, under a modernising banner, here are five measures he might try.

House of Lords reform: stage two

Labour's stage one reform has left 92 hereditary peers still governing by right of birth. A further 17 who were hereditaries have been made life peers. Therefore, the 695-strong upper house remains Conservative, using its natural majority to defeat Labour in some 30% of votes.

Labour wants to go further, but its problem is that its supporters do not want a Lords capable of challenging the elective dictatorship that springs from the Commons. Ministers therefore want only a few elected peers; (Lord) John Wakeham's Royal Commission on Lords Reform suggested a mere 65-130. With the public overwhelmingly in favour of election, William Hague is dallying with outbidding Mr Blair, by making half the House elective.

If Labour wants to modernise but resists election, it should worry less about who is in the Lords than about how the chamber operates. Lords' procedures are antediluvian, with the intricate details of bills formally debated in the main chamber; no speaker to keep order; and governance more suited to a private club than a legislature. A root-and-branch reform could create a truly effective second chamber. To symbolise it, the government might well go beyond Wakeham, stripping not only new Lords but also existing political appointees of their archaic titles.

Legalise dope

Jack Straw, Labour's home secretary, is probably the only 1960s undergraduate who has always been against cannabis. But the public is now leaving him adrift: 61% of them, according to a MORI poll in 1999, thought it was not very, or at all, harmful and 57% of those with an opinion thought it should be legalised. Decriminalisation was also proposed in 2000 in a report from the Police Federation (gulp….).

David Lipsey: political commentator and member of the House of Lords.

Cannabis is freely available and widely used by the young: a third of those under 30, according to the Police Federation. Possession of cannabis accounts for between 75% and 85% of drugs busts. Though a majority of offenders are now cautioned, some are jailed. All of which amounts to a huge waste: of prison space, of police time and of young people whose careers may be tainted by a criminal record. There are some signs that Mr Straw, a keen student of public opinion, is softening his line on soft drugs and a shift towards decriminalisation may yet follow.

Reform communications regulation

A revolution is sweeping through telecommunications, both technically (with phones, computers and television becoming indistinguishable) and competitively (with the industry dominated by international giants). Yet British telecommunications regulation has not faced up to change. Telephones are regulated by one kind of regulator, OFTEL, concerned essentially with competition. Commercial television is governed by another kind of regulator, the Independent Television Commission (ITC), which also meddles with content. If a commercial television company makes an offensive programme it can be censured by two different bodies: the ITC and the Broadcasting Standards Authority. Television advertising is pre-vetted but e-mail advertising is not. In other words, it is a mess.

The government knows this. For two years it has been consulting about reform (though matters are complicated by the fact that the European Union wants to get in on the act).

Mr Blair's government has always run scared of broadcasters, from BSkyB's Rupert Murdoch to the BBC, tending to talk tougher than it acts. So it remains to be seen whether it will dare go for the radical solution: a single regulator for competition, which might or might not embrace a single regulator for content.

Votes in local government

Mr Blair's government talks a good game about restoring local government: mayors for the big cities, following London's example, best-value rules to stop it wasting money and new internal structures. But apathy is the main problem in local government, with just 28% voting in 2000's elections. That apathy springs from a voting system that tends to lead to one-party, often corrupt administrations. So in Newham, London, Labour holds all the seats on 60% of a tiny vote. In notorious Hull it won 18 of the 20 seats contested with 57% of the vote. Which is where the problem lies: John Prescott, Labour's deputy leader, who is in charge of local government, is a Hull MP and wants to protect his party's local power. Mr Prescott should be told forcibly to get modern, or move over.

Transport

The government announced a £120 billion ten-year plan for transport investment in July 2000: and about time too. Much of the money will go to Britain's trains, which, contrary to popular myth, have boomed since privatisation. There will be no new roads, though there will be lots of by-passes and widenings which Joe Punter may find indistinguishable from new roads.

Road usage has to be rationed somehow: by congestion or by price. The government has experimented with the latter, allowing cities to charge commuters and hoping to raise £2.7 billion a year as a result. But Downing Street has ruled out motorway charging as too politically sensitive. Even the utility companies, daily threatening Britain's motorists with a collective nervous breakdown by their endless digging of holes, do not have to pay for the congestion they cause. Government may discover quite soon that, though charging is unpopular, not charging will be unpopular too.

Britain THE WORLD IN 2001

The coming of e-government

Matthew Symonds

> **2001**
> A voluntary contribution stakeholder pension starts in April. It will provide more people with an option for a second pension and a more secure retirement.

In 2001 a few governments around the world will start to embrace their citizens by intelligent use of the Internet. It will be the beginning of a revolution that will profoundly change the relationship between citizen and state: a more efficient, more humane, more responsive system of government will slowly start to emerge.

Until now, most governments have seen their job as creating a benign environment in which the hoped-for economic and social benefits of the Internet could unfold, rather than actively harnessing the fancy new technology for their own ends. As monopoly suppliers of services they had little to fear from being "Amazoned" by some new web-based competitor. Thus the risk/reward ratio for public servants tempted to dabble with the Internet was unattractive compared with their counterparts in the private sector.

But quite suddenly, that attitude has changed. The big IT vendors have stepped up their efforts to prove that by applying much the same (rapidly maturing) technologies and principles that are fuelling the e-business revolution, the business of government can be similarly transformed.

The potential benefits of e-government are just too great to ignore. If big companies are making procurement savings of up to 20% by putting their supply chains on the web, why shouldn't government departments?

But if cost reduction is one important motivation, so too is the pressure to respond to rising expectations of service. Most people transact with government because they have to rather than because they expect to enjoy it. But that doesn't mean it has to be as dismal an experience as it usually is. If the same 24/7 availability and convenience, fast delivery, customer focus and personalisation that the best businesses offer on the web became the norm in the public sector, the calculation is that it would not just make life better, but it would fundamentally change the way people view government itself.

One of the problems in dealing with government is the sheer complexity. The average developed-economy government has up to 70 different departments and agencies. Even relatively straightforward matters such as registering a birth or declaring a bankruptcy can require interacting with multiple agencies.

The Internet can provide a solution. Increasingly, governments are realising that it is not enough for departments to do their own thing on the web, posting a bit of information here or an online form there, each website with a different look and feel. What are needed to create fully "joined-up government" are fully fledged Internet portals—public-service equivalents of consumer portals such as Yahoo!—that can provide a one-stop shop for all of a citizen's needs. A portal of this kind, called eCitizen, has recently launched in Singapore, while others in Austria and Britain (UK Online) will soon open. In other parts of Europe, and in America and Australia, where government is organised on federal lines, local government has been leading the way with multi-functional portals.

Singapore's eCitizen is seen by many as a model to be adapted. All government agencies have adopted a common technology infrastructure and the same modules for form-filling, payment and security. The result is a single, consistent user interface that has adopted the metaphor of a citizen journeying through life.

All a user has to do is say which event on the journey is being faced—a change in marital or employment status, the purchase of a house, the beginning of military service, payment of taxes—and the site will smoothly package the necessary information, generate the appropriate forms and provide a secure means of exchange. The citizen does not have to know anything about the way government is organised: the complexity lies behind the scenes. The next stage is personalisation, allowing rapid access to frequently used services and an online record of the individual's previous dealings with government.

The new order
Global company earnings, % average increase 2000-01
Source: HSBC

- Telecoms wireless: 45
- Internet: 37
- Telecoms equipment: 29
- Computer hardware: 23
- Telecoms fixed-line: 22
- Software: 20

However, fully fledged e-government, which even Singapore is still some way from, will be hard to achieve. The huge scale of government operations, the difficulties of handling the kind of public/private partnerships that are increasingly favoured for implementing major IT projects, the requirement for thousands of inefficient processes to be re-engineered if the technology is to be allowed to strut its stuff, and the sheer effort of cultural transformation all make e-government fundamentally more challenging even than e-business.

True e-government will rest on four legs:
- A secure government intranet and central database that reaches across all departments.
- Electronic delivery of services from government to people by means of a one-stop portal.
- A government e-marketplace where departments can advertise their requirements and suppliers bid.
- Digital democracy: governments must use the web to make their actions more transparent and themselves more accountable. Eventually, they will offer collaborative legislation and voting online.

And what of the drawbacks of e-government? There is just one really. Vastly more efficient governments will know much more about us. The exponential increase in the ability of e-governments to gather, store and mine data about their people can be put to bad as well as good uses. Wise e-governments will go out of their way to ease well-founded worries about civil liberties and privacy. For e-citizens to be happy, e-governments will need to be eternally vigilant. □

Matthew Symonds: IT and communications editor, *The Economist*

e marketplaces

WHAT A GREAT LOCATION FOR AN E-MARKETPLACE.

Introducing the new e-marketplace alliance: IBM, i2 and Ariba. E-commerce expertise, procurement, auctioning, supply chain know-how, and resources to implement on a global scale. There to provide an effortless link between buyers and sellers over the Web. Whether you buy or sell steel or plastic, cars or cargo capacity. It's b2bx3.

ibm i2 ariba

www.ibm-i2-ariba.com or call 0870 010 2530

IBM and the e-business logo are trademarks or registered trademarks of International Business Machines Corporation. Ariba and i2 are registered trademarks of Ariba, Inc. and i2 Technologies, Inc. respectively. e-marketplaces is not the name of a product or service of either IBM, i2 or Ariba. © 2000 IBM Corporation. All rights reserved.

Britain THE WORLD IN 2001

Chris Patten, European commissioner for external affairs, calls for a more political European Union in 2001

Success is not always loveable

"Europe needs a constitution in order that Europe's citizens can remain in control. The first move will be made in 2001"

By any reckoning, the European Union has filled the sideboard with trophies. Beginning with the overwhelmingly important tasks of securing peace—alongside the Atlantic Alliance—and making the first halting steps towards prosperity in the war-ravaged countries of Western Europe, it has flourished to fulfil and conceivably to exceed the most visionary dreams of its founding fathers. Standards of living have soared; the menaces of the cold war have been defeated; and "ever closer political union" has been nurtured by treaties and institutions. So much success. So why no applause?

It will not only be in Britain that the audience sits on its hands in 2001, though there the degree of disenchantment has become so great as to inhibit the effective pursuit of the national interest. No politically defensible alternative vision to a constructive role in Europe will be offered for Britain, yet constructiveness itself will be regarded as the next worst thing to treachery. Criticisms will be heard elsewhere. What's wrong?

To some extent the problem is similar to that affecting other international organisations. For all the reality of globalisation, the nation state remains the basic political unit. People feel that their primary loyalties are to their country. But they recognise rationally that in order to protect national well-being, their states have to share decision-making in certain areas. This involves a dilution of sovereignty that appears to be acceptable to most people. The trouble is that the institutions created to implement policies where sovereignty has been pooled find it difficult to attract the enthusiastic commitment of the people in whose name they act, and therefore the credibility of those institutions is attenuated.

It should be easier for the European Union to deal with this problem than the World Trade Organisation, the International Monetary Fund or the World Bank. After all, the countries that make up the European Union have a rich tradition of winning political consent through democratic development. But we have failed miserably, and that failure could be exposed more clearly as the Union pursues the vital task of enlargement and accepts as members almost as many states as at present comprise it.

The problem is not a reluctance to surrender sovereignty. Most people have an intelligent sense that sovereignty is not like a deposit in the bank. It is fluid and relative—as difficult to nail down as jelly on the ceiling. Take those European countries outside the Union which regard it as their biggest market. They have theoretically the sovereign independence to make all their own economic decisions. But how many of the decisions made in Brussels—regulating this or that part of our single market—can they actually avoid? Usually, they find themselves in practice bound by rules that they had no part in shaping. The issue is not sovereignty. It is democracy.

For Europe's citizens, despite the enhanced powers of the Strasbourg Parliament, the Union will seem too bureaucratic, too centralised, too opaque, too closed to public accountability. That may be partly unfair. But it is what people will think over the coming year.

Be more political, not less

Politicians have regularly (and increasingly ill-advisedly) played down the political dimension of the Union. Sometimes we have sought refuge in the argument that it is a unique creation, that nothing like it has been constructed before, that we should simply go with the flow rather than try to work out what exactly the European Union should be for. Giuliano Amato's description of the Union being like an unidentified flying object, destination unknown, has been quoted with approval. Wherever we're heading, we're sure it'll be an agreeable destination.

While there may have been in the past a case for such Aristotelian pragmatism, I believe that it is no longer either wise or politically acceptable. Nor can we continue to sit out the conceptual debate about the nature of Europe and the nature of the institutions that should preserve and enhance its spirit.

There seems to be an open and shut case. If you don't advocate with passion a coherent and workable vision of Europe, you leave the field open to those who at best offer an unrealistic prospectus and at worst destructive jingoism.

So we need to define where European countries want and need to pool sovereignty, what powers should be handled at the national level or below and how the exercise of Europe-wide powers can be open and subject to the sort of viable democratic checks and balances that will earn public acceptability—for example, through the greater involvement of national parliaments in Europe's institutions.

Europe needs a constitution, not in order to define its unlikely destiny as a super-state, but in order to describe within this grouping of nation states who should do what, and how Europe's citizens can remain in control of the whole process. The first move towards a constitution will be made in 2001. This constitution should recognise that the European nation state endures and will continue to do so, thereby reassuring many of our citizens disquieted by what they perceive as perpetual constitutional changes.

This is an enterprise that needs to breathe democratic vitality into our political life and requires as well an awareness that the great political challenge of the past century—the reconciliation of France and Germany—has been achieved. The task now is different but certainly no less demanding: to anchor the liberated nations of the old Soviet empire in a liberal democratic community, and to make Europe whole once again, and genuinely free. ☐

E-MARKETPLACES ARE THE ULTIMATE MANIFESTATION OF THE POTENTIAL OF E-BUSINESS

E-marketplaces are Web-based trading networks that have the potential to reshape every industry. They eliminate bureaucracy and red tape, and streamline procurement and supply chain management. The result is lower transaction costs, more customers, and faster time to market. What's being sold? Steel by the ton, power by the megawatt, widgets by the million – negotiated, bought, sold and scheduled online. In the 21.2.2000 issue, *Forbes ASAP* forecast, "Net markets eliminate the barrier of geography, create order out of chaos by matching buyers with sellers, and wring time and cost from the process.... Even the most glowing projections may not be bright enough." But while recognising the possibilities of e-marketplaces is easy, actually putting one together that fits your business, your industry, your technology infrastructure and the needs of your extended organisation is a significant undertaking.

INTRODUCING THE E-MARKETPLACE ALLIANCE: IBM, i2 AND ARIBA

"The b2b dream team has been created to bring e-commerce solutions and Internet trading exchanges to market."—*Morgan Stanley*

Now, three of the biggest names in e-business have joined forces to build the most comprehensive, integrated e-marketplaces the world has ever seen. Best-of-breed solutions that combine the innovation, reliability and resources of three companies. i2 brings proven collaborative e-commerce solutions for buying, selling, designing, planning, fulfilment and content management. Ariba provides leading b2b applications, commerce services and dynamic trade for marketplaces. And IBM, perhaps the most trusted name in e-business integration and infrastructure, security and reliability, brings its experience in building mission-critical systems.

IT'S HAPPENING AT AN ASTOUNDING RATE

IDC projects that, this year alone, b2b transactions will account for 78 per cent of the $272 billion in worldwide e-commerce revenue. The Gartner Group forecasts that e-marketplaces will capture $2.7 trillion – or 37 per cent of b2b transactions – by 2004. The word is out: get in the e-marketplace game or find yourself in danger of being cut completely out of your own market.

AN E-MARKETPLACE FOR EVERYONE

There are two key types of e-marketplace. Vertical e-marketplaces are organised around a commodity (like plastics) or an industry (haulage, for example). Horizontal markets typically focus on one buyer offering customers a more efficient procurement system, based on supplier relationships (e.g., financial services). A vertical or horizontal marketplace can also be public or private. Public e-marketplaces are open to many buyers and sellers, while private e-marketplaces are based around a single company's links to trading partners.

EXPERIENCE COUNTS

A successful e-marketplace requires working through the quirks of companies, of technology, and of industries. The dental equipment industry does not work like the electronics industry or the financial services industry.

IBM, i2 and Ariba have more experience than anyone else in this field. We've implemented more than 300 b2b e-marketplaces, across multiple industries, throughout the world, for major clients. The e-marketplace alliance can help you become part of an established marketplace or implement one of your own.

JUST LOOK AT WHAT WE'RE DOING

We're setting up a *Worldwide Retail Exchange* that features more than 30 retailers (including Kmart, Gap Inc., Jusco Japan and Marks & Spencer) whose combined sales total over $500 billion. We're helping to build *e2open.com*, which will let thousands of computer, electronics and telecommunications companies plan, manage and execute supply chain transactions online. And *RubberNetwork.com*, composed of six of the largest companies in the tyre and rubber industry, has just selected the IBM, i2 and Ariba alliance to implement its global purchasing and procurement marketplace.

OPEN MARKETS NEED OPEN PLATFORMS

Industry expertise isn't the only thing we offer. Our strategy is designed around an open platform. That means buyers and suppliers can leverage their existing IT investments to connect with virtually anyone, anywhere.

WHAT CAN WE DO FOR YOU?

The IBM, i2 and Ariba alliance offers proven, scalable solutions that address all these issues and more. We can help you figure out what you need, design a complete end-to-end solution and implement it on a global scale.

You'll find more information on the e-marketplace alliance at www.ibm-i2-ariba.com Or call us at 0870 010 2530.

ibm
i2
ariba

making the sky the best place on earth
AIR FRANCE
www.airfrance.com
L'Espace Affaires.
You can come from far away and arrive fresh.
Member of SKYTEAM

THE WORLD IN 2001

Europe

The single currency: The euro in your pocket 42 / **European Union expansion:** The triumph of nations 42
Germany: Surprises itself 43 / **Shopping in Germany:** Open sesame 46
Brian Beedham: It really is a new world now 47 / **France:** French magic 48 / **Benelux:** Forecast 48
Italy: Modern Italy's old-fashioned ways 49 / **The Nordic countries:** Forecast 50
Spain: Unceasing violence 50 / **Ireland:** Forecast 51
Eastern Europe: A dappled continent 52 / **Russia:** Gloom or boom? 55
Tennis: Russian racketeers 56 / **Turkey:** Forecast 56

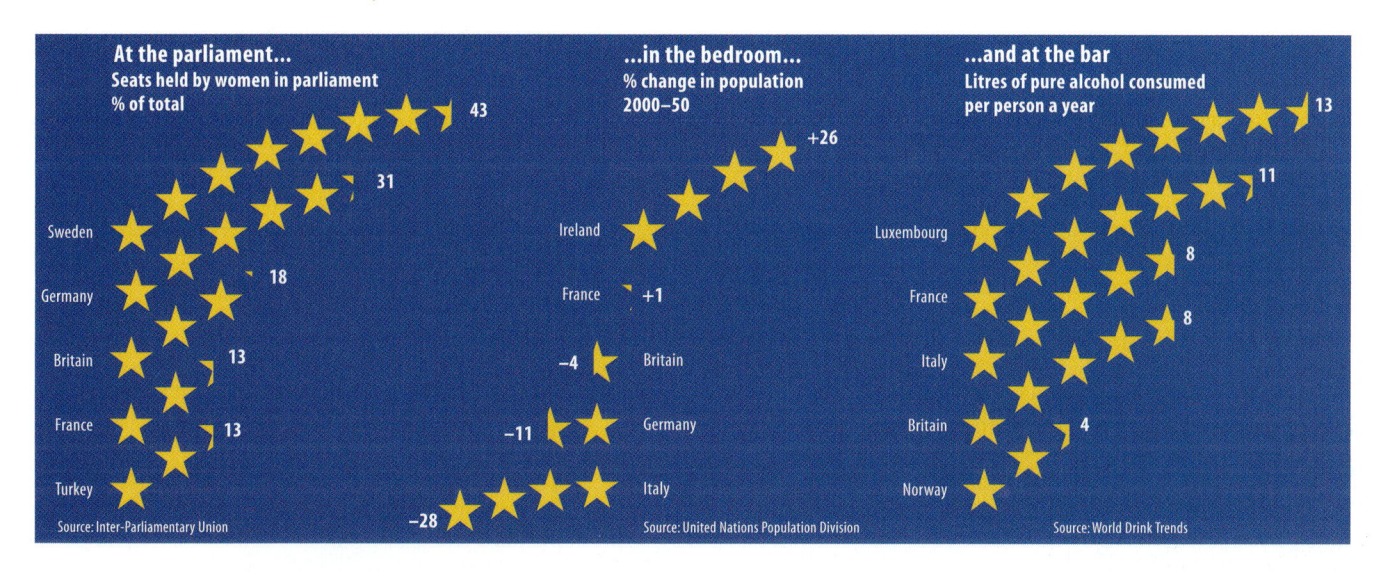

At the parliament...
Seats held by women in parliament, % of total

Sweden 43
Germany 31
Britain 18
France 13
Turkey 13

Source: Inter-Parliamentary Union

...in the bedroom...
% change in population 2000–50

Ireland +26
France +1
Britain −4
Germany −11
Italy −28

Source: United Nations Population Division

...and at the bar
Litres of pure alcohol consumed per person a year

Luxembourg 13
France 11
Italy 8
Britain 8
Norway 4

Source: World Drink Trends

Europe's busy year

Robert Cottrell *Brussels*

And then there were 12. Greece will usher in the new year by joining Europe's monetary union on January 1st, undeterred by the few ups and many downs of the euro in its short life to date. Denmark's rejection of the currency in a national referendum leaves only Sweden and Britain to decide whether they, too, will be joining the monetary union any time soon. Denmark's "no" may lead Sweden to delay the referendum that was once pencilled in for 2001 or 2002. Britain will decide how and when after a general election pencilled in to most diaries for May.

As they ponder the euro question, Swedes will have plenty of chances to study the EU and its workings at close quarters. Their country holds the presidency of the Union for the first half of the year, before handing the job on to Belgium. The biggest task for the Swedish presidency will be to give new momentum to the process of enlarging the Union into Central and Eastern Europe. The Union is deep into detailed negotiations with 12 candidate countries. Most of these are now pressing for firm dates—if not for their accession to the EU, then at least for concluding negotiations. Sweden sympathises with them, and as Union president it will be in a strong position to argue their case. The timing of the next enlargement will be a main item for an EU summit in Gothenburg in June.

Sweden will also be pressing other EU countries to think more about what it calls the "Northern dimension" of the Union's foreign policy. This means, mainly, trying to improve relations with Russia, so that Russia will co-operate more readily with the EU in dealing with regional problems, such as those of the environment and of organised crime.

At an "informal" summit in March, also hosted by the Swedes, EU leaders will review a series of bold measures for liberalising European markets in public utilities and service industries. They agreed on these in principle a year earlier in Portugal. Now they have to implement them. One big aim will be to complete the liberalisation of all the EU's telecommunications markets by the end of 2001. That should mean more competition in the industry, and thus cheaper phone calls.

Another, more distant, goal is to equip the EU with a single air-traffic control system, in place of 15 national ones. The European Commission reckons this move could halve the number of delayed flights. A decision even in 2001, of course, would not become a reality for many years thereafter. European air travel will remain a misery in the year ahead, a reminder of what an uncoordinated place Western Europe was in many other ways before the advent of the EU and its single market.

The year should also bring encouraging news for travellers by road. The European Commission looks set to take a decision that will make cars cheaper almost everywhere, by allowing more international competition among dealers. Until now, manufacturers of cars have been allowed to block the free sale of vehicles across national borders within the EU. They won this exemption from the usual rules of the single market by claiming that cars needed to be tied to local dealers for reasons of after-sales service, and with it safety. But these arguments are widely seen now as a cover for price-fixing. The car mak-

> **2001**
> Switzerland will move a step closer to the EU. Seven bilateral agreements reducing barriers to trade and freeing up access to Swiss labour markets come into effect.

Robert Cottrell: *Financial Times*

41

ers' privilege expires in 2002. The commission will decide in 2001 whether to renew it. Few expect it to do so.

Issues of immigration and asylum will climb up the agenda when Belgium takes over the presidency of the Union at mid-year. Europe's open borders are obliging EU governments to discuss immigration and asylum policy at the Union level. Belgium wants to accelerate the movement towards common policies in these areas, and plans a big conference on the subject in the autumn.

Belgium will also want to boost the role of the "euro group" of finance ministers from the eurozone, the caucus that becomes, with the accession of Greece, the "euro 12". Belgium has a strong position here because, by a quirk of the calendar, it holds the presidency of the euro group for the full year. Sweden would have taken the chair in the first half-year. But it is not a member of the eurozone, so it is disbarred. A bigger role for the euro group means more statements from finance ministers about how well the European economy is doing and, in consequence, how the euro ought to be doing.

The euro group will also be busy hatching schemes for the common regulation of Europe's securities markets. These are becoming more closely integrated, thanks in large part to the stimulus of the common currency. Financial-market regulation could as easily be discussed among all 15 EU countries. But Britain has made clear in advance its opposition to any new common regulator. So pushing the discussion forward in the euro group will offer other countries a convenient way of avoiding any British blockage.

Throughout the year, the EU will maintain its regular output of high-flying rhetoric and grand theological rumination about "the future of Europe". Romano Prodi, president of the commission, promises a white paper on the "governance" of Europe for May, which will try to explain how the various tiers of Union, and national and local government, should rub along with one another.

2001
The Mont Blanc tunnel re-opens. No more detours through Alpine passes for thousands of European drivers between Italy and France.

The biggest talking point of the year will be whether Europe needs a fully fledged constitution: at present it scatters its constitutional law through several long and tedious treaties that nobody reads or understands. President Jacques Chirac of France is in favour of a constitution. Some other leaders agree. The principle appeals to Euro-federalists who want to give more power and legitimacy to the institutions of the Union. It also appeals to some conservatives, such as Mr Chirac, who want to limit explicitly the powers of the Union and to reassert the powers of nation states. That breadth of support makes a constitution an idea whose time will soon have come.

When they meet in December 2001 at a summit to close the Belgian presidency, leaders will be ready for a political agreement on the need for a constitution, and they may fix a roadmap for arriving at it. □

The triumph of nations

Charles Grant

In 2001 the EU's governments will tackle the big, existential question posed by Joschka Fischer, Germany's foreign minister, and France's President Jacques Chirac during the summer of 2000: how can the Union maintain its coherence, effectiveness and democratic legitimacy when it has expanded to around two dozen states? Both those politicians answered their own question by calling for an avant-garde group of EU members to establish a constitution for a highly integrated Europe.

It is easy to be cynical about the pace of the EU's enlargement into Central and Eastern Europe. After all, for the past ten years the likely date of the entry of the first new members has always been "in five years' time". But the process has built up an unstoppable momentum. During 2001 the EU will agree to set a date—perhaps 2005—for the entry of the best-prepared applicants.

That date will focus minds on the need for radical institutional changes in the next round of treaty revision. Britain and France will push for a more "inter-governmental", as opposed to supranational, system of governance. The trend of the past few years has been for the European Council (the regular summits of prime ministers) to give a lead in areas of growing EU involvement, such as defence policy, police co-operation and economic reform.

Tony Blair will argue that this trend offers a means of tackling the "democratic deficit": the voters should see that democratically elected leaders are in charge of the EU. He will propose that the European Council should enhance its role as Europe's visible, strategic authority, setting a direction for the various

Charles Grant: director of the Centre for European Reform

The euro in your pocket

Most people expect to part with large sums of money over the Christmas and New Year holiday season. But in the dozen countries of Europe's monetary union, as 2001 draws to a close, people will be preparing to part with entire currencies. "National monetary units will cease to exist at midnight on December 31st 2001", as the European Commission puts it. On January 1st 2002, brand-new euro banknotes and euro coins will start circulating. National notes and coins will cease to be legal tender soon after. The single currency, which has existed in electronic form since January 1st 1999, will have its physical form too.

For everything to go right, the countries of the monetary union will need to pump 50 billion euro coins and 15 billion euro banknotes into their economies almost literally overnight. They have been printing and coining the stuff since mid-1999, stockpiling it in secret vaults. National central banks, acting on behalf of the European Central Bank, will make the first advance deliveries of notes and coins to high-street banks in September 2001. High-street banks will pass the notes and coins on to shops and other commercial customers between September and December. Individuals will be able to buy small advance quantities of euro coins from mid-December.

The stage will then be set for what the European Central Bank hopes will be a smooth handover at midnight—and what many retailers fear will be utter chaos by morning. □

institutions to follow.

This chimes with the Gaullist tradition that has favoured a "Europe of nation states". The smaller countries, together with Germany and Italy, have in the past opposed this model. They have wanted a stronger commission and European Parliament. The smaller countries, in particular, have seen the commission as their protector against the bossy bigger countries.

In the coming years, however, the British-French approach to institutions is likely to gather support. One reason is that Germany is becoming less *communautaire*. The Länder are fearful of their powers ebbing to Brussels. Gerhard Schröder is no fan of the commission. And even the EU-friendly Mr Fischer has refrained from defending the commission and the parliament. The second reason is that the commission has still not recovered from the forced resignation of the entire college of commissioners in April 1999. Romano Prodi became president in September 1999, faced with the hugely difficult task of restoring the commission's standing. By the end of 2000 he had failed to do so. The commission now lacks the credibility or self-confidence to demand a larger role in the EU's institutional structures. The third reason for the decline of the *communautaire* case is the widespread acknowledgment that the EU's greatest challenges are now external. The single market and the single currency have been built. But the Common Foreign and Security Policy (CFSP) is embryonic. And if Europe is to integrate in such a sovereignty-sensitive area, it will happen on an inter-governmental basis or not at all.

So there will be a consensus among the governments that the European Council, rather than the commission, should set the EU's agenda. And also—against the wishes of the European Parliament—that national parliaments should play a role in EU decision-making. There will be agreement that a European Senate, consisting of national parliamentarians, should act as an upper chamber.

There will also be a discussion on how to reform the rotating presidency. At present, members take it in turns to manage the EU for six-month periods. This discontinuity maddens the EU's partners and is a highly inefficient method of running business. One proposal is for high-profile individuals, such as Javier Solana (currently "Mr CFSP") to represent the EU to the world and chair meetings of ministers. Another would have each Council of Ministers elect one minister as president. A third proposal would group two small members and one large one into "team" presidencies for two-year periods.

The scheme of Mr Fischer and Mr Chirac for a European constitution—in which a sub-group of the member-states would agree on a legal document that defined who does what at the European and national levels—is unlikely to work. However, there could be support for a non-binding, political declaration, specifying which policies should be handled at which level. The point would be to reassure voters that the EU is not going to grab ever more powers from member-states. □

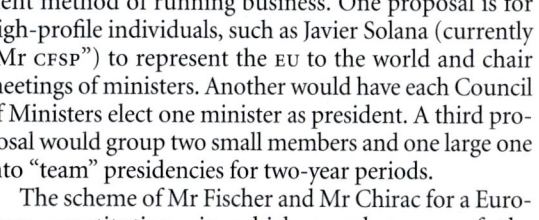

> **2001**
> The Berlin Jewish museum will open in September. Its metal zig-zag architecture provides a telling memorial.

Germany surprises itself

Barbara Beck

Who says the Germans are set in their comfortable ways? The coming year will see profound changes in the way Europe's largest economy is run, and all of them will be for the good. Last summer the Social Democrat chancellor, Gerhard Schröder, manipulated a reluctant Bundesrat (the upper house of parliament, where his government lacks a majority) into supporting a tax-reform package that many consider the most radical in Germany's post-war history. The tax changes are designed to make the German economy more flexible and more competitive. Over the next five years, they should lop around DM56 billion ($25 billion) from German tax bills, and in 2001 alone they are expected to lift GDP by nearly half a percentage point. The top rate of corporate tax will be cut from 40% to 25% at the start of 2001, though with local taxes and other levies on top companies will still be paying up to 39%. Germany's confiscatory top rate of income tax, which had already been trimmed from 53% to 51% in 1999, is due to come down further in stages, to 42% over the next five years.

For German big business, however, perhaps the most important change will be the abolition of capital-gains tax on the sale of company cross-holdings, currently levied at 50%. This will not be implemented until the start of 2002, but big companies are already trying to find ways—for example, using derivatives—to start unwinding their holdings earlier. The value of these cross-shareholdings is huge, probably well above $200

Barbara Beck: surveys editor, *The Economist*

PUBLICIS

However far you're going, teamwork makes the difference. As a client of UBS, you know that you can rely on an integrated network of financial specialists working around the clock, around the world. A partnership that offers private banking, investment banking, asset management and private equity. A small step for you, a giant leap for your finances. The Power of Partnership.

Visit us at www.ubs.com

Success is more than ego and publicity.

UBS

Financial Services Group

Europe THE WORLD IN 2001

Life's pleasures come to Schröder

billion. In recent years they have become less of an asset and more of a liability, but the capital-gains tax discouraged companies from unwinding them. The reform is expected to trigger wholesale restructuring and a move towards a more Anglo-Saxon system of corporate governance. It will give Germany an economic edge.

In scoring this victory, Mr Schröder established himself as a consummate political wheeler and dealer. The same qualities now seem likely to help him achieve another important reform, that of pensions, which eluded his Christian Democrat predecessor, Helmut Kohl. This reform is urgently needed because the rapidly ageing German population relies primarily on the state to provide generous retirement pensions. These are funded on a pay-as-you-go basis, so as dwindling numbers of workers have to maintain growing numbers of pensioners, either pension contributions will have to go up to unacceptable levels, or pensions will have to be cut. To avoid this unpalatable choice, Mr Schröder's labour minister, Walter Riester, is proposing to strengthen Germany's declining private-pensions sector by giving employees the option of putting up to 4% of their gross incomes tax-free into a private pension scheme. The proposal would have the further advantage of giving Germany's financial markets a welcome boost. If Mr Schröder can pull it off, mid-way between federal elections, he will begin to look hard to beat.

Regional elections are due in March 2001, when voters in two large states, Baden-Württemberg and Rhineland-Palatinate, will go to the polls. The first is a rock-solid Christian Democrat stronghold, but in the second the Social Democrats have a slender lead over their rivals, so the outcome there will be seen as a pointer for the federal election in the autumn of 2002. For now, Mr Schröder seems to be gaining ground.

He has also presided over a German economy that has been doing increasingly well. Year-on-year GDP growth in 1999 was only 1.5%, but the figure for 2000 is estimated to be nearly double that, and 2001 should carry on at much the same level. Much of the buoyancy in the economy has come from increased trade, helped by the weak euro. That has been good news for exporters, but the German public, reluctant to lose its beloved D-mark, is now even less enthusiastic about the introduction of euro notes and coins due at the start of 2002. Still, inflation looks set to remain low, at around 1.5% in 2001, and stronger growth is beginning to show up in lower unemployment figures. For Germany as a whole, the proportion of people out of work dipped below 10% in 2000 for the first time in many years, and looks set to drop below 9% in 2001—just in time to put voters in a good mood for the federal election the following year.

As he enters the final straight for the national race, Mr Schröder can take comfort from German voters' well-documented preference for continuity. In the entire history of the Federal Republic, through 14 elections, they have only ever booted out one incumbent chancellor: the Christian Democrat Kurt Georg Kiesinger in 1969. □

Open sesame

For German shopaholics, 2001 might just bring some welcome relief after decades of deprivation. Germany's archaic shop-opening hours will move a little closer to what consumers want. It seems remarkable that in Europe's biggest market shoppers' wishes should have been ignored for so long. The problem is not a lack of shopping facilities: in food retailing, for instance, selling space per head of population in Germany is around twice the figure in France or Britain. It is just that the opening hours seem designed to suit the shops, not the customers. Until fairly recently, a law dating from 1956 compelled all shops to close punctually at 6.30pm during the week and 2pm on Saturdays, just when working people might think of popping into their local supermarket. A cautious reform in 1996 allowed shops to stay open till 8pm (though not many do), and until 4pm on Saturdays. If the latest liberalisation goes through, people will be able to indulge their shopping urges until 10pm during the week and 8pm on Saturdays. Some German states may leave it to local authorities to draw up their own rules.

In the past, attempts at comprehensive reform have been foiled by an unlikely alliance between the trade unions, keen to protect their members from exploitation, and the churches, anxious to keep Sundays and religious holidays as days of rest and contemplation. But a change in attitudes is being spearheaded by Germany's once-communist east, which attaches less importance to religious observance, and where high unemployment has made employees far more flexible. Shops and department stores there have been experimenting with creative solutions of sometimes doubtful legality, such as labelling all merchandise as "tourist souvenirs", which by law can be sold outside conventional hours. And in stations and airports, where shops are allowed to stay open to provide for travellers' needs, new shopping centres now stand ready to sell almost anything.

However, most Germans prefer their rules cut-and-dried. Polls suggest that nearly half the population wants to see an end to all restrictions from Monday to Saturday. That day may be coming closer. Nearly half also say they would like to see the ban on Sunday trading relaxed, yet not even the boldest reformers are proposing to throw Sundays wide open to Mammon. □

THE WORLD IN 2001 Europe

Expect the world's balance of danger to shift radically, says **Brian Beedham**, associate editor of *The Economist*

It really is a new world now

"The tally of separate countries—around 190 now—could be heading for the 300s before long"

For more than ten years, the world's politicians have been happily agreeing that the cold war is over; and yet they go on acting as if it were still icily with us. In 2001, they may at last have to face up to some of the ways in which the world has been radically changed by the collapse of communism after 1989.

Realisation number one has to be that the relationship between Russia and the West no longer holds the centre of the stage. The ideological war between communism and free-market democracy has ended, and with it has gone the idea that they are the rival models between which the rest of the world has to choose. New powers are beginning to emerge—above all China, to Russia's east—and so are new areas of potential conflict involving some of these new powers, such as the energy-rich, politically primitive deserts and mountains of central Asia.

After 1989, the struggle between Russia and the West has passed into history, as the struggle between France and Britain did after 1815. There will be moments when the old adversaries have minor spats, as post-Waterloo Britain and France occasionally did. But they will more often prefer to help each other, as Britain and France increasingly worked together against the rise of that new power to France's east, Germany.

This could be put to the test quite early in the new year, if America decides to push ahead with its attempt to build an anti-missile shield. The Russians will not like this, because it is yet another reminder of their post-cold-war weakness. But it presents no real danger to them, because in this new world—unless they improbably try to reassert their control over Eastern Europe—there are not going to be many arguments between Russia and the West, and certainly none fierce enough to lead to a nuclear confrontation.

The proposed anti-missile shield, if it can be made to work, is designed to protect the Atlantic democracies against some future Saddam Hussein, and perhaps against a mid-century Chinese superpower. The Russians have no more real cause to worry about it than France had about some impressive 19th-century British advance in naval technology. It is a pity that Russia's politicians (and some of Europe's) have been so slow to grasp this. Now is their chance to do so.

The second great change brought about by the melting of the cold war's ice will be the break-up of some of the countries which that ice unnaturally held together. The cold war was beginning just when the empires assembled by the European powers in the 18th and 19th centuries were coming to their end. Many of the new countries that emerged from those ex-empires were an implausible mixture of different races, languages and religions. If they stayed intact for so long, it was partly because either the Soviet Union or the Atlantic alliance wanted the support of their governments, and was willing to let those governments use rough methods to keep their countries in one piece. Now that the helpful external hand has gone, some of them will not stay in one piece.

One post-imperial amalgam that may start to come apart in the next year or so is Indonesia. A country of 17,000 islands and 210m assorted people spread over an area nearly as big as the United States, Indonesia under half-blind President Abdurrahman Wahid is now in the second faltering year of its first more or less democratic government. Its eastern and western extremities are claimed by breakaway rebels; a religious civil war bloodies its northern Molucca islands; its new president has no sure grip over the country's parliament, its army or the corruption he inherited from the Suharto dictatorship. Indonesia is heading to where the Soviet Union and Yugoslavia have already gone.

There are other places where the cracking noise can be heard: Sri Lanka, the Philippines, bits of the Arab world, maybe Malaysia, conceivably Pakistan, certainly whole swathes of Africa. The global tally of separate countries—74 in 1946, around 190 now—could be heading for the 300s before the new century is very old.

And the third great change? It has already begun. Because the two big alliances did not want fingers poked in the ribs of their local friends, the cold war also artificially prolonged the old definition of "sovereignty", which said that what went on inside a country's borders, no matter how dictatorially brutal, was nobody else's business.

This studied inattention could not long survive the cold war's end. As television and the Internet reveal to the world what a dictator is doing to his own people, outsiders are likely to say that he should be stopped from doing it; and technology has given the outsiders the means, economic and military, of trying to stop him.

The Kosovo war of 1999 told Serbia's Slobodan Milosevic that he could not go on suppressing the Kosovars, a separate people from the Serbs. The Serbs' overthrow of Mr Milosevic last October was also helped by outsiders. This time they did not have to use force. But NATO's bombing of Serbia in the Kosovo war had already undermined Mr Milosevic. Now Europe and America, by telling him that he could not ignore his election defeat, strengthened the anti-Milosevic majority's determination to defy him. The outsiders were saying that what happened in Serbia was their business too.

There are of course dangers in this redefinition of sovereignty; the rules of legitimate intervention have still to be clearly spelled out in a way that ordinary people everywhere can understand and support. But the dangers are smaller than the possible outcome—the end of dictatorial immunity, the worldwide elimination of the old baronial principle. How much things will be changed, in so many ways, by what happened in 1989 is at last becoming plain. □

Watch your back, Jacques

French magic

Jean Daniel — Paris

As with all democracies, the future of France will be determined by its electoral calendar. The country's army of politicians is preparing for municipal elections in March. Then comes the all-important presidential election in 2002, in which the conservative incumbent, Jacques Chirac, will seek a five-year term, challenged by the leftist prime minister, Lionel Jospin. And then, in 2004, there is the European parliamentary election, the first to be held after the arrival of the euro in the pockets of the French.

In all this, the country's politicians will seek one thing above all: to be popular. And who can blame them? One cannot claim that popular consensus is a sign of democracy and then criticise politicians who make popularity a political priority. So the French centre will win the day, pushing to the margins both the old intellectual lags who cling to notions of socialism and the thoroughly discredited far-right, epitomised in recent years by the crass leadership of Jean-Marie Le Pen.

But the French man in the street who will epitomise the centre—and who is more like his European neighbours in behaviour and attitude than he might like to think—is profoundly bored of politics. At a recent referendum to reduce the presidential term from a too-long seven years, 70% of the voting public could not be bothered to vote. In France, where politicians take themselves and their role seriously, this constituted an affront to every part of the political spectrum.

Nonetheless, the referendum passed and it will change the future political landscape. It will shorten the length of time that individuals stay at the top of French politics: François Mitterrand was president for 14 years; Mr Chirac first held high political office over a quarter of a century ago. And it will soon bring to an end the very French and highly problematic system of cohabitation, under which a president and a prime minister of different parties occupy the highest positions of state with different, but equally valid, electoral mandates.

The French public is blissfully indifferent to much of this for one reason: the country is flourishing. Look to this continuing in 2001. The *carré magique*—the magic square of the French economy—is robust: production is growing, unemployment is declining, prices are stable and exports exceed imports. It is rare to find success on all four economic fronts simultaneously. Big industry foresees 12% growth in investment in 2001 and 2002. Demand has never been as strong nor consumer spending as buoyant. To top it all off, with the rising tax revenues that stronger growth brings, the government will be able to reduce its deficit to FFr106 billion ($14 billion), some 1% of GDP.

So where does the problem lie for the future? It lies in the euro. The creation of a single currency was revolutionary. But it was also a way of postponing decisions on shared political institutions. France bided its time by as-

Jean Daniel: editor, *Le Nouvel Observateur*

BENELUX

FORECAST

The Netherlands will be among the best countries in which to do business over the next five years. Wim Wok's ruling "purple" coalition is popular, the labour market flexible and the banks efficient. Solid consumption and investment have driven economic growth above 4% in 2000. This will continue as one of the most intelligently organised countries flourishes.

Official unemployment will be only 2% but this hides a secret army of potential workers. The Netherlands' participation rate (the share of people working or looking for work) is well below that of many other European countries. More Dutch people will soon be in work. A comprehensive tax reform in 2001, and initiatives to tap this pool of labour, will help restrain wage demands, and keep inflation down. Expect a shift from direct to indirect taxation. The government will win a general election in 2002.

Belgium will be strutting the international stage in 2001, enjoying a moment in the limelight. It will enjoy a year-long presidency of the "euro group" of finance ministers from the 12 eurozone countries. Hand in hand with France, the prime minister, Guy Verhofstadt, will seek to empower the group. Success will mean more of a two-tier Europe as euro-members pull together.

Influence will also be boosted by Belgium's six-month presidency of the EU starting in July. Mr Verhofstadt will want to put poverty reduction and unemployment on the agenda. He would like to see the percentage of Europeans living below the poverty line fall from its current 18% to 10% by 2010.

Back at home, economic growth will slow, after a burst of 4.1% in 2000, to 2.6%. Unemployment will drop too, but only to 10.6%. While their prime minister leads Europe, some Belgian firms will be suffering Brussels' wrath. Interbrew and Alken Maes will be defending themselves from EU accusations that they operated an illegal cartel in the beer industry.

Mr Verhofstadt himself will be busy promoting competition in one of Europe's most over-governed countries. He will be overseeing privatisations: 2001 will see sales in the telecommunications sector as well as, perhaps, in railways. Ten million Belgians will be more interested in reform of the police and judicial system, after a series of scandals.

While these have caused much national shame and soul-searching, one great source of pride in 2001 will be the royals. Watch out for the glamorous Crown Prince Philippe and his new wife Princess Mathilde on the front cover of your Sunday newspaper supplement. □

GDP GROWTH (%)	1999	2000	2001
Belgium	2.5	4.1	2.6
The Netherlands	3.6	4.3	4.0
Luxembourg	7.5	5.7	4.9

EIU COUNTRY ANALYSIS AND FORECASTING

serting that economic and political institutions operate on a different logic. This is not the case: the euro's dependence on the dollar clearly indicates that competition between America and Europe presupposes political control of the currency. It is with political decisions that France will attract investment, reduce social charges, increase citizen participation and motivate profit-sharing schemes for employees.

The coming years will be decisive and, with the debate on federalism growing ever more fierce, France is at the heart of these difficulties; at the heart, but perhaps also at the head of those who wish to triumph. Although in Britain no major politician or newspaper wishes even to address the future problems of Europe—and few would carry much influence in any event—in France these matters are taken seriously. French proposals for the future management of the euro and the EU may not always be right; they may not be accepted. But at least they are made—and, by being made, set the agenda.

How can we maintain the famous *exception française* which so irritates foreigners, above all the Anglo-Saxons? Although the phrase will keep its potency, the words that underpin it are changing. Arrogant words like *la grandeur* have been exchanged for more modest ones such as *l'ambition*. France still wants to protect itself from rapid Americanisation in the food, fashion, film and television industries. But this should be seen not as a quixotic war to retain the past but as an opportunity to renew creativity. France's sporting triumphs have helped integrate the immigrant populations and led to a new national pride. Paris is close to becoming as alive and happening as London two years ago or Madrid ten years ago.

In foreign politics an equilibrium is being sought between France's role as a medium-sized power on the international stage and its wish for independence. From time to time, France favours the Russians, Chinese and even the Iraqis against America and Britain. But this flirtation is without great consequence. No one is more openly *occidental* and more secretly *atlantique* than the French. Do not expect to see this change. □

Modern Italy's old-fashioned ways

Beppe Severgnini *Rome*

Italy is going to be a lively place in 2001. The first four months of the year will be dominated by the general election campaign, which will be a very Italian contest between the rich and the handsome. Opinion polls say that Silvio Berlusconi, 64, media-to-football tycoon, will return to Palazzo Chigi, the prime minister's office in Rome, where he had been briefly in 1994. His opponent will be Francesco Rutelli, mayor of Rome since 1993, a tall 46-year-old with a broad smile and easy manners. The rowdy centre-left coalition picked him after dumping prime minister Giuliano Amato, hoping that Mr Rutelli's youthful charm and television skills will be easier to sell than the accomplishments of five years and four governments.

From January to April, Italians will talk a lot. But not much will happen. No major legislation will be passed; no foreign-policy initiative is likely to get under way. Expect last-minute attempts by the left to regulate Mr Berlusconi's many conflicts of interest; and there may be proposals from Mr Berlusconi for a new electoral law. No one will succeed. Italy will go to the polls with a candidate who owns half the country's television (while the left has a discreet hold on the other half). It will still keep the unhappy electoral law that allows political parties to join forces in order to win first-past-the-post contests—only to be at each other's throats the day after the election.

The excitement will come in the spring. Italy's much-needed reforms cannot be delayed any further—and it is likely that the new government will try its hand at some of them. A winning right will start with devolution, something the Northern League (once again allied to Mr Berlusconi) sees as a priority; it will push for tax and employment reform. A winning left may also try something bold in the labour market. In the past four years, 90% of

Berlusconi crosses his heart and hopes to die

new jobs have been part-time or temporary; and with youth unemployment at more than 50% in the south, it is no use pretending that old-style, full-time, trade-union jobs will materialise. A review of Italy's over-generous pensions is also due for 2001, and the country's professional guilds (and resulting closed shops) are supposed to be tamed as well. No one will dare to touch these issues before polling day. But after the election, someone might (and ought to).

Italy's rebound, though, will not come from above. Civic society and the business world, once they have come to terms with their new political masters, are going to take the lead, as usual. Italy's problems—red tape, ferocious lobbies, lack of infrastructure—are not going to go away. But Italy's talents—resourcefulness, creativity

Beppe Severgnini: columnist for *Corriere della Sera* and Italy correspondent for *The Economist*. His latest book is "Manuale dell'imperfetto viaggiatore" (Rizzoli)

Europe THE WORLD IN 2001

THE NORDIC COUNTRIES

FORECAST

The four Nordic countries—Denmark, Finland, Norway and Sweden—all have flourishing economies and rising prosperity. Yet in their different ways they are all perplexed about a common issue: their respective relationship with Europe. The Danish referendum in September 2000, in which voters narrowly rejected membership of the single currency, ensured that the soul-searching will go on there. (But remember: it took them two votes to accept the 1992 Maastricht treaty.)

Sweden will assume the EU presidency in the first half of 2001, its first stint in the job since joining the EU in 1995. The Swedish government will push for greater transparency of EU institutions and decision-making, issues close to the heart of Swedish voters. A successful presidency could then boost the government's campaign for euro membership.

Euro membership is not on the Norwegian agenda. But the 2001 general election, due in September, will put the issue back on the map. The governing, pro-European Labour Party, which is expected to stay in office, is likely to push for a third referendum on EU membership in the next parliament. But its leader, Jense Stoltenberg, will be criticised by Carl Hagen, leader of the populist Progress Party, to spend some of Norway's enormous budget surplus. This will stand at 10% of GDP, a result of North Sea oil revenues. Responsible Mr Stoltenberg worries that spending too much will trigger inflation. Norway is one of the few countries to have handled its oil wealth well.

In or out of the euro, the Nordic economies will all experience falling unemployment and solid growth, boosted by strong exports to the euro area and also by confident consumers at home. In Finland and Sweden, the dynamic IT and electronics sector will make a big contribution to the economy. Finland's Nokia accounts for nearly 4% of the country's GDP. The oil and gas industry will remain the driving force of the economy in Norway. These are all highly international industries that will draw the Nordic countries ever closer to the heart of Europe in 2001. □

GDP GROWTH (%)	1999	2000	2001
Denmark	1.7	2.6	2.4
Finland	3.5	5.2	4.3
Iceland	4.5	4.1	2.5
Norway	0.9	2.7	2.2
Sweden	3.8	4.3	3.9

EIU COUNTRY ANALYSIS AND FORECASTING

---

and a certain laid-back attitude—are well suited for the new economy. "*Piccolo è bello*" ("small is beautiful"), the rallying cry of Italy's entrepreneurs, will allow more and more young people to start their own Internet-based businesses.

A question mark hangs also over e-commerce. Italians have no tradition of mail order, distrust credit cards, love cash and adore the social side of shopping in *vie* and *piazze*. If you add slow deliveries, you can see what Internet shopping is up against. Business-to-business, on the other hand, looks set to grow and is expected to reach $50 billion in 2003.

Overall economic growth will stay above 3%, while unemployment (currently at 11%) is likely to decline slowly, unless some major legislation affects the labour market. Foreign direct investment may not pick up for some time (currently it creates less than 10% of GDP; in the United Kingdom, with a similar GDP per head, it produces 27%). The reason? A maze of administrative regulations and a cumbersome legal system frighten off investors. But Italian goods will remain popular. The Milan stock exchange, which last year extended its normal hours to satisfy online traders, will move in step with its European counterparts. More companies will be floated, expanding choice for millions of small investors.

This will affect corporate Italy. Many patriarchs will leave; new figures will emerge. Some will be the children or grandchildren of the founders (you will hear more about young Berlusconis and Benettons). Others are executives with American MBAs and stints as management consultants under their belts. Several will leave their well-paid jobs, cash in their stock options and do their own thing. New companies (such as Tiscali and e.Biscom) are going to expand, at home and abroad, while big players such as Enel, Eni and Telecom Italia will use the wealth generated by their monopolies (on electricity, oil-and-gas and telephones) to launch into new ventures. A new television group is going to emerge. Telemontecarlo (a recent acquisition by Telecom-Seat), will start eroding the duopoly of Rai (public television, which sooner or later will privatise two channels) and Mr Berlusconi's Mediaset.

But old habits will die hard. Expect Italy's top businessmen to put too much faith in their political mentors, and to resist reform. State-owned companies worth 300,000 trillion lire ($135 billion) must still be privatised; others have been partly privatised, but the state still has control. Silvio Berlusconi's likely return to power will complicate things further (imagine what will happen when television frequencies and telecommunications licences are handed out). And Italy's *nuova economia* will still be based on commercial ventures more than research and innovation. Therefore, expect Italy's brain-drain to continue, with people moving to the United States and Northern Europe.

What about Italy's legendary *sommerso* (the hidden world), which accounts for 27% of the economy, according to Confindustria, the industrialists' association? Well, in 2001, as always, tax authorities will chase tax-evaders, who will claim they must dodge taxes in order to stay in business. The demands of the fiscal system are indeed excessive, and regulations are suffocating. If people don't pay their taxes, though, the rules won't change; but if the rules don't change, people won't pay their taxes. It is a vicious circle that would have delighted Pirandello. But it is not worthy of a modern country. □

2001
The leaning Tower of Pisa, saved from collapse, will stand tall for at least another 350 years. Visitors can try it from June.

Juan Luis Cebrián: founder and publisher of *El País*

Unceasing violence

Juan Luis Cebrián — *Madrid*

During the 19th century, Spain was all the rage among English intellectuals, many of whom wrote chronicles of their journeys in the country, influenced to the point of ecstasy by "Tales of the Alhambra", by Washington Irving. They sought to discover the mystery of a land that maintained an overseas empire of considerable scale while succumbing, at the same time, to the legacy of a seven-century-long war with Islam. For millions of present-day travellers, the mystery of Spain still involves violence. Tragically, 2001 will be another year soured by tension in Euskadi, the Basque homeland.

Violence by ETA, the Basque separatist group will mask a brilliant economic performance. The good news for the prime minister, José María Aznar, is that Spain's economy will grow at 3.5% in 2001, just above the EU average. The budget deficit could be eradicated. The bad news is that inflation will grow by more than expected. As with every country in Europe, high oil prices will create big problems for Spain. The important energy, telecommunications and pharmaceuticals industries will be liberalised. And though the merger of two electricity companies, Endesa and Iberdrola, will temporarily give them control of 84% of Spain's electricity, full competition even in this sector will arrive in 2003. The government will retain approval powers over any mergers that affect more than 25% of a market. Alongside the rest of Europe, Spain has already brought down taxes. Corporate income and capital-gains taxes will fall. Tax credits will also be granted for research and development.

¡Basta ya!

National attention will be focused on the ETA problem. Mr Aznar shows signs that he has a strategy but many people doubt that it is the correct one. The terrorist group multiplied its attacks and assassinations throughout 2000. Although there have been periods of greater terrorist activity, especially during the late 1970s, there has never been such visible confrontation among the Basques themselves.

The existence of political autonomy in the region has done nothing to stop the violence. Basques are divided equally by their sympathy and antipathy to the idea of independence. This is due in good measure to the turnaround of the Basque National Party (PNV), a conservative group with Christian Democrat roots and moderate leanings, which has been governing the region almost continuously since the inception of democracy. The PNV has dealt dangerously with representatives of ETA. Indeed, it has gone as far as signing political agreements with the terrorists.

These undermined their loyalty to the Spanish Constitution and to the Autonomous Statute by which Euskadi has been ruled for two decades. Mr Aznar has now cut all ties with his former PNV allies—at the time he needed them to form a majority in the Madrid parliament—and will seek to undermine them further in their own homeland. He hopes that 2001 will afford him the opportunity of ousting the PNV leader, Xabier Arzalluz,

Hands up if you want it to stop

from the Basque regional government. The strategy has been one of head-on confrontation between the political leaders of Spain and the Basque region. The conflict has been exacerbated by street riots and political disputes. If Mr Aznar's People's Party wins in the next Basque elections (it came close last time), then he would gain some influence. But even if he were successful, the Basque issue would not go away.

Politicians, journalists, judges, businessmen, soldiers and policemen have all suffered the effects of the violence, and a wave of pessimism has begun to take hold. The national mood in Spain is grim. The real problem is that there is no plausible solution—either political or military—in sight. Ulster has some hope in the year ahead, and a political plan to go with it; the Basque country has none. Almost half a century after making its appearance (having been as active during the present democracy as in the former dictatorship) ETA will continue to darken the horizon of Spain's political and cultural life throughout 2001. □

2001
Spain will turn back over 1m illegal immigrants from North Africa. But Western Europe, including Spain, needs more foreign workers—75m of them over the next 50 years. Not parasitic but symbiotic.

IRELAND

FORECAST

Every year since 1995, Ireland's economy has grown at near double-digit rates. How long can this extraordinary boom last? Many international analysts expect a hard landing in 2001. As inflation soars, credit growth rockets and property prices reach the stratosphere, they say a bust cannot be far off. But the Irish, convinced their luck will hold as they live it up like never before, dismiss these foreign concerns. They have good reason to remain optimistic.

After a decade of falling unit labour costs the economy is hyper-competitive. As a result, high wage inflation will not seriously threaten competitiveness in 2001. Credit expansion, though strong by international standards, is slowing. Moreover, private-sector indebtedness is still well below levels in other rich countries. What about those stratospheric property prices? The commercial property market, in particular, is a cause for concern, but not—yet—a recipe for disaster. Irish eyes should keep smiling in 2001.

As the economy avoids a crash, the centre-right coalition government of Fianna Fail and the Progressive Democrats will struggle to stay aloft. Buffeted by the revelations of sleaze which are emerging from two judicial investigations into corruption, the minority government, which spent much of 2000 hanging on by its finger nails, is unlikely to last the year. With both of the investigating judges due to report by mid-2001, the government will not survive if the conclusions are half as damning as many expect them to be. Such is the ongoing rate of revelation that the crisis may well come to a head even sooner.

The most likely winners in any early election will be the two big opposition parties, Fine Gael and the Labour Party, though this combination will probably need the support of independent parliamentarians to govern. But with near total agreement across the political spectrum on the big issues, there will be little change in policy. □

KEY INDICATORS	1999	2000	2001
GDP growth (%)	9.8	9.4	7.1
Inflation (%)	1.6	5.4	3.8
3-month money market rate (%)	4.7	5.6	5.1
Current account (% of GDP)	0.3	-0.1	-0.2

EIU COUNTRY ANALYSIS AND FORECASTING

Europe THE WORLD IN 2001

A dappled continent

Jonathan Ledgard *Prague*

Europe will come to the uncomfortable realisation in 2001 that its former communist countries have developed into two distinct regions: Central Europe, consisting of Poland, Hungary, Slovakia, the Czech Republic and Slovenia, give or take Croatia and the Baltics, and Eastern Europe, itself an unsatisfactory term for the rag-tag band of little or no hopers to the south and east. Central Europe will become more prosperous in 2001; Central Europeans will buy new, locally built cars, and drive them on new roads from new industrial estates to new hypermarkets, with, perhaps, a pitstop at a new McDonald's along the way. Eastern Europe will attract more foreign investment but remain poor and worryingly distant from the European Union enlargement process.

Poland will dominate Central Europe in 2001, although domestic uncertainties will damage market confidence and weaken its currency, the zloty. Even so, the Polish economy will grow at a perky 5% or so. Polish hopes of joining the EU any time before 2004 will stumble over the vexing question of agricultural subsidies for Polish farmers. The minority government of Jerzy Buzek, which tottered along for much of 2000, will finally collapse when it has to present its budget in the spring. Leszek Miller's reformed Communists should win the resulting early election, probably in April or May. That need not be a cause for concern; Mr Miller's economic and foreign policy decisions will be as circumscribed by market considerations and an eagerness to please the EU as were his predecessors'. Ordinary Poles' proclivity to spend far more than they can afford on flashy gear, however, could lead to a spate of personal bankruptcies. That same desire for the new and fashionable should, at the same time, keep Poland the most culturally inventive and stimulating of former communist countries.

The rest of Central Europe, all former chums in Austria-Hungary, will make fair speed in their bid to join the EU. The Czech Republic, self-confident from hosting IMF/World Bank bankers and containing their attendant anarchist rowdies, will regain its position toward the front of the pack of EU hopefuls. The Czech economy should grow by over 4%, after three years in recession. New tax incentives, a central location in Europe and low labour costs will bring in over $6 billion of foreign direct investment; the highest per head in the region. The Czech government will not, yet, learn how to be dynamic, but it will remain stable. Slovakia's fractious coalition government will also survive, if only because the reforms it has undertaken have made it so unpopular it dare not risk an election. Slovakia's grossly mismanaged state industrial concerns will be restructured; Slovak banks will be better run. Even so, Slovakia will remain the weakest of Central European countries and is unlikely to make the first group of EU entrants.

Hungary will be the steady star in the Central European firmament. Budapest will dominate Hungary, to the disadvantage of its provincial towns. Economic growth will slow slightly to around 4%. The economy will be hit by the weak euro, damaging exports, and the high price of oil. The coalition should keep its populist tendencies in check; if it does not, the central bank will impose tighter monetary policies. Slovenia, Hungary's next-door neighbour, will have an even better year, despite its squabbling and surprisingly mediocre politicians. A former prime minister, Janez Drnovsek, should be back at the helm. Despite the potential for political feuds, legislation related to the EU will be fast-tracked through the parliament. Already the richest of Central European countries, Slovenia will profit from overdue privatisation of state monopolies. On environmental issues, the Alpine statelet will be a model for other former communist countries.

A new border, named the Belgian curtain for the country which hosts the EU, will follow a line from the Baltic to the Black Sea. It will be imposed, this time, from the West. Central European countries, together with Romania and Bulgaria, will impose visas on the citizens of Ukraine, Belarus and Moldova. Those three East European countries will have a risible year, although Belarus may get rid of its authoritarian regime. Not one will push through reforms necessary to begin mending their pathetically broken and corrupt economies. If a drought persists, some rural areas will suffer famine. The brightest and best on the wrong side of the Belgian curtain will smuggle themselves westwards in ever larger numbers.

Romania is on the right side of the Belgian curtain, just about, but 2001 will be a testing year. A disciplined Romania would have great potential, but then discipline has never been a Romanian strong point. A return of the populist Ion Illiescu for another stint in the presidency, and suc-

---

2001
Georgia sees its future with Europe. Problem: it is still partially occupied by Russian troops. Two bases will close in 2001. Presidents Shevardnadze and Putin will argue about the two.

Jonathan Ledgard: Central and Eastern Europe correspondent, *The Economist*

The long haul to prosperity

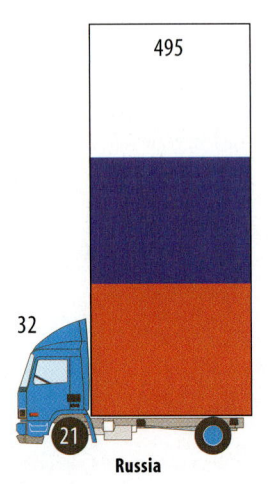

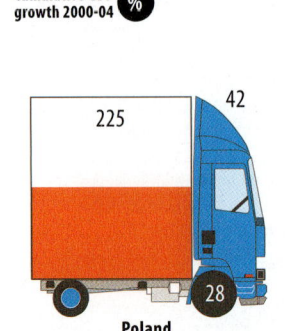

Total exports 2000-04, $bn
Foreign investment 2000-04, $bn
Cumulative GDP growth 2000-04, %

Russia: 495 / 32 / 21
Poland: 225 / 42 / 28
Czech Republic: 222 / 25 / 20
Hungary: 206 / 9 / 24

Total EU imports from Central and Eastern Europe in 2001 €35bn

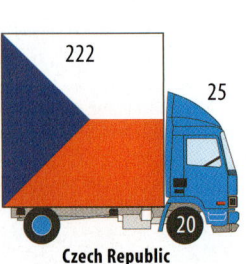

Source: EIU

NOURISH YOUR MIND, YOUR BODY, AND YOUR INSATIABLE DESIRE FOR ALL THINGS FREE.

Earn up to 5 Free Bonus Nights or 12,000 Bonus Miles when you join Gold Passport and stay at Hyatt 15 November–28 February.

STAY 3 NIGHTS
Earn 1 Free Weekend Night or 2,000 Bonus Miles

STAY 6 NIGHTS
Earn 2 Free Weekend Nights or 4,000 Bonus Miles

STAY 9 NIGHTS
Earn 3 Free Weekend Nights or 6,000 Bonus Miles

STAY 15 NIGHTS
Earn 3 Free Nights or 8,000 Bonus Miles

STAY 20 NIGHTS
Earn 4 Free Nights or 10,000 Bonus Miles

STAY 25 NIGHTS
Earn 5 Free Nights or 12,000 Bonus Miles

To join Gold Passport, visit www.goldpassport.com or call (0845) 758-1666 in the UK or (49) 180 593-8800 in Germany. Or contact your nearest Hyatt Worldwide Reservation Centre.

HYATT GOLD PASSPORT
Membership Makes a World of Difference.

To qualify, you must join Gold Passport, provide your account number at check-in and pay an eligible rate. Current members must sign up for the promotion. Qualifying nights must occur between 15 November 2000 and 28 February 2001. Only one credit will be given per member, per night, regardless of number of rooms. Award nights do not qualify. The maximum award you can earn is 5 free nights at participating properties or 12,000 bonus miles regardless of the number of nights you stay. After 15 April 2001, you will receive the Award for which you qualify. Award may be redeemed for room rate only at participating properties, subject to limited availability, during a limited time period. Or Award may be redeemed for miles in a participating airline by 15 September 2001. Miles are subject to the terms and conditions of each participating airline program. Mileage award amount will vary for participating airline partners with frequent flyer currency other than miles. These airlines include Aeroméxico,® LanChile, Qantas Airways and Southwest Airlines. Other restrictions apply. For complete details and conditions visit www.goldpassport.com or call 1-800-51-HYATT. This promotion is subject to the terms and conditions of the Gold Passport program. Hyatt Hotels and Resorts® encompasses hotels and resorts managed, franchised, or leased by two separate groups of companies—Hyatt Corporation and its affiliates and affiliates of Hyatt International Corporation. ©2000 Hyatt Corp. American Airlines® is a registered trademark of American Airlines, Inc.

Participating Airlines: Aeroméxico,® Alaska Airlines, All Nippon Airways, America West Airlines,® American Airlines,® British Airways, Cathay Pacific Airways, China Airlines, Continental Airlines, Delta Air Lines, Korean Air, LanChile, Lufthansa, Midwest Express Airlines, Northwest Airlines,® Qantas Airways, Qualiflyer, Singapore Airlines, South African Airways, Southwest Airlines, Thai Airways International, TWA,® United Airlines, US Airways℠

Sign of Progress

Nonferrous and precious metals are a must in modern industries indispensable to today's technologies.

Norilsk Nickel is one of the world's biggest producers of base and precious metals and the largest supplier of nickel and palladium in the world.

The metals are mined and produced by Norilsk Nickel subsidiaries, Norilsk Mining Company and Kola Mining Metallurgical Company – leading enterprises of the Russian economy.

High quality of products, customer-oriented approach and timely deliveries worldwide make Norilsk Nickel a reliable supplier.

Products of Norilsk Nickel are fundamental to industrial progress.

NORILSK NICKEL

Norilsk Nickel JSC
Usadba Center, 22 Voznesensky Per.,
Moscow, 103009, Russia
Tel: +7 (095) 915 82 75 Fax: +7 (095) 915 83 85
E-mail: rao@nornik.ru http://www.nornik.ru

Base metals
Tel/fax: +7 (095) 787 76 42
Precious metals
Tel/fax: +7 (095) 915 83 07

cess for his centre-left party in parliamentary elections, could undo attempts of more sober technocrats to keep down wages and shut down loss-making state industries. Inflation and the current-account deficit will remain high, but the Romanian economy is expected to grow by 3% thanks to booming exports. Bulgaria, Romania's smaller and less flamboyant neighbour to the south, should grow at about the same rate. It will also attract more foreign investment but not enough to offset high unemployment. Nor will demoralised Bulgarians match Romanians for civic participation or entrepreneurial spirit.

During 2001, the Gypsy question will emerge as a serious obstacle to Central Europe's bid to join the EU. Gypsies, or Roma, will continue to flee to the EU, citing racism. At home, a few will be beaten to death by racists for the colour of their skin; many more Gypsy children will be denied proper schooling. Life expectancy for Gypsies will fall, while illiteracy rates and the number of Gypsies behind bars will rise. Unemployment will remain chronically high. Housing stocks in Gypsy communities will deteriorate alarmingly. Tuberculosis will make a comeback in poorer villages; a meningitis epidemic may not be far behind.

Despite all this, Gypsy leaders will not find common cause; their ethnic political parties will remain too fractured and self-serving to press for the civil rights of their constituents. The underlying demography of Gypsies will vex bean-counters in Brussels and become an unsavoury populist issue within the EU for opponents of enlargement; at the current rate of growth Gypsies will outnumber Slovaks in Slovakia by 2060 and will sink its

Russian gloom or boom?

Edward Lucas *Moscow*

This will be another miserable year for most Russians, as they stay more or less as poor, unhealthy, badly housed and badly governed as they were in 2000. Oddly, that may be a good thing. It is only when the costs of cronyism and disorganisation become blindingly clear that Russians will ditch their idiosyncratic habits and try to do things the way that happier countries do.

A sliver of good news in 2001 will be that Russia may have become stable enough for the carrots and sticks of capitalism to start working, at least in some bits of the economy. A handful of Russia's big companies may try selling their shares in New York. The idea that the difference between good and bad management may be several million dollars in the pockets of those responsible is a novel one in Russia, but powerful when it sinks in—so far, the thinking has been mainly about how much managers can loot, and how quickly. Equally, a really badly run Russian company now has a better chance of being taken over by a competitor.

This will spread only slowly, but the sight of even a few big companies that do well because they are better run will send powerful signals to their competitors. Some smaller Russian companies will be showing that it pays managers to compete on price, quality and efficiency rather than on their ability to bribe the right bureaucrat. Last summer's reform of the tax code, although incomplete, will allow ambitious managers to make 2001 the year they concentrate on building their business rather than dodging the tax man. Foreign investors are beginning to come back. Most are manufacturing for the local market, but some will start thinking about making clothing and other labour-intensive goods for export. If this happens, it will be a big step forward: Russia's skilled and cheap labour force has been largely cut off from the world economy by the monumental costs and difficulties that the country imposes on most businesses.

But there is still a huge way to go. Without a drastic reform of the bankrupt, badly run banking system, Russia's economy will never fire on all cylinders. Although Russia's new entrepreneurs have tremendous energy, imagination and flexibility, they are still weak on impor-

Sorry, the future is running late

tant skills like managing money, time, things and people. And even if Russia's laws are becoming a bit more sensible, Russian bureaucrats are not: poorly trained, ill-paid, unsupervised, they remain one of the greatest curses on the country's future.

Good and bad businesses alike face two other great dangers. One is that the country is simply falling apart. The decay of Russia's pipelines, electricity cables, roads, bridges, railways and hospitals is accelerating. Often badly built in the Soviet era, and with little maintenance since then, the infrastructure is collapsing. The one certain prediction for 2001 is that pipeline leaks, fires, floods, power-cuts, building collapses, industrial accidents and catastrophic failures of public services will be regular and depressing. In effect, Russia's economy is racing against time. If the internationally competitive bits can grow fast enough, there is just a chance that there will be enough money and oomph to keep Russia as an advanced industrial society. If not, the grim, primitive, vodka-sodden life of much of the countryside will gradually become the norm, rather than the exception.

The other great danger is Russia's politicians. The country has long been cursed by impatient rulers wanting quick results. The best that President Vladimir Putin can do for his country is to bash relentlessly away at the

---

2001

Russia finally reverses Stalin's collectivisation of farmland. Expect private farms to become legal and, therefore, to change hands. Remember the needless slaughter of the Kulaks.

Edward Lucas: Russia correspondent, *The Economist*

Europe THE WORLD IN 2001

Russian racketeers

Matthew Glendinning

There will be three great Russian tennis players doing the rounds in 2001. Starlet Anna Kournikova may never win a major tournament but she has already caught every eye. Marat Safin, charismatic and strong, will dominate Paris and Wimbledon in 2001, having beaten Pete Sampras in the United States Open. This was no fluke. He will repeatedly be a finalist and familiar on every television screen. And look out for 18-year-old Elena Dementieva, a Muscovite. She has already surpassed Miss Kournikova's achievements by reaching the semi-finals of the women's United States Open.

Characteristic of the new Russian confidence, Miss Dementieva is far from overwhelmed by the West. Speaking of her two weeks in Flushing Meadows, New York, she said: "Transportation bad, food bad, big tournament that's okay, but this place is a little crazy."

There will be a number of other new prodigies on the world tennis circuit: Australia's Lleyton Hewitt and Ecuador's Nicolas Lapentii are two to watch.

Watch out also for a wonderfully talented 14-year-old black player, Jamea Jackson, daughter of former American footballer, Ernest Jackson.

Matthew Glendinning: features editor, *Sport Business*

Safin's a sure hit

---

things that keep it poor: the weak legal system, the bad bureaucrats, corruption and organised crime. But he may have other plans, or be forced to look for some quick fixes. The modest reforms of 2000 happened in the best possible financial weather, with a high oil price and a very cheap currency. The coming year is unlikely to be so friendly. The good bits of the economy are still too small, and too weak, to support the rest. When the next crunch comes, Mr Putin will be tempted to start bossing business about and printing money, with disastrous results.

Vladimir Putin's thuggish and duplicitous side will also cause worries among Russia's neighbours in 2001. A chilly calculation of Russian national interest has replaced the boozy backslapping of the Yeltsin era. Russia seems to have accepted, at least for now, that it has little chance of halting the Baltic states' shift back to Western Europe. But the Kremlin's efforts will concentrate all the more on the rest of the former empire: Central Asia, the Caucasus, and the western states of Ukraine, Belarus and Moldova.

In all three of these, expect to see plenty of mischief-making and muscle-rippling as Russia reminds its former captives who is boss. Russia's three big levers are security, energy and visas. The central Asian countries are worried about Islamic terrorism. Even if this is stoked by Russia, as some suspect, it is only the Kremlin, not the United States, that can supply the military might needed to protect autocratic regimes in places like Uzbekistan. The energy weapon is lethal against countries with no oil and gas of their own. As countries like Ukraine and Moldova shiver this winter and next, Russia will drive an ever harder bargain. The Kremlin will make Russian citizenship as attractive as possible for people in places like Georgia and Azerbaijan—the only two former Soviet republics that are still clearly allied with the West. Russia's relative prosperity makes it a magnet for people from the former empire. By being tough with visas and generous with passports, Russia will undermine its neighbours' national identity and tie them ever closer to Moscow.

> **2001**
> Destroyed by Bosnian-Croat shells in 1993, the 500-year-old Mostar bridge in Bosnia-Herzegovina will be rebuilt.

TURKEY   *FORECAST*

In 2001, Turkey will embark on the second year of an ambitious three-year IMF programme and yet another year of trying to catch up. Turkey is still struggling to tame inflation—a task most emerging markets successfully tackled in the 1990s. The wage packets of 500,000 public-sector workers will come up for renegotiation. A high public-sector wage settlement scuttled the previous IMF agreement in 1995, and another over-generous deal would throw the country's economic plans badly off course. Turkey has a better chance this time as the three-way left-right-centre coalition tends to agree on economic policy. Sumer Oral, the finance minister, has promised one-digit inflation by the end of the year. He will not make it. Lower inflation would unmask problems in the banks. Although the World Bank will come through with a large loan for restructuring the sector, rapid consolidation will be required to maintain public confidence.

But if the government is going to survive beyond a second year—a feat virtually no Turkish government has achieved for a decade—it will also have to steer its way around some tough issues. Most difficult will be management of tensions between the coalition, the new head of state (the independent-minded President Ahmet Necdet Sezer), and the politically intrusive military as they tussle over the role of Islam in Turkey's system. The generals will not relent in their campaign to eliminate Islam's influence on Turkish politics. And although the coalition will generally do their bidding, it will be a reluctant partner. Islam is still a major vote-winner.

Turkey will also be looking to catch up on its bid for EU membership. Turkey was finally accepted in 1999 as a candidate for EU accession, but the offer will lead to serious negotiations only if Turkey first meets the EU's standards on human rights. Top of the list will be greater freedom for Turkey's minority Kurdish population and the abolition of the death penalty. But a repeal of that would be contentious: it would allow the jailed leader of the Kurdistan Worker's Party, Abdullah Öcalan, to escape the threat of execution.

KEY INDICATORS	1999	2000	2001
GDP growth (%)	-5.1	6.0	4.3
Inflation (%)	65.1	54.2	25.6
Current account (% of GDP)	-0.7	-4.5	-4.2

E·I·U EIU COUNTRY ANALYSIS AND FORECASTING

Industries collide. Billions change hands. New world orders emerge.

Where does the Old Economy meet the New Economy? In The Deal Economy. Every day, corporate players, lawyers, money movers and entrepreneurs are making the deals that are changing the world. We invite you to be a part of it.

Welcome to the Deal Economy.

The Deal
The Daily Deal · TheDeal.com

To subscribe, call 0.207.956.2463 or email: subs@TheDeal.com

The moment of truth is when the best price is yours.

At Instinet, we don't hold a portfolio or take a position in any of the securities we handle for clients.

We're neutral. Objective. Yours.

So you never worry about us competing with your trades, or taking a position against you or giving you some nonsense about spreads. No spreads here.

Our only goal is to help you get the fastest trade at the best price — and handle all the follow-up automatically.

Perhaps that's why thousands of institutions worldwide use Instinet to electronically access some of the broadest, deepest — most liquid — trading opportunities around the globe.

With all those institutions at your fingertips every day, you have a greater possibility of finding a buyer or seller when you need one.

The fact is, we pioneered electronic brokerage over 30 years ago. Since then, we've helped U.S. pension funds and mutual funds save billions of dollars — three billion last year alone.

For more information, call our international freephone number +800 INSTINET (+800 4678 4638) or visit www.instinet.com

Instinet
A REUTERS Company

Nothing comes between you and the best price.^{SM}

As an agency broker, Instinet does not come between its clients and the best price. We do not commit capital, make markets or make profits on spreads. ©2000 Instinet Corporation, all rights reserved. INSTINET and the INSTINET marque are registered service marks in the United States and other countries throughout the world. Instinet Corporation is member NASD/SIPC, and Instinet UK Limited is regulated in the U.K. by the SFA.

THE WORLD IN 2001

North America

Economics: **Time for the party to wind down** 60 / Prisons: **Two million behind bars** 62
Richard Daley: **A tale for all cities** 63 / Mexico: **The eagle and the fox** 66
Farming: **A cornucopia of trouble** 66 / Families: **When did you last see your father?** 69
Gridiron: **Football in your face** 70 / Security: **When defence looks like attack** 70
The environment: **Nature strikes back** 71 / Canada: **Canadian-ness** 72

What augurs after the inauguration?

Morton Kondracke *Washington, DC*

Can it get any better than this for the United States? The economy is in the midst of its longest growth run ever. Poverty and unemployment are at their lowest rates in three decades. The federal budget, once in deficit by hundreds of billions of dollars each year, is now in surplus by like amounts. Crime, teenage pregnancy rates and welfare rolls are all down and real wages, home ownership, school test scores and charitable giving levels are all up. America is the dominant power in the world, militarily, economically and culturally. Its companies and icons are everywhere, yet its soldiers—although targets of terrorism all over the world—are nowhere engaged in combat.

Yet into this paradise has come a note of sourness. When America's 43rd president is sworn in on Saturday January 20th, many Americans will feel unable to share in his moment of triumph. The disputed election, and the bitterness of the days of indecision in arriving at the result, have ensured that the administration will get off to an unhappy start, just as the economy is slowing.

The evidence also suggests that though Americans may be contented with their condition, they are by no means satisfied. Americans would not be Americans if they did not think things could be better than they are. And they do. Various polling organisations have asked their favourite question to test the public mood: are things basically headed in the right direction, or are they off on the wrong track? The balance is right track, 46% and wrong track, 41%.

What could possibly be wrong? Senator John McCain, a Republican, backed by many of the country's editorial pages, asserts that the United States political system has become fundamentally corrupt because parties and candidates increasingly depend on unlimited "soft money" contributions from corporations and labour unions to get elected. There is truth in that and the administration should address the problem.

The disquiet in America, however, is not with Washington politics, no matter how justified that might be, but with the quality of domestic life. It is an embarrassment that 42.5m Americans, 7.5m more than in 1992, are without health insurance—a government-guaranteed benefit in most of the industrialised world. And it appears morally wrong that in 1998 the United States ranked 12th in the world for life expectancy and 30th in infant mortality.

The surge in employment also has its downside: overwork and a crunch on family life. More than 70% of women with children under 18 have jobs, 32% of American employees work more than 40 hours a week and the average number of leisure hours enjoyed each week by adults has declined from 24.3 in 1975 to 19.5 in 1997. Even as their incomes rise, workers feel stressed. And, often, their children are being raised by television sets or by their peers. The market for breakfast cereals, for example, is in decline: getting milk, spoon and cereal together in a bowl every morning is too taxing a feat of co-ordination—and anyway few families meet around the breakfast table anymore.

For all the prosperity, there is a rising suspicion of the motives of capitalism and the altruism of its bosses. As reflected in media reports, think-tank studies, congressional hearings and campaign rhetoric, Americans are worried that their privacy is being invaded by credit-card companies and Internet vendors, their medical care is being impaired by greedy insurance and pharmaceuticals companies, and racial minorities are being unfairly targeted by the legal system.

It is this widespread sense that social injustice still abounds amid all the prosperity that undermined what should have been overwhelming support for the incumbent, Al Gore. It also forced both candidates to promise to fight, in their different ways, to change the country.

Both Mr Gore and Mr Bush campaigned on the premise that although conditions in the United States have improved markedly over the past eight years, much

---

2001
State legislatures will redraw the boundaries of 435 districts for the House of Representatives. Expect many of them to be altered for partisan gain: against the law but too tempting to resist. Because Americans are moving west New York will lose five House seats, and California will gain nine, over the next 20 years.

Morton Kondracke: executive editor, *Roll Call*

North America THE WORLD IN 2001

work needs to be done to secure and extend the prosperity, improve the nation's education system and guarantee the solvency of the Social Security (pensions) system. The economy has given Congress and the new president an expected $4.6 trillion surplus over the next ten years with which to do the work. They have agreed to use $2.4 trillion of it to pay down the national debt. How to divide up the other $2.2 trillion between tax cuts and spending on health and education initiatives is one of the big issues of 2001.

The House of Representatives, still under Republican control, would like to legislate substantial, across-the-board tax cuts; Social Security reforms that allow younger workers to invest a part of their retirement taxes in private markets, and the channelling of new health benefits through private-insurance companies rather than the government. It won't all be plain sailing, however: the Senate is split evenly between the Republicans and Democrats, and it takes 60% of votes to pass legislation. That may prevent the passage of campaign-finance reform to curb the power of money in elections.

Although it was not a high priority for voters or candidates in the election campaign, foreign policy will preoccupy the new president. Congress and he both agree that the defence budget needs to be increased. A good trick would be to maintain national missile defence as no more than "a research programme". That might help minimise conflict with Russia and China over the issue.

Washington's relations with Beijing will undoubtedly be smoothed by the disappearance of the annual review of China's normal trade relations in Congress. The entry of the last major communist country into the World Trade Organisation in 2001 will be one of the major legacies of the Clinton administration. But when he first arrived in Washington, Bill Clinton took a different line, hoping to use trade sanctions as a lever to force improvements in human rights in China. The Chinese government reacted badly—and it would do again. If Congress presses in 2001 for a return to such an aggressive approach, the president, whatever his instincts, would be wise to continue encouraging trade.

Mr Clinton was accused of having no consistent foreign policy. The new president will undoubtedly face similar criticism. Whether he chooses an activist foreign policy that intervenes when American "values" are under threat, or a more conservative one that commits troops only when American "interests" are at stake, he will face the same dilemma: the kinds of problems the world throws up cannot be so easily classified. The Middle East is explosive; success in brokering peace evaded even Mr Clinton. His successor lacks his combination of political *savoir faire* and charm. Resurgent nationalism in Russia will present new challenges. And the thawing of relations between North and South Korea will require a sensitive yet firm approach.

As the president faces the world, however, he has this going for him: he inherits a country at the height of its power, yet without the innocence that possessed it at a similar moment after the second world war. His administration will be liberal by nature yet, by the nature of America, conservative and wary of excessive government. In his heart he must fear that with things so good, they can only turn more fragile in 2001. ◻

Time for the party to wind down

Zanny Minton-Beddoes Washington, DC

From cameo to starring role
US inflation, %

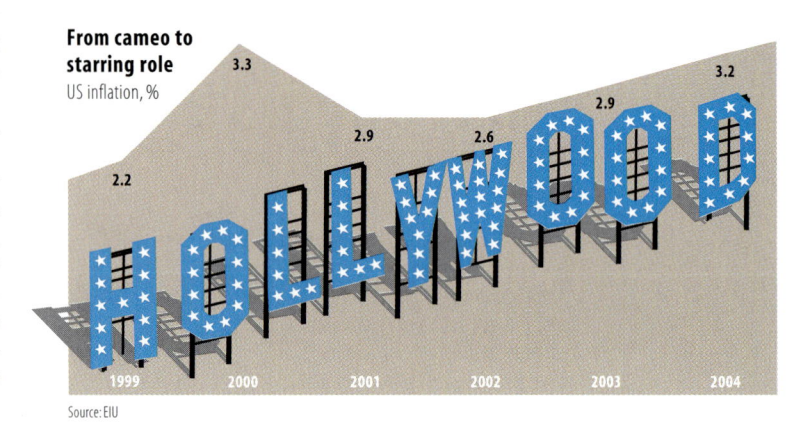

1999: 2.2
2000: 3.3
2001: 2.9
2002: 2.6
2003: 2.9
2004: 3.2

Source: EIU

In recent years, America's economy has led a charmed existence. Growth has consistently been higher than forecast, yet inflation has failed to accelerate sharply despite record low unemployment. Towards the end of 2000, the boom slowed to a more sustainable pace, but without the "hard landing" that many foretold. Cassandras looking for America's crash have been consistently disappointed.

This sparkling performance is partly due to the extraordinary strength of the "new economy". Productivity growth, in particular, has been more spectacular than all but the most starry-eyed techno-fiends suspected. In mid-2000 American workers, outside agriculture, were producing almost 6% more stuff per hour than they had been a year earlier. As a result of this productivity growth, unit labour costs remained low and firms' profits remained high even though pay packets were swelling.

Good fortune has also played its role in keeping the party going. In 2000 the biggest surprise was the fact that foreign investors kept pouring money into America's economy, even as the current-account deficit reached, and broke, historic records. By mid-

Land of the very very rich
Number of American households with net assets of more than $1 million

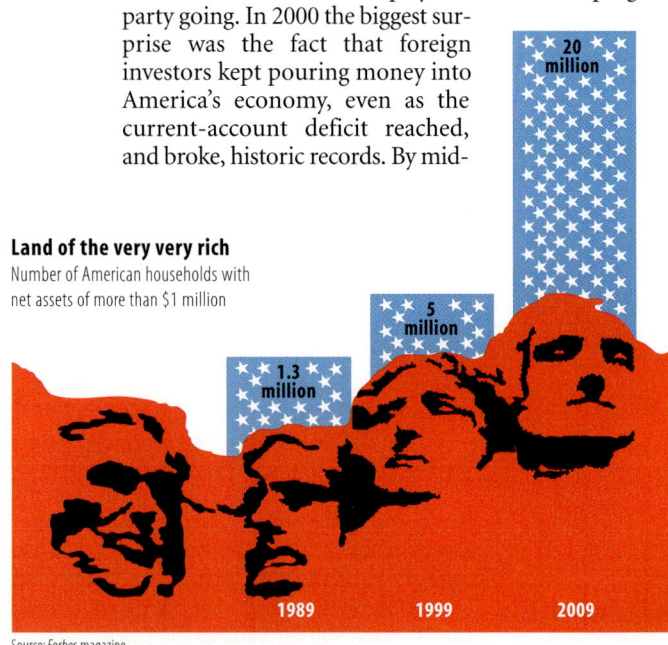

1989: 1.3 million
1999: 5 million
2009: 20 million

Source: *Forbes* magazine

2000 the current-account deficit—the broadest measure of the country's trade imbalance—hit 4.3% of GDP. Yet investors' lack of confidence in the euro, enormous confidence in the Federal Reserve and seemingly inexorable appetite for American assets meant that the money kept pouring in and the dollar stayed strong.

In 2001, however, the tables will turn. The glories of the new economy will no longer be powerful enough to dull the impact of rising wage pressure and high oil prices. And faced with a yawning current-account deficit, foreigners will become leery of buying ever more American assets. But, with luck, there will not be a sudden crash, a massive dollar crisis or a deep recession. More likely is a gradual, but nonetheless uncomfortable, shift: squeezed corporate profits, jitters on Wall Street, worries over inflation, and a moderately weaker dollar. By the end of 2001, the American economy will still look strong—at least compared with others—but it will seem less invincible. It will be clear that the next few years will require a painstaking process of unwinding imbalances, in particular the current account deficit.

By historical standards, and compared with other industrialised countries, growth will still be robust in 2001. Consumption will slow in the winter months as high oil and natural-gas prices make Americans face unexpectedly high heating bills. But by the spring, the irrepressible shopping instinct will be back. Investment will slow from recent torrid levels. (In the first half of 2000 business investment in equipment and software rose by almost 20%.) Nonetheless, GDP growth will still be close to 4%.

The gradual slowing of economic growth will also be reflected in less rosy productivity figures. Although productivity gains will remain strong, they will not reach the levels of 2000. Labour productivity will rise by around 3%, compared with over 4% in 2000. Wages, in contrast, will continue their gradual, but inexorable, upward march as the labour market remains tight (unemployment will continue to hover around 4%). Hourly earnings could rise by over 5%. That means unit labour costs—or the cost of a worker relative to the output he produces—will rise quite sharply. As a result profit margins will be squeezed and core inflation will creep gradually upwards. The mixture of lower growth and a lacklustre stockmarket could dampen foreigners' appetites for American assets. And that could prove to be the economy's Achilles heel.

Foreigners call the shots

In the past couple of years the American economy has increasingly relied on foreign funds to finance its investment and consumption booms. Strong corporate investment coupled with falling personal savings (which reached an all-time low of minus 0.4% in mid-2000) means that America's private-sector financial deficit has been reaching record highs. Earlier in the expansion this was largely covered by improved government finances.

Gradually, however, ever more of the private-sector financial deficit is being covered by foreign capital inflows.

Funding even moderate growth in demand will require considerable foreign capital. According to economists at Goldman Sachs, an investment bank, demand growth of 4% in 2001 (compared with 5.7% in 2000) would still imply a private-sector financial deficit

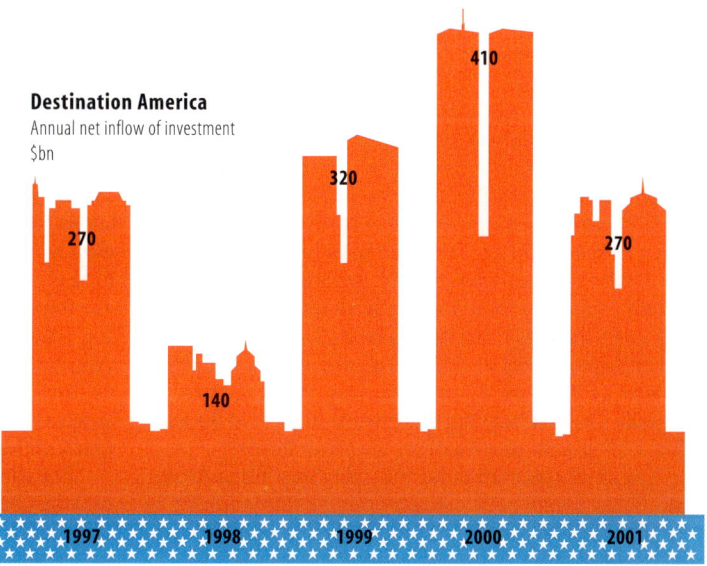

Destination America
Annual net inflow of investment
$bn

270 140 320 410 270
1997 1998 1999 2000 2001

of 7% of GDP. If foreigners do not provide this capital, the impact on growth, asset prices and the dollar could well be substantial.

In a paper recently presented to the annual gathering of central bankers at Jackson Hole, Wyoming, Maurice Obstfeld, an economist at the University of California at Berkeley, and Kenneth Rogoff from Harvard University, argued that for the current account quickly to reach balance, the dollar would need to depreciate by more than 24%, perhaps even over 40% in real terms. A gradual adjustment, where the current account returned to balance over a period of three to five years, would demand a real exchange-rate adjustment of 12%.

There are good reasons to expect the more gradual, and favourable, scenario. Foreigners' love affair with American assets has not been speculative, but has consisted in large part of long-term financial flows (including a lot of direct investment), based on productivity improvements that are increasingly evident. These are unlikely to dry up overnight.

Nonetheless, history is full of sudden current-account reversals due to investor panic and exchange-rate crises. Remember East Asia in 1997. Much will depend on policymakers' aptitude. A loose fiscal policy—whether it comes from irresponsible tax cuts or from excessive spending—will increase the need for foreign capital to fund American demand, and could easily spook investors. Monetary policy will have to steer a careful course: keeping the lid on price pressure without precipitating a sudden slowdown. Any mis-step and the Federal Reserve could face the unenviable combination of rising inflation, falling asset prices and a falling dollar. America's economy in 2001 will need good policy and, every bit as important, another dollop of good fortune. □

2001
The biggest waste of taxpayers' money in 2001? What can beat the $40 billion to be spent in America's "war against drugs"? Result: the number of young people taking illicit drugs will rise to nearly 30%. The price of marijuana and cocaine will fall to record lows.

Zanny Minton-Beddoes: Washington correspondent, *The Economist*

North America THE WORLD IN 2001

Two million behind bars

Sebastian Mallaby — Washington, DC

Two million Americans will be locked up behind bars by the end of 2001: the biggest civilian incarceration in history. This means that America, with 5% of the world's population, will have 25% of its prisoners; its rate of incarceration will exceed that of every other country that keeps statistics, with the possible exception of miserable Russia. The question is whether the 2m milestone will prompt the rethink that America's penal policy deserves, or whether it will slip by unnoticed. The American incarceration rate not only exceeds that of other industrialised countries by between five and eight times; a generation ago, it would have been unthinkable even in the United States. In 1960 America's inmate population (counting those locked up in long-term prisons plus short-term jails, but not counting illegal immigrants and minors) stood at 333,000 and over the next two decades it rose at a comparatively modest pace to 474,000. The quadrupling that ensued in the two decades after 1980 has no precedent in American history.

The chief explanation for this crazy leap lies in America's failed drugs policy. Nearly one in four inmates is serving time for some kind of drug offence, meaning that the number of incarcerated drug offenders in 2001 will be roughly equivalent to the entire inmate population of 1980. There will be 100,000 more people imprisoned in America for drug offences than all the prisoners in the European Union, even though the EU has 100m more people. In California the number of drug offenders behind bars has increased a staggering 25-fold since 1980.

The direct cost of locking up drug offenders in 2001 will come to nearly $10 billion, but the indirect costs are just as frightening. These begin with the effect on America's anguished race relations. Surveys show similar drug usage rates for young blacks and whites, but black drug offenders are far more likely to go to jail. This discrimination, coupled with higher black incarceration rates for non-drug crimes, causes more than one in ten black males in their 20s and early 30s to be locked up. In Texas, where the prison system grew faster than that of any other state during the 1990s, nearly one in three young black men is under some form of criminal justice control (counting those on parole and probation as well as those incarcerated); in some cities, like Washington, DC, and Baltimore, half or more were.

This rate of penalisation tears at the social fabric of inner cities. One in ten black children has a parent in prison, and is in turn more likely to experience neglect, poverty and later on delinquency. But high penalisation rates have political consequences too. In all but four states, prisoners who have been convicted of felonies lose the right to vote; in 12 states, a felony can result in lifelong disenfranchisement. As a result of these rules, there are states, particularly in the South, where a quarter of the black male population is permanently disenfranchised. As older, pre-prison-boom blacks die, the share of the disenfranchised will go up. 2001 will see further progress towards the time when a third of the nation's black males are voteless.

But the scariest cost of all is one that America has only just begun to reckon with. This is the cost of releasing tens of thousands of prisoners once their sentences have been completed. Since less than a tenth of prisoners are serving life sentences, the dramatic spike in incarceration is going to be followed inexorably by a similar spike in release rates. Admittedly, the people coming out will be older than the people going in, and older people are generally less likely to be criminal. But the prisoners being released are unlikely to slip back easily into society.

Half a century ago, rehabilitation was a primary goal of America's penal system. During the past couple of decades, however, the aim has simply been to get bad guys off the streets. The fading of the rehabilitation effort means that, if those guys were indeed bad when they went in, they are likely to be worse when they get out again. More prisoners are spending more time in crowded and degrading conditions, and often in various forms of high security detention. So one sad prediction for 2001 is that the newspapers will carry stories of ex-inmates emerging from years of semi-isolation to commit blood-curdling murders.

These horror stories could be the trigger for a rethink of incarceration policies. Already, several states have begun to question the use of imprisonment in dealing with the drug problem. Michigan has modified its mandatory sentencing system by shying away from mandatory life sentences. The chief judge in New York state has announced a reform effort to get 10,000 offenders out of jail and into drug treatment. Even if the passing of the 2m mark does cause the penal system to break the surface of public debate in 2001, don't expect much change. America has committed itself to a strange policy from which it will be hard pressed to back down, however grim the consequences of its continuation. □

2001
Watch out for 2001's blockbuster movie: "Lord of the Rings". Thirty years of cult readership should guarantee filled seats and sequels. We'll all be speaking elfish.

Sebastian Mallaby: editorial page staff, *Washington Post*

I'm a troubling statistic

Richard M. Daley, mayor of Chicago, spells out six universal rules for running a successful city in 2001

A tale for all cities

"The best cities will be as diverse as possible. The narrow ones, resisting immigrants and minorities, will fail"

Although each of the world's mayors will face different challenges in 2001, there is one that will be common to us all: how to balance the immediate needs of our residents with the long-term investments—reaching far beyond our political tenure—needed to assure a prosperous future. I set out here the rules that I will be following as I try to make Chicago America's most flourishing city.

1. Challenge the status quo

Cities are fast-moving things. The conventional wisdom of even the recent past is not a good guide to even the immediate future. Mayors must be willing to spend political capital on keeping themselves up to date. They must be ahead of the curve, of their constituents and their critics. The strategies needed to improve today's quality of life in a city, and to invest in the future, may not be politically popular.

2. Education matters most

The vibrancy of any city in, say, a decade's time will depend disproportionately on the quality of education it gives to its future citizens. Everything depends on this: the economy, the tax base, the cultural life, the future levels of employment or of crime are driven by the quality of a city's schools. The urgency of this mission increases each year, as technology advances. Those who are victims of educational failure now will fall further and further behind. The successful cities of of the future will undoubtedly be those that have successful schools today.

In 1995 I sought and was granted responsibility for Chicago's public schools. Once, our schools were called the worst in America. Now—after only a few years—our reform efforts are taken as a model for the whole country.

Our first, most controversial, step has been to end the policy of social promotion—of promoting a child to the next grade because of his or her age, regardless of whether or not the child has the skills required. Children who do not pass their exams are required to attend summer school. Each year more children have graduated from summer school and moved on to the next grade. Second, we returned to teaching the basics—reading and writing, mathematics and science. Today, although we have much more to do, test scores are up significantly. Third, we have made schools safer. All our schools have metal detectors. We inspect lockers and we ban gang-related clothing. Fourth, we persuaded our local taxpayers to invest over $2 billion, more than any city in America, to build new schools and renovate existing ones.

3. Execute well

Executive competence matters much more than political posturing. Residents must have confidence that local spending is managed well and directed to their needs. In Chicago our tax base is mostly local. Our taxpayers work hard for their money. We want to make sure they get the most from every dollar we spend.

Chicago was among the first cities in the country to privatise the delivery of certain services. One result of privatisation is that while our budget has grown 53% in the past ten years, the number of city employees (excluding the police) has increased by just 200.

Even in our country's strong economy, we have been sensitive about raising taxes, especially local property taxes that affect homeowners. In fact, even with our self-imposed limit on increases in property taxes, we could have raised another $600m. We chose not to. High taxes can thwart a city's development.

4. Invest in the quality of life

For the past 40 years, the trend in urban America has been the flight of people from cities to suburbs. In Chicago we have made it a priority to improve the quality of life in order to keep working families in our city, as well as encouraging others to return.

To that end, we've invested more than $6 billion since 1989 to improve our neighbourhoods, starting with safety. Now, after years of losing population, families are returning. The investments have paid off. As people return, so the tax base grows. While our city's crime rates have been dropping for eight years, it didn't happen by accident. In part, it happened because Chicago executed aggressive strategies to fight gang, drug and gun crime. We have hired more than 1,000 new police officers.

5. Grow a varied economy

As our city has grown, our strategy has been to create a more diverse economy that can withstand cyclical downturns. Many of the food and durable-goods industries that for years have been Chicago's foundation are still here. Our financial-services industry is second only to Wall Street. Chicago is the transportation hub of our country. And our convention and tourism industries are still growing.

We are working hard to add information technology to the mix with a city-wide fibre-optic infrastructure.

6. Diversity is strength

The key to a good city is diversity. People of every religious, ethnic and sexual orientation proudly call our city home. Diversity is strength. A successful city is a cosmopolitan city. In other parts of the world people (and mayors) find this hard to accept. But look around. The best cities in 2001, from London to Los Angeles, will be as diverse as possible. The narrow ones, resisting immigrants and minorities (however defined), will fail.

We have encouraged people to get involved in their communities and to take responsibility for their own quality of life. Chicago today is better off because hundreds of thousands of people are involved in its citizenship. They indeed are the new city bosses. □

It took him
five years to build
a local business.
He's taking it global
at light-speed.

With the Optical Internet Lucent is creating, a business knows no boundaries. We're building all-optical networks that are four times faster than today's—with the speed and capacity to connect local markets to global markets. So businesses large and small can serve new customers anywhere in the world. Change the way people communicate, and you change the way they do business. Lucent Technologies. We make the Internet move at light-speed.

Expect great things.

Lucent Technologies
Bell Labs Innovations

www.lucent.com

©2000 Lucent Technologies

North America THE WORLD IN 2001

21st century Fox

The eagle and the fox

Mark Mazzetti — *Austin, Texas*

Mark Mazzetti: Southwest United States correspondent, *The Economist*

Mexico experienced a political earthquake in 2000, one felt on both sides of the Rio Grande. Vicente Fox's victory in Mexico's presidential election brought an end to 71 years of rule by the Institutional Revolutionary Party (PRI) and silenced doubters around the world who questioned the health (or even the existence) of Mexican democracy. In large part, Mr Fox was swept to victory by the force that from time to time overcomes any democracy: the people's desire for change. In 2001, he has the chance to silence another set of critics: those who question whether real change is possible.

He takes office only on December 1st, just seven weeks before America's new president is installed in the White House. So nothing of substance can happen before 2001: thereafter there will be high hopes that these two large, disparate and awkward neighbours will use the year to improve their relations. Nothing is more important to the United States than that Mexico should speed down the road to open markets, decent human rights and the rule of law. For Mexico, one of the world's great cultures, 2001 presents the chance to grow up, to put behind it the childish politics of the emerging world and accept the standards of the best.

One of Mr Fox's first objectives will be to root out the corruption within the government and judiciary that has long undermined the rule of law within Mexico. Having spent much of his career outside government, and without having to carry the baggage of the PRI with him, Mr Fox is in a position to undertake a thorough house cleaning. More than anything else, a sustained war on official corruption would help stimulate foreign investment in the Mexican economy, investment that has bypassed Mexico in the past from fear of widespread fraud. If Mexico wants to get to the next level of commercial sophistication, there has to be judicial reform.

Such reform would be a first step toward Mr Fox's pledge to transform the Mexican economy. The man who once headed Coca-Cola's Mexican operations talks boldly of infusing government with a business sensibility, complete with benchmarks to track performance. To fulfil his pledge, he will necessarily have to look north, seeking cooperation from the United States to expand the role of institutions such as the North American Development Bank. Mr Fox has proposed to increase the bank's capital from $450m to $10 billion.

As both countries know, no real progress in bilateral relations can be made without progress on two specific fronts: drugs and immigration. The war on illegal drugs has often fuelled suspicion and resentment on both sides of the border, with each country blaming the other for taking steps that are counterproductive to the overall effort. The United States has helped little on this front, with

A cornucopia of trouble

Charles Wheelan — *Chicago*

In February, the National Corn Growers Association will recognise the winner of its corn-yield competition, which it proudly bills as the "World Series of farming". Last year's winner, Francis Childs of Manchester, Iowa, coaxed an average 394 bushels per acre from his land, roughly three times America's average corn yield. The agronomics are impressive; the economics are more sobering. Might America's staggeringly productive farmers be sowing the seeds of an agricultural glut?

Average corn yields in the United States climbed 15% per acre between 1989 and 1999; a bushel of corn fetched 20% less at the end of the decade than at the beginning. Net farm income slid from $53 billion in 1996 to $45 billion in 1999. Many American farmers made money in recent years only because Congress, feeling flush, voted them $22 billion in direct cash payments.

The burgeoning supply of everything from soyabeans to hogs shows no signs of slowing. America's Freedom to Farm act in 1996 took government out of the business of farming, allowing farmers to plant "fence row to fence row". The industry has been steadily consolidating into larger, more productive farms; 3% of farmers will produce 50% of farm output in 2001. And the farmers themselves are getting more clued up. Some 30% of farmers will use the Internet to gather information on everything from weather to genetically modified seed.

Meanwhile, as countries like Brazil and Ukraine adopt even rudimentary technological improvements, their yields will improve, dumping more supply on the market. The answer, farmers reckon, lies in boosting world demand. Trade liberalisation, such as the beef and citrus agreement with Japan, can prise open foreign markets for American farmers. Farmers would also like to see food taken out of America's foreign-policy arsenal. Without sanctions American farmers could sell 60 billion bushels of corn a year—the entire annual production of the state of Tennessee—to Iran and Cuba.

The biggest boost in demand will come from moving the world's poor into the middle class, where they will consume not only more food, but more meat, which is a high value-added product. Indeed, American meat exports have been growing at 15% a year while bulk food exports have been flat. In future, turning out bountiful harvests will be the easy part. □

Charles Wheelan: Midwest United States correspondent, *The Economist*

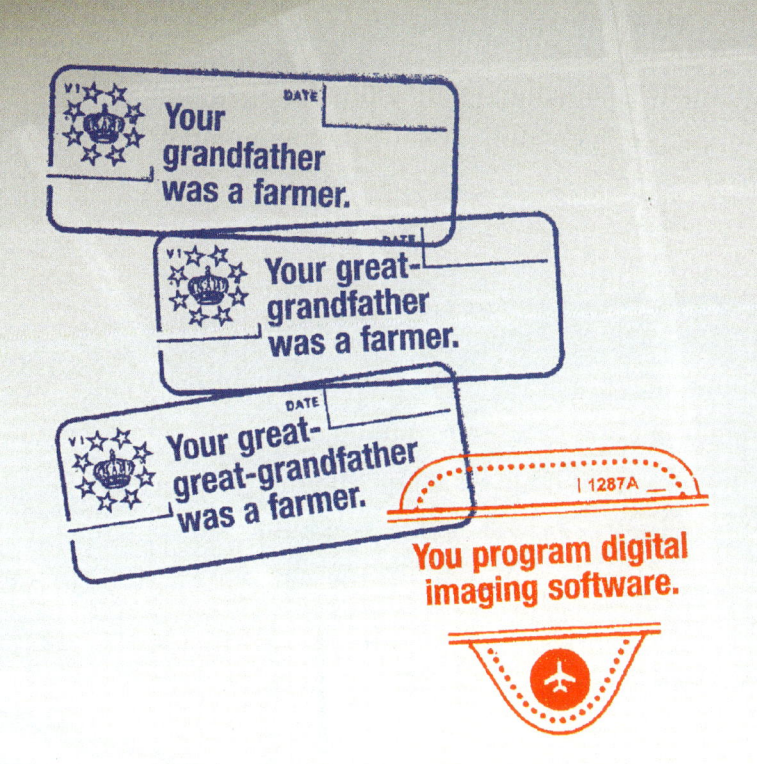

Your grandfather was a farmer.
Your great-grandfather was a farmer.
Your great-great-grandfather was a farmer.

You program digital imaging software.

In this day and age it's never been easier. You can book your own ticket online, check flight status via SMS text message and travel paper free by using E-ticket. What would your grandfather say?
Life is a journey. Travel it well.

UNITED AIRLINES
A STAR ALLIANCE MEMBER

www.unitedairlines.co.uk

We deliver anywhere within a 12,450 mile radius.

Every day we have your business mail flown direct to hundreds of destinations worldwide. That way you can always be sure it will get there fast. So however much international mail you send, send it world class. For more information visit www.royalmail.com/global

SEND IT WORLD CLASS

Royal Mail

Congress requiring an annual certification process to determine whether foreign nations are fully co-operating in the anti-drug effort. According to Kevin Middlebrook, director of the Center for US-Mexican studies at the University of California at San Diego, the annual certification is perceived abroad as an "interventionist attitude by the country that does most to underwrite the market for illegal drugs". While the annual certification is popular on Capitol Hill, a pledge by the United States to amend the process would generate goodwill south of the border. But when will America ever accept the obvious: that it is the demand of its own people, not the supply of others, that keeps the drug trade flourishing?

The United States could also extend an olive branch on the issue of immigration. Illegal immigration will exist as long as the wage gap between the two countries exists. Nevertheless, the United States could go along with Mr Fox's request for more temporary work visas, allowing Mexican agricultural workers to enter the United States during the growing season.

For its part, Mexico will promise greater enforcement at the border to prevent illegal immigration, along with more bilateral co-operation between the border agencies of both countries. During his visit to the United States and Canada in August, Mr Fox talked about a future for North America that more closely resembled the European Union model, complete with open borders and greater economic integration. Both President Bill Clinton and Prime Minister Jean Chrétien of Canada greeted the idea with scepticism, saying publicly that such a proposal was not viable given the economic disparity among North America's nations. Mr Fox is not so naïve as to think such a dream can be realised right away. On the contrary, he is shrewd enough to know that when bargaining it is best to ask for more than you expect to get.

Mexico wants to be viewed as an equal partner in the continent's future. This is already beginning to happen, as the reduction of trade barriers brought about by NAFTA has made North America's three big countries economically interdependent. Since NAFTA was passed in 1993, California's exports to Mexico have more than doubled, to $10.8 billion annually, and the stream of trade running through Texas continues to swell.

To be sure, the United States has historically been able to dictate the terms of its trade relations with Mexico, yet the importance of the Mexican market to American producers can only help Mexico's bargaining position in future negotiations. Moreover, the burgeoning population of Mexican-Americans (who now account for 67% of America's Latino population) has changed the country's political landscape, and politicians are taking care to pay deference to America's neighbour to the south. Mexico-bashing is now a fast track to electoral disaster.

Taken together, these factors will no doubt allow Mr Fox a political honeymoon that will last throughout 2001. His election victory gave him a mandate for change, and consequently he will be given time to effect that change. Both at home and abroad, there are great expectations for the Fox presidency. On the night of his victory, people paraded through the streets of Mexico City chanting, "Don't fail us! Don't fail us!". No doubt there are many in Washington who privately will be whispering the same thing. ◻

2001
America's 2.6m overworked nurses are leaving their hospitals in droves. The shortage will be most acute just when millions of ageing baby-boomers will be in need of care.

When did you last see your father?

Jonathan Rauch   Washington, DC

In 2001 America's National Center for Health Statistics will release a remarkable figure that will receive virtually no public attention. For many years, the proportion of American children born out of wedlock—the illegitimacy ratio—has been rising. The increase has been gradual but inexorable. To judge from preliminary estimates released in late 2000, in 2001 the illegitimacy ratio will reach 33%. That is, one in every three American children will be born to an unmarried mother.

This milestone is both less and more important than it may at first appear. It is less important inasmuch as, sooner or later, the one-third mark was bound to be reached, and inasmuch as that particular level is by itself of no special significance. On the other hand, the figure is momentous in the deeper sense that the trends underlying it are, at last, coming into focus after several decades

It's easy for you, you've got a daddy

of confusion and flux. The new patterns that American family structures are settling into after the turmoil that began in the 1960s are diverse, rich and very complicated; and they can be described in many ways. Perhaps, however, a particularly revealing description is to say that a new de facto class system is emerging, one based not on wealth as such, nor on colour, but on marriage.

In 1965, the black illegitimacy ratio that so alarmed America was 26.3%. Between that year and 1994, the rate for blacks rose to about 70%, and thereabouts it has stayed. The consequence is that there are entire American districts, notably in central cities, where marriage and stable fatherhood are all but unknown to black children. However, there is more to the story. In 1965, the illegitimacy ratio among whites was 4%. Again judging from preliminary estimates, in 2001 the government will declare that in 1999 the white illegitimacy ratio, for the first time, exceeded the 26.3% figure that seemed so out-

Jonathan Rauch: Brookings Institution

landish among blacks in 1965.

Unlike the black figure, the white illegitimacy ratio has not stopped rising, but in the 1990s its rate of increase markedly slowed. And so a picture emerges. It seems likely that the first decades, at least, of the new century will be ones in which married parenthood is rare among blacks and optional among whites. Half of American high-school seniors now say that having a child without being married is experimenting with a worthwhile lifestyle or does not affect anyone else.

On the latter score, they are certainly wrong. In some Scandinavian countries, marriage seems often to be replaced by stable, marriage-like cohabitations: marriages in all but name. Such does not seem to be the pattern in America, where cohabitations tend to be brief and unstable. Unmarried fathers usually vanish quickly from their children's lives; a third of children living with an unmarried mother have had no contact with their father during the past year, and fewer than 40% saw their fathers once a week. By now the consequences of unmarried parenthood are well known: the children are twice as likely to drop out of secondary school, twice as likely to become teenage (generally unmarried) parents, one and a half times as likely to be idle rather than employed.

Less well known is that being white or relatively well-to-do does not necessarily mitigate the ill effects. Two social scientists, Sara McLanahan and Gary Sandefur, report that "the chances that a white girl from an advantaged background will become a teen mother are five times as high, and the chances a white child will drop out of high school are three times as high, if the parents do not live together." Where poverty is concerned, marital status is a sharper and brighter line of demarcation than colour. More unmarried black mothers (nearly 70%) than unmarried white mothers (about 45%) are in poverty; but both groups are poorer by far than two-parent families of either colour (about 12% of black married families and 6% of white ones are in poverty). And so the rise of two cultures, a prospering one in which marriage and two-parent families are taken for granted and a floundering one in which they are exotic, brings with it omens of a new sort of class divide: one that appears to be new not only to America but to the modern world. □

> **2001**
> The United States will grant 200,000 H-1B visas for high-tech workers for each of the next three years. Almost double the number issued in 2000.

Football in your face

Gridiron—American football—is the country's most popular sport, and the National Football League is the king of the televised game. But 2001 will see a challenge to its power. The eight-team Xtreme Football League, backed by the NBC television network in partnership with World Wrestling Federation Entertainment, will begin play on February 3rd 2001 in major cities throughout the United States.

The new league wants to return gridiron to its "tougher roots". The Xtreme Football League has already decided on the "brand and emotional values" the teams will represent. New Yorkers may be interested to know that the New York/New Jersey Hitmen are already an "aggressive, relentless, in-your-face and hard-hitting team". Memphis are characterised as Maniax—"the plural of maniac"— while Orlando have been dubbed the Rage. The National Football League will hope that the 35th Super Bowl, to be played in Tampa, Florida, on January 28th 2001, will offer strong enough entertainment to see off its rivals. The high-spending Washington Redskins are our bet to win. □

I'M A LONESOME COWBOY

When defence looks like attack

Bruce Clark

National security is the prime responsibility of the president. And as he settles into his desk at the end of January, he will get a nasty surprise. What he will discover is that the threat to American territory from non-conventional weapons is real and growing, not just a political bogeyman as it must have seemed on the campaign trail. But such dangers cannot be kept at bay by anything so simple as a giant anti-missile shield over the United States, even if that proves technically possible. And any steps that America might take towards building a shield, however modest, will have huge, unpredictable consequences for its relations with traditional friends and former enemies.

It would all be simpler, perhaps, if long-range rocket assaults were the most promising way to attack the United States with non-conventional weapons. They are not. Suicide attacks by terrorists in trucks, or even short-range rockets lobbed towards America from a boat or a submarine, seem far more probable. And there is the growing likelihood of high-tech terrorism bringing America to a halt through spreading a computer virus. There is no silver bullet to deal with those murky threats, except increased vigilance at home and abroad by American security services.

Still, rocket attacks by unpredictable states such as North Korea, Iran and Iraq may soon (well, within a decade or so) become technically possible; and that will put huge pressure on any American leader to make such attacks technically impossible by developing a way to in-

THE WORLD IN 2001 **North America**

Nature strikes back

Americans, an ever more suburban and cocooned people, will have some strange encounters with nature in 2001. Many species of wild animal, such as racoons, skunks, possums and rats, are learning to thrive on the detritus of human development. Indeed, the white-tailed deer has proved to be the consummate "edge species", plunging in public esteem to the level of vermin. So beloved were these deer once that residents in America's north-east paid guards to keep hunters off their property. Now they pay hunters to cull the herd.

The reason is Lyme disease, a potentially serious bacterial infection spread to humans by ticks carried on the adult deer. The incidence of Lyme disease will have climbed from several hundred cases in the early 1980s to 15,000 cases in 2001 as human populations increasingly interact with the burgeoning deer populations that host and spread disease-bearing ticks. "It all comes down to man encroaching on nature—or nature encroaching on man—however you want to look at it," says Lyle Petersen, an infectious-disease specialist at the Centers for Disease Control and Prevention.

Meanwhile, globalisation and a taste for world travel will continue to put Americans in contact with some of the world's most exotic micro-organisms. There is an old adage in medicine that when a doctor hears hoofs, he should not think zebras. Yet it was an astute clinician in New York who recently diagnosed West Nile encephalitis. The disease had not previously been documented in the western hemisphere. West Nile is a potentially fatal virus spread to humans by the bite of an infected mosquito. Cases have since turned up in seven states, causing a handful of deaths. It is not clear how West Nile reached America, though it is probably not a coincidence that the disease first presented itself in Queens, not far from two international airports, reckons Dr Petersen.

Watch out, Bambi's about

West Nile is a prototype for what is happening to many diseases worldwide at a time when travellers and cargo (including exotic animals) move quickly around the globe. Indeed, West Nile was not the first disease to leap continents. In the early 1990s, there was an outbreak of the Hanta virus among Navajo Indians in the south-west. The virus, named after a river in Korea and never before documented in the western hemisphere, caused 50 to 100 deaths. The disease is spread by contact with the urine and faeces of mice, whose population had exploded when El Niño brought abundant rain to the desert.

The United States regularly sees cases of other dread diseases, such as malaria and dengue fever, among returning travellers and immigrants. The public-health challenge lies in preventing these diseases from spreading once they arrive. The mosquito that carries dengue fever, *Aedes aegypti*, is common in the American south-east. These public-health concerns were the impetus for the International Conference on Emerging Infectious Diseases, which will meet again in 2002. There is also a fear that America is not adequately prepared for the threat of bioterrorism. The skills necessary in dealing with an outbreak of serious disease—surveillance, epidemiology, research and communication—are the same whether the agent is introduced on a rat swimming across the Rio Grande or in a suitcase sneaked through Kennedy airport. □

---

tercept them. Under a law signed by his predecessor, the incoming president will be obliged to develop, as soon as possible, a system for defending America against ballistic-missile attacks. But given the technical difficulty of stopping a missile in mid-flight, which of the half-dozen approaches on offer is the most promising? The issue, artfully parried by Bill Clinton, will not go away. In 2001 and well beyond, it will seriously strain both the Atlantic alliance and the whole system of international diplomacy. And the terms of the *pax americana* which holds sway in most of the world may have to be radically revised. As America puts more emphasis on protecting its own territory, it may be less inclined to rely on far-flung overseas bases and fickle allies. In the short term, the new president will have to decide whether, after a spate of embarrassing failures in the past year, he should plough on with a series of tests for a land-based system, which is designed to defend America from a limited attack by stopping missiles far above the atmosphere.

He must also decide whether it is worth trying to renegotiate and preserve the Anti-Ballistic Missile (ABM) treaty, under which America and Russia pledge to remain vulnerable to each other's rockets. Regardless of his own political impulses, the president will feel pressure from American hawks to scrap the ABM treaty at once. At the same time, he will hear loud warnings from Moscow and Beijing that such a move would trigger an acute international crisis. With its coffers boosted by rising oil prices, and anti-western sentiment seething away in Moscow, the Russian leadership under Vladimir Putin can be expected to fight hard. For example, Russia may unveil a more menacing military doctrine, further upgrading the role of battlefield nuclear weapons in defending its frontiers—including its western border with NATO.

In the end, as both sides know, there are limits to the Kremlin's bargaining power. Even if its economy improves sharply, Russia will not have the money to maintain a long-range nuclear arsenal of the current size for much longer. So American proposals for deep cuts in both sides' forces, in return for Russian consent to a limited anti-missile system, will start to look attractive. But Russia's political bosses, still smarting over their loss of global influence, will not willingly permit America to erect defences that neutralise their only remaining token of superpower status, a huge nuclear arsenal. So expect some loud snarls from the Bear.

Mr Putin may woo America's European allies, especially Germany, by refining his hitherto vague proposals

2001
At the Kyoto conference on climate change, America agreed to cut carbon dioxide emissions by 7% from their 1990 levels by 2010. They will not make it—between 1990-1998 emissions grew 11.5%.

Bruce Clark: defence correspondent, *The Economist*

2001
Four billion people will tune in for the 8th IAAF athletics world championships, in Edmonton, Canada. Sydney's winners will seek to burnish their reputations; losers will seek revenge.

for a joint approach to warding off missiles from rogue states. With a mixture of blandishment and threats, he may point out that Russia's importance as a supplier of oil and gas to Europe could grow as energy prices rise. West European leaders will react sceptically; but their electorates, and business communities, may be more impressed. Meanwhile, China, while not a party to the ABM accord, will scream even louder about its demise—threatening to increase and improve its puny long-range nuclear arsenal even faster than it is doing already. And that in turn could draw China's rival, India, into a regional nuclear arms race.

When the new American secretary of state holds a first set-piece meeting with NATO counterparts, probably in May, the United States will be faced with a barrage of anguished and contradictory messages. Some Europeans—the British and Danes, for example—will be fretting about their own increased vulnerability to missile attack if their territory is used for radar stations linked to an American shield. Others may voice the old fear that an America bent on hunkering down beneath a protective umbrella is not likely to take many risks for its allies. (The opposite case—that a well-defended America would be a bolder ally—can also be made.) Other Europeans may be angling for a share of technology and defence contracts.

The new administration will try to buy some political space by ordering a fresh review by security pundits of emerging missile threats and how to deal with them. To the delight of hawks, the study will look into a much wider variety of national missile-defence systems than have so far been considered: space-based, airborne and, above all, sea-based solutions as well as land-based ones—or possibly some combination of all these approaches. Very probably, one of the study's conclusions will be that sea-based interception of missiles a few seconds after they are launched, when they are still "big, hot and slow", is a more promising concept than using land-based interceptors to stop rogue rockets in space.

To the dismay of hawks, the president will do his best to preserve the ABM treaty in some form—given the serious consequences of tearing it up. On the face of things, securing Russia's assent to a sea-based system will be virtually impossible; after all, Mr Putin has responded with a firm *nyet* to the very modest treaty changes which Mr Clinton had proposed. On the other hand, Mr Putin seems pragmatic as well as tough, so a grand nuclear bargain between America and Russia is still worth a try. ☐

Canadian-ness

Canadians will have little to complain about in 2001. Their economy will be one of the best in the world. It will grow more than 3%. Any recession is at least four years off. Unemployment will fall, again, in 2001. And the United Nations will, yet again, name Canada as the best country in the world for overall human development. Not the most exciting of plaudits perhaps, but a compliment nonetheless. The icing on the cake will be that even the separatists in Quebec will be quiet.

Jean Chrétien, the prime minister and leader of the Liberal Party, will celebrate his 38th year in politics in 2001. He will start the year in good spirits, with a general election in late 2000 safely under his belt. Support for his Liberal Party will be strong for two reasons: the booming economy and his answer to the tricky question of what constitutes "Canadian-ness".

Mr Chrétien believes Canadian-ness involves social justice and tolerance, values he embodies. His recent spending on health and education has given substance to this rhetoric. And with the coffers bursting—the federal budget will be C$7.5 billion ($5 billion) in surplus in 2001—he can also afford to give to other worthy causes.

Stockwell Day, the leader of the opposition Canadian Alliance, would like to make

It's fun being a Canadian

Canadian-ness all about smaller government. But many voters find him too American. The federal government in Washington takes only 31% of America's GDP in taxes. Canada remains much closer to Europe in its belief in big government: its government takes 41%. (Americans, in contrast, believe in big pay packets—per capita GDP in Canada will be $24,400 in 2001. Americans will be half as rich again.)

However charismatic, Mr Day will not be a serious threat. At least not until the economy goes pear-shaped. Mr Chrétien's more serious worry in 2001 will be calls within his own party for his retirement and the elevation of Paul Martin, the finance minister behind the economic miracle, to the top job.

Apart from Mr Day, the only Canadians in for a painful 2001 are those having to fly. Over half of Canada's domestic routes are monopolised by Air Canada or one of its subsidiaries. The firm controls 90% of the country's domestic-flight revenues. 2000 was scarred by their delays, cancellations and corporate arrogance. The government could bring relief to fliers if it carries out its threat to allow full foreign competition in 2001.

If tax is one area where Canada likes to keep its distance from the United States, then foreign policy is one where the two countries are inevitably linked. Relations are usually dominated by trade, but in 2001 the two countries will talk about defence as well. Canada cannot but be sucked into America's plans for building a continental missile defence shield. The Canadian government will be asked for a financial contribution (not really needed) and moral support (crucial, Washington believes, if it is going to justify the project to the rest of the world). Canada is likely to want to minimise its involvement, and a commitment to its traditional detection role would probably be enough. It will be a reminder that Canadian-ness must always have a bit of American-ness mixed in. ☐

The Middle East: The Middle East's misery 74 / **Peacekeeping:** Tough love 75
Peter Singer: How are your morals? 76 / **The Gulf:** Forecast 79
Latin America: Gets a taste for wealth 79 / **Brazil:** Has Brazil's moment come? 80
Africa: Africa's darker shades of black 81 / **Egypt:** Forecast 81
Afghanistan: Where's the world's worst? 82 / **The future:** Letter from 2050 84

THE WORLD IN 2001

International

Let me through, I'm non-governmental

NGOs: New Gods Overseas

Adam Roberts

2001
Expect America and Iran to re-establish diplomatic relations. They were cut off 22 years ago.

Adam Roberts:
The Economist

On Earth Day in April 2001, a crop of protesters against GM plants will scatter turf and turnips across the streets of Europe's cities. In Quebec, Canada, an "anti-capitalist convergence" against free trade in the Americas will attract Nike-wearing youths to kick in the windows of McDonald's, a burger chain. The activists' year will start in January, at the World Economic Forum's meeting in Davos, Switzerland, and continue through the year with more Seattle-style whistle-blowing wherever television cameras lurk.

This is the extreme side of a growing, and generally positive, phenomenon: influential activists and their NGOs. Non-governmental organisations will become more numerous, prominent and powerful in 2001 than ever before. Now, 30,000 international ones exist; 50 years ago there was just a handful. Domestic ones are counted in the millions: there were almost none ten years ago in Russia, now there are 65,000; in America, 8% of workers are employed by some sort of non-profit group; in Zambia, they sprout up so quickly that newspapers explain "how to spot a fake NGO." As trust in political parties and companies declines, as governments funnel more money through charities and as the Internet gets cheaper, the numbers will grow even faster.

In poor countries they will multiply especially fast. An NGO is an efficient tool with which to harvest donor money. Rich governments have lost their appetite for handing over cheques to poor, corrupt and dictatorial regimes. So they hand them to NGOs instead. And not only money passes hands. In 2001 large numbers of expatriate (usually white) workers will be dispensing the aid and giving assistance. A white person representing a European government in, say, Africa (or an American official in Latin America) may be labelled a colonialist. But someone working for an NGO has less such baggage.

Many of these organisations are political institutions: they have an agenda. They also have an eye on publicity. In the wars, accidents, natural disasters and world summits of 2001, they will jostle ever more fiercely before the cameras. Some of the best advice and analysis of the year's Balkan troubles in and around Serbia especially will come from specialists like the International Crisis Group, whose reports fly ever thicker and quicker through the ether. The flags and landcruisers of relief agencies will be prominent at floods and man-made famines in parts of Africa and southern Asia. Where mundane, but just as deadly, poverty strikes, aid groups will get more money for their work: between 1994 and 1997 the European Union's aid spending via NGOs rose from 47% to 67% of the relief budget. The upward trend will continue.

Far harder to measure is their power. On some issues

International THE WORLD IN 2001

(GM foods, animal rights, global warming, racism) they will set the agenda for public debate. They will be particularly active at the world conference on racism in South Africa in September. In the lead up to the Rio+10 conference in 2002 (a decade after the world's environmental conference in Brazil in 1992), green groups will shift attention from current topical issues, such as poor-country debt, to rich-country concerns, such as the depleting ozone layer. One sign of clout is how much annoyance they will cause. Australia's touchy foreign minister, Alexander Downer, for instance, has berated activists supporting Aborigines for ignoring the "primary role of democratically elected governments and the subordinate role of non-governmental organisations". Russia, Serbia, Mexico, Zimbabwe and many other African nations routinely weigh in against groups they see as threats or as agents of western imperialism.

Globally, the bigger ones such as Oxfam, Care, Médecins Sans Frontières, Greenpeace and Amnesty are already more influential than some smaller governments. They have large budgets and highly skilled staff. (Some, such as Bernard Kouchner of Médecins Sans Frontières, and Olesegun Obasanjo, formerly of Transparency International, flit between jobs in government, in the UN and in NGOs.) Some will try to broker peace deals, most likely in civil wars such as Sudan's, Sri Lanka's and Sierra Leone's. Others will learn to work closely with armies, especially during disasters. They will also get a greater say in the UN: some already want to exert their influence to help pick new heads of UN agencies.

Idealism + Cash = Activism

Governments and political parties may retreat yet further: international networks of single-issue NGOs already mimic multi-issue political parties. But the more interesting development to watch in 2001 will be relations between NGOs and businesses. Here lie the greatest rivalries and attractions. As brands become more important to companies, NGOs' power grows accordingly. Oil companies know—think of Shell in Nigeria—how bad publicity hurts business.

In Sudan a Canadian oil company, Talisman, now tries to work with local NGOs to avoid accusations that it is helping to fuel the civil war. Monsanto and Greenpeace will clash more over modified foods in 2001, as will NGOs and arms exporters in Eastern Europe. Animal-rights activists have already turned on corporations and their directors. More responsible NGOs now talk of codes of conduct. They know that their own brands and images are vulnerable too.

But clever businesses will attempt to co-opt NGOs. Already some businessmen, such as Bill Gates and George Soros, wield money and power in the voluntary sector. Fund-starved volunteers rarely resist such munificence, even if large donations from a single source threaten independence. In aid, private flows of capital to poor countries already massively outweigh official aid: expect more private investors to team up with aid-NGOs (with good reputations) in emerging markets. Despite the clashes on Earth Day, at the G8 and the next meeting of the World Bank, NGOs will be needed ever more as partners in the coming years; and they, in turn, will need private money. Welcome to the real world. □

2001
Visionary or lunatic? Libya's Colonel Muammar Qaddafi will declare the creation of a United States of Africa in March. Oil money will buy some fawning.

The Middle East's misery

Roula Khalaf

Arabs and Israelis will struggle to reach a comprehensive peace agreement in 2001. But the signatures of statesmen will mean little to those on the dusty streets. Palestinian teenagers, living in miserable conditions and without hope of jobs, are scarcely going to stop throwing bricks because Yasser Arafat asks them. And that section of Israel's religious society—a large minority—that spurns any idea of peace or compromise answers to an authority other than the government. Violence, chaotic and brutal, will never be far away. There will be times when there is a lull in the storm: it will not pass, however, in 2001 or indeed the next decade. Israel's problems need to be seen in the context of a growing unease in the Middle East. Of the 163m Arabs living in countries that border the Mediterranean region between Morocco and Syria, a staggering 91m, or 56%, will be under 24. No country's economic growth or political system will be able to cope with this onslaught. The longer the unrest in the Palestinian territories, the more Arab governments will come under pressure to react. Public opinion in the Arab world, which has been enraged by the violence in the West Bank and Gaza Strip, could also turn against the region's existing governments.

Ehud Barak's negotiations with Syrians and Palestinians in 2000 may have come to little but they had the merit of breaking taboos. He acknowledged the need to relinquish to Syria virtually all of the Golan Heights and he agreed, at least in principle, that Palestinians have the right to share Jerusalem. But he underestimated the resolve of Arab leaders and the fractiousness of his own government. Who can be an effective leader of Israel? Was ever a country so divided? One swathe of its society emulates California in its liberalism, education, entrepreneurialism and high-tech savvy; the other swathe is fundamentalist and reluctant to relinquish 4,000-year-

Roula Khalaf: Middle East editor, *Financial Times*

Different ideas of paradise

old customs.

Bashar al-Assad, Syria's new 35-year-old leader, could prove more forthcoming than his father on water-sharing arrangements for Lake Tiberias, but he will be as adamant about sovereignty over the northern shore of the lake—the issue that broke the back of negotiations in the past year. Yasser Arafat, the Palestinian leader, will remain desperate for a peace agreement but unlikely to make concessions over sovereignty of Muslim holy sites in Arab East Jerusalem. Israel's border with Lebanon will be more volatile if peace negotiations with Syria are not revived. At the same time, however, Mr Assad will be careful to avoid a flare-up in violence. Anti-Syrian feelings in Lebanon, a country under the control of Syria, will be on the rise, putting pressure on the government to withdraw its 35,000 troops. At the very least, Mr Assad will be forced to rebalance Syria's economic relationship with Lebanon and make the Syrian presence more discreet. At home, his focus will be on consolidating his rule and reining in the competing intelligence services. He will take steps to promote foreign investment in Syria, but liberalisation measures will come up against vested interests in the military and intelligence establishment.

For Gulf monarchies too, economic management will be the top priority. Rulers in the region will use the windfall from high oil prices in 2000—Middle East oil producers are estimated to have earned as much as $200 billion from oil during the year—to replenish foreign-exchange reserves and pay down debt. With the strain on government finances reduced, the effects of the oil boom will begin to trickle down. Payments of arrears to the private sector in Saudi Arabia, for example, should revive the sluggish economy. The kingdom can be expected to open its gas sector to foreign oil companies and to promote foreign investment in non-energy sectors. But Crown Prince Abdullah, now running the daily affairs of the kingdom on behalf of his ailing brother, King Fahd, will face competing pressures. Rival members of the ruling family will want an expansion in spending, on military purchases, for example, and a more gradual pace of reform. With the unemployment rate running at around 15%, daring structural adjustment will be needed to promote the private sector.

The sanctity of sanctions

The demands of the baby-boomers, the result of the past three decades of fast population growth, will be the main difficulty facing rulers across the region. Most serious will be the pressures in Iran. The reformist president, Mohammad Khatami, remains immensely popular. He should easily carry the presidential election in 2001. But as the past year has proved, popular legitimacy does not necessarily translate into practical change in Iran, where

Tough love

Peacekeeping is back in vogue. The United Nations' peacekeeping budget for 2001 is $2.6 billion, the most for six years. There will be more than 40,000 peacekeepers stationed around the world. The biggest deployments will be in East Timor, an operation that should shrink in size as a new government is established there late in the year, and in Sierra Leone. A peacekeeping force will be set up in Eritrea and Ethiopia, where Kofi Annan, the UN secretary-general, hopes to send 4,200 troops.

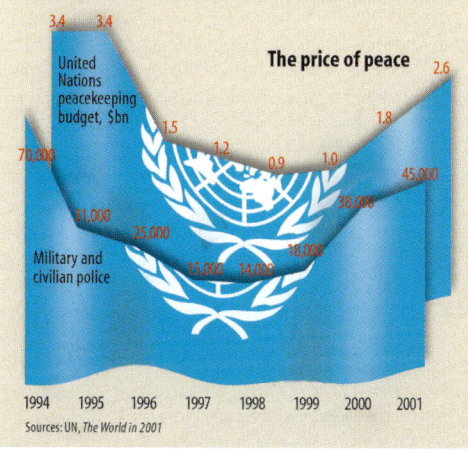

The UN wants the troops that various governments lend it to be better trained, better equipped, and to have a mandate actively to engage those who break peace accords. That would break the principle of neutrality that has underpinned peacekeeping in the past 20 years. Since troop-contributing governments will be suspicious, it is unlikely that the year will witness much "peace-enforcement".

Another thorny question will be who pays for this peacekeeping renaissance. The United States wants to renegotiate its peacekeeping contributions from 30.5% down to 25% of the budget. Other countries are unlikely to want to pay more.

The result: Mr Annan will have his hands full in 2001 trying to keep the peace among United Nations members. □

The price of peace
United Nations peacekeeping budget, $bn: 3.4, 3.4, 1.5, 1.2, 0.9, 1.0, 1.8, 2.6
Military and civilian police: 70,000, 31,000, 25,000, 19,000, 14,000, 18,000, 38,000, 45,000
1994 1995 1996 1997 1998 1999 2000 2001
Sources: UN, *The World in 2001*

the conservative clerical establishment retains the levers of power. The power struggle between reformists and conservatives will intensify, risking further polarisation in Iranian society. Mr Khatami will be caught between the conservatives afraid of reform and the young generation clamouring for change. His attempt to navigate this minefield will lead him to focus on economic reform, on which reformists and conservatives can find consensus. Iran's international rehabilitation is another area of agreement which will be more vigorously pursued. In particular, relations with the United States will improve, leading to the likelihood of a lifting of sanctions in 2001. Iraq will not be as lucky. United Nations sanctions will be maintained, with no big change expected in American policy. However, support for the ten-year embargo will erode and the sanctions regime will become more difficult to enforce. Saddam Hussein will try to create a crisis over the American and British bombings of the northern and southern no-fly zones.

In North Africa, relations between Algeria and Morocco will remain strained over the disputed Western Sahara. The UN, which has been planning a referendum on the fate of the territory, will grow increasingly impatient with Morocco and the Algeria-backed Polisario Front. But this will not bring the parties to an agreement.

In Algiers, the power struggle between President Abdelaziz Bouteflika and powerful army generals will deepen, resulting in gridlock and a more severe social crisis. The level of violence should remain stable, however, with attacks concentrated in rural areas. In Morocco, King Mohammad's honeymoon will end and Islamists outside the political structure will put on pressure for a deepening of political reform. The young monarch's hope is for a pick-up in the economy, which would alleviate the pressure of unemployment, now running at 20% in urban areas, and reduce the risk of social unrest. □

2001
The host of the Olympic Games in 2008 is chosen by a vote in Moscow in July. Paris, Istanbul, Osaka, Toronto and Beijing are competing. Expect tales of Athens, host in 2004, floundering with its preparations, amid incompetence and corruption.

Peter Singer, DeCamp professor of bioethics at Princeton University, raises three points that will challenge our ethical behaviour in 2001

How are your morals?

"Free trade is too important to be left to the economists"

Perhaps the best indication of the significance of the three issues I have singled out for attention is to look briefly at those I have had to reject. These include:
• Reducing our output of greenhouse gases to prevent climate change that will, among other things, inundate the farming land of tens of millions of poor people in delta regions in Bangladesh and Egypt.
• Saving chimpanzees, gorillas and orangutans from being pushed into extinction in Africa and Indonesia and, more generally, ameliorating our ruthless exploitation of all other sentient beings.
• Preserving our planet's dwindling biodiversity.
• Remembering that nuclear weapons have not gone away.

The three issues that are more significant, or more urgent, are:

1. Poverty

At the United Nations Millennium Summit the South African president, Thabo Mbeki, said that "the poor of the world stand at the gates of the comfortable mansions and palaces occupied by each and every king and queen, president and prime minister privileged to attend this unique meeting." There were no reports of leaders inviting the homeless to take over their vacant guest rooms, but the General Assembly passed a Declaration setting a series of ambitious and specific targets to be met by 2015. The most important was to halve the proportion of the world's population who suffer from hunger and lack safe drinking water.

The first and greatest ethical challenge of 2001 will be to take practical steps towards meeting this target. Debt relief for the world's poorest nations will be a start, but the target will not be met without reversing the long downward spiral in the proportion of their wealth that rich nations give to foreign aid. For the United States to give barely 0.1%—yes, that is just one-tenth of 1%!—of its GNP as foreign aid is a complete disgrace. (And even that overstates the situation, because the largest recipient is Israel, hardly one of the poorest nations.)

2. The AIDS scandal

Globally, AIDS has now caused more than 20m deaths and orphaned 13m children. There are 35m people living with HIV/AIDS, and there will be more than 5m new infections in 2001 alone. A catastrophe of barely imaginable proportions is unfolding in southern Africa. Botswana now has more than 35% of the adult population HIV positive. In South Africa the figure is 20%, or 4.2m people, and still rising sharply. Neither the increase in new infections, nor the deaths of those already infected, is inevitable. Uganda, one of the worst-affected countries in the early 1990s, has brought its infection rate down sharply by a strong educational campaign. For the leaders of countries with high infection rates, the ethical challenge is to do the same, and for the rich nations, to finance those efforts.

The most direct ethical challenge to us in the rich nations, however, arises from the fact that we have the drugs to treat HIV/AIDS, but the overwhelming majority of the infected people in the poor nations cannot afford to buy them. Are we going to stand by and watch millions die when we have the drugs that can save their lives? Do the leaders of the NATO nations who chose military intervention in Kosovo think the lives of Kosovars are more precious than the lives of Africans? The number of AIDS victims in Africa is thousands of times greater than the number of victims of Serbian "ethnic cleansing" in Kosovo. When massacre threatened in Rwanda, countries with the capacity to intervene did nothing. Bill Clinton has since acknowledged that this was the greatest moral failure of his presidency. Now, in Africa, greater loss of life is occurring, but there is more time to intervene. For the rich nations to do too little, too late, would be a much more clear-cut moral failing than their inaction in Rwanda.

Without ignoring the logistical problems of getting the drugs to the people who need them, the first step is to allow the developing nations to produce the drugs themselves at a fraction of the cost they now have to pay. When South Africa first mooted this proposal, the United States threatened a trade war to protect the proprietary rights of the pharmaceuticals corporations. After AIDS activists dogged Al Gore at every campaign stop, the United States has shelved that threat, but the drug companies are now suing the South African government to stop it going ahead. If they win, the chief executives of those pharmaceuticals companies will have the deaths of millions of men, women and children on their hands.

3. Reforming the WTO

Not everyone thinks that globalisation is an unalloyed blessing. Through all the rhetoric, there is a critique of the WTO that must be taken seriously. The WTO dispute panels refuse to allow nations to use trade sanctions to protect environmental values. They have consistently refused to allow nations to prohibit the sale of products created in an unacceptable way. So tuna caught in a way that drowns dolphins has to be treated the same as tuna caught in a way that avoids killing dolphins. If this kind of thinking still prevails when the European Union's ban on the battery cage for laying hens comes into effect, the WTO is likely to say that Europe cannot stop the import of eggs from countries where hens are jam-packed into bare wire cages.

These issues ought not to be resolved in this manner. Free trade is too important to be left to the economists. The ethical challenge is to meld the benefits of free trade with the values that the WTO now leaves out of the equation. □

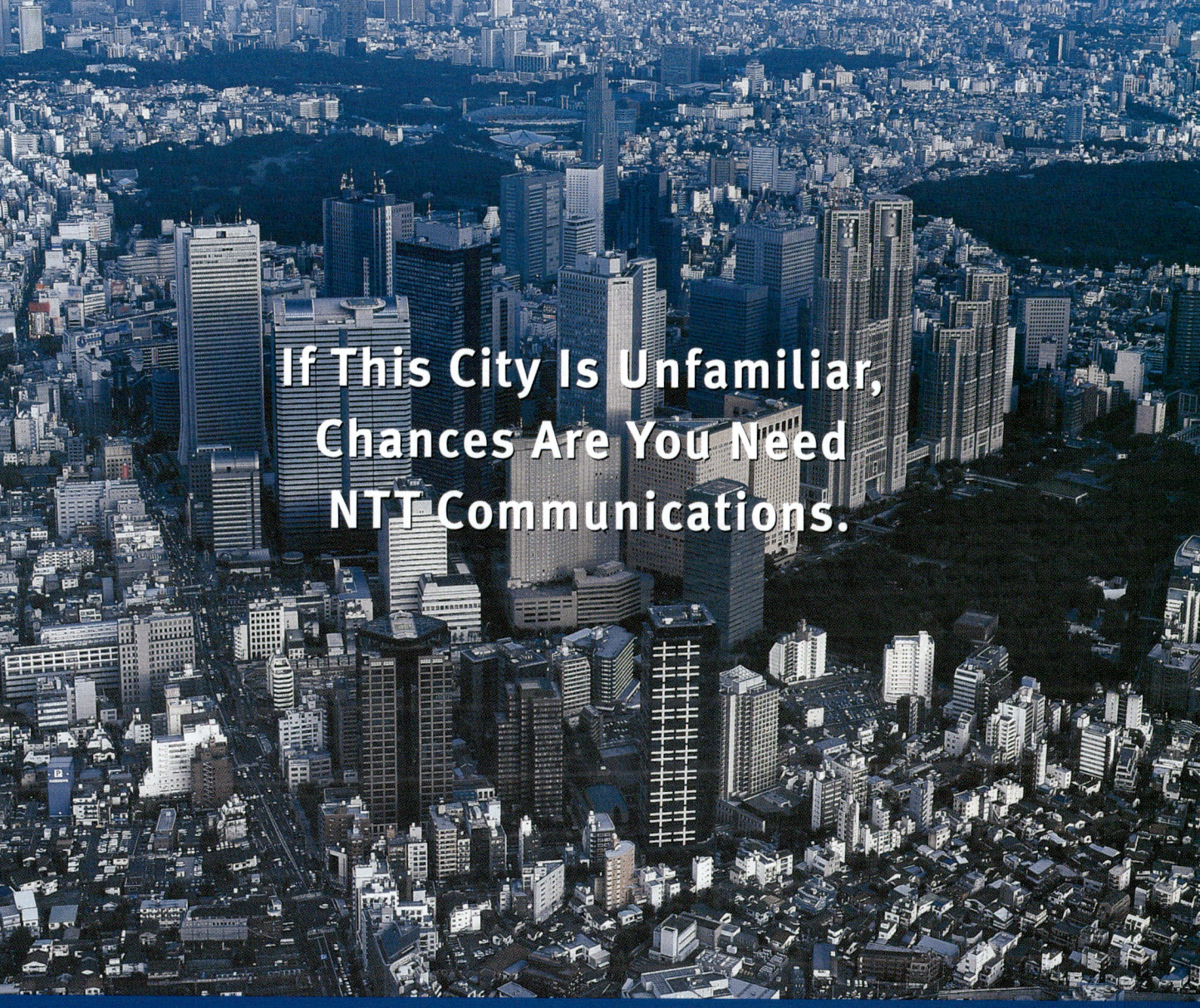

If This City Is Unfamiliar, Chances Are You Need NTT Communications.

Recognize this city? It's in Asia. Here's another hint: A lot of global companies do business here. If you're feeling left out, try getting connected with NTT Communications. As Japan's leading telecommunications company, NTT Communications can provide your business with everything it needs to stay ahead of the competition, including our one-stop network solutions service: *Arcstar*. Currently serving 25 major cities around the world and available in 53 countries, Arcstar can develop the network solution that's right for you. And with special focus on IP (Internet Protocol), Arcstar offers top-quality, high-speed and secure access to the Internet. So when it comes to connecting to Tokyo, or anywhere else in the world, connect with NTT Communications. **Your trusted partner in Network Solutions.**

Global Connections From East to West.

NTT Communications

www.ntt.com/world

Tokyo Osaka Seoul Beijing Shanghai Taipei Hong Kong Hanoi Bangkok Manila Kuala Lumpur Singapore Jakarta Sydney London
Brussels Paris Geneva Düsseldorf Frankfurt Milan New York Washington D.C. Virginia San Francisco Los Angeles Rio de Janeiro São Paulo

NTT Communications Group: NTT Australia +61-2-9231-5677 / NTT Korea +82-2-3446-2030 / NTT Taiwan +886-2-2547-2561 / NTT Hong Kong +852-2521-0688 / NTT MSC (Malaysia) +60-3-8311-2000 / NTT Singapore +65-438-3101 / NTT Communications Thailand +66-2-236-7527 / Beijing Rep. Office +86-10-6590-9200 / Shanghai Rep. Office +86-21-5835-8211 / Manila Rep. Office +63-2-888-2481 / Hanoi Rep. Office +84-4-825-9258 / NTT Europe London Head Office +44-20-7977-1000 / Paris Office +33-1-4076-0660 / Düsseldorf Office +49-211-164-700 / Frankfurt Office +49-69-1338-9670 / Milan Office +39-02-5821-5303 / Geneva Rep. Office +41-22-798-3840 / NTT America +1-212-661-0810 / NTT do Brasil Telecomunicacoes Ltda. +55-11-253-0108

Visit our virtual tour @ www.dubaiairport.com

800 metres of total tranquillity

Ease of movement, unhurried efficiency. That's what 800 metres of world class architecture gives you. An airport designed around you and your every need. You probably won't notice half of the systems and measures we've put into place to make passing through our airport so effortless, but you will feel the difference.

If only all airports were like this.

DUBAI INTERNATIONAL AIRPORT

Where the world connects

THE WORLD IN 2001 International

THE GULF

FORECAST

Celebrations in May of the 20th anniversary of the Gulf Co-operation Council (embracing Saudi Arabia, Kuwait, Bahrain, Qatar, Oman and the UAE) will be long and lavish. The reason: the dramatic recovery in oil prices. Dark warnings of fiscal and exchange-rate crises have been drowned out by fat budget and current-account surpluses. Watch out for tensions within OPEC, especially if the price of oil remains high.

In the region's largest economy, Saudi Arabia, many policymakers will be tempted to drift back into old ways, by cloning meaningless civil-service jobs for an ill-trained population. But a growing number of dissenters, including a younger generation of Saudi princes, argue that the only way to create sustainable development, and the job opportunities to feed a rapidly growing workforce, is to engage in the global economy. A more energetic push for membership of the World Trade Organisation, along with a greater encouragement of foreign investment, will be one by-product of their growing influence.

In other countries, the arguments have already been won. Qatar will continue with its ambitious gas-based industrialisation project, while pruning back royal perks and other subsidies. Women have already been granted electoral emancipation. Expect further lively political debate—much of it to be aired on Qatar's fearless Al-Jazeera satellite station. Kuwait, too, will seek to create a more pertinent, private-sector career path for its western-educated and Internet-savvy graduates. Dubai will set the standard for what a modern, open, ambitious and entrepreneurial Arab state can look like.

Some foreign-policy issues will aggravate this harmony. Saudi Arabia and Iran will pursue their cautious détente, but Iran's dispute with the UAE over three tiny Gulf islands will put a drag on full rapprochement. Further arguments over Iraq will erupt if Saddam Hussein either dies (he is said to have cancer) or makes mischief over oil. Meanwhile, the prospects for a customs union look as distant as ever. □

GDP GROWTH	1999	2000	2001
Saudi Arabia	0.5	2.5	3.0
Bahrain	2.5	4.0	4.0
Qatar	0.2	4.3	4.6
Kuwait	-2.4	1.5	2.5
United Arab Emirates	2.5	5.0	5.5
Oman	0.3	3.4	2.4

EIU COUNTRY ANALYSIS AND FORECASTING

Latin America gets a taste for wealth

Michael Reid

For Latin America it will be a year of steady economic growth. Inflation will fall: indeed, in 2001 all of the main economies in Latin America may record single-digit inflation, for the first time since the 1930s. It will be 12 months blissfully free of major presidential elections, when politicians can settle down to practical things, like making democracy work. Despite its shaky hold on some poorer Andean countries, democracy will emerge strengthened across the hemisphere by the end of the year. But economic growth will still not be strong enough to slash poverty rates, nor to provide a feel-good factor.

Overall, the region will find it harder to grow any faster in 2001 than the 4.5% it managed in 2000. But growth will be more evenly spread. Mexico's red-hot economy will cool, in line with that of the United States, and with falling oil prices. After expanding at more than 7% in 2000, the highest rate since 1981, Mexican growth will fall to a respectable 4%. But further south, expect faster growth in Brazil to help other countries too.

Poor export performance will remain an obstacle in Latin America. The search for new markets lies behind the region's interest in a Free Trade Area of the Americas (FTAA). That will be the main topic of discussion when 34 western hemisphere leaders (all of them, except Cuba's Fidel Castro) meet in Quebec in April for the third summit of the Americas. It will be an opportunity for Latin America to press its claims on the new administration in Washington. But the FTAA negotiations will only take on any urgency after the Quebec meeting if the United States' Congress approves legislation granting the president fast-track negotiating authority for trade deals.

The other big subject in Quebec will be Colombia. By April, a new army brigade trained by the United States will be nearly ready to go into action in Colombia's southern lowlands, the source of much of the world's cocaine. The brigade's target will be the drug industry, but also the anti-government guerrillas. Do not expect dramatic results. Colombia will see no release in 2001 from its nightmare of kidnaps and extortion by the guerrillas, and massacres of civilians by right-wing paramilitaries. Expect no significant progress towards peace until after a successor to President Andres Pastrana is elected in 2002.

Elsewhere, hopes of change are higher—and nowhere more so than in Mexico. After his historic defeat of the Revolutionary Institutional Party (PRI), Vicente Fox begins his presidency on December 1st at breakneck pace: he will clean up venal police forces, and push through constitutional changes that will give more power to local government. But President Fox will find that governing is harder than campaigning. He faces resistance in Congress, and from vested interests. That resistance may even

Michael Reid: Americas editor, *The Economist*

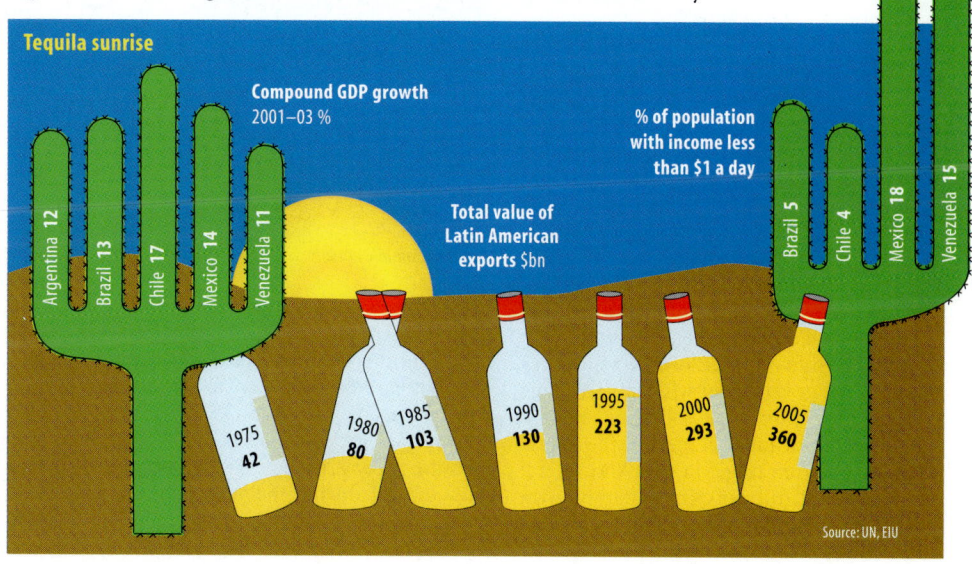

Tequila sunrise

Compound GDP growth 2001–03 %

Argentina 12, Brazil 13, Chile 17, Mexico 14, Venezuela 11

Total value of Latin American exports $bn

1975: 42; 1980: 80; 1985: 103; 1990: 130; 1995: 223; 2000: 293; 2005: 360

% of population with income less than $1 a day

Brazil 5, Chile 4, Mexico 18, Venezuela 15

Source: UN, EIU

79

International THE WORLD IN 2001

be violent, but only in isolated cases. Mexican politics will be noisy, but in that they will at last resemble those of democracies anywhere.

Against the background of a slowing economy, Mr Fox will push through a tax reform aimed at raising government revenues, and spending on health and education. He will probably have to settle for incremental changes in the tax system. Neither will he find it easy to get congressional approval for another reform, aimed at allowing private investment in electricity and oil. Expect him to win this argument, even if not in 2001. In August, President Fox will face an early test of public support for his rule in an important election for governor of the border state of Baja California, held by his PAN party since 1989. The PRI, for its part, will not split formally, but it will atomise in practice, with Mr Fox receiving pragmatic support from some of its technocrats and state governors, while diehards resist change. The power of these diehards is not to be underestimated. One-party rule (by the PRI, of course) had been a way of political life in Mexico for three generations. Something so culturally ingrained—and so comfortable—will not just fade away.

Elsewhere, change will be more gradual. Argentina will continue to be a worry. President Fernando de la Rua will muddle along. His fragile centre-left Alliance will probably hang together. He will hope that the economy will at last revive enough for him to avoid a drubbing from the opposition Peronists in a congressional election in October. Growth in Brazil and a weaker dollar should help Argentina's exports, allowing the economy to expand by 4%. But improvements in wages and employment will still be painfully slow. Should growth, or fiscal discipline, falter, Argentina may yet need emergency aid to prop up its fixed exchange rate.

In Chile, a more vigorous economic recovery, with growth at over 5% in both 2000 and 2001, will help another centre-left government, that of Ricardo Lagos, to win a congressional election in December 2001. General Augusto Pinochet may do his country a service by quietly dying; if not, human-rights cases against him will drag on in Chile's courts.

Peru faces an uncertain year. Expect the fresh election promised by the president, Alberto Fujimori, to be held in April. Alejandro Toledo, Mr Fujimori's opponent in the flawed election of 2000, will be a strong candidate; but a host of other contenders will emerge. The armed forces will hover in the background: a coup is possible, but unlikely. ◻

Has Brazil's moment come?

Mike Reid

Brazilians will at last see some of the benefits of the economic reforms of the past few years. They will take a rosier view of their president, Fernando Henrique Cardoso—and will fret about who might replace him in an election due in 2002. After growth of almost 4% in 2000, Brazil's economy should expand by 5% in 2001, the best result since the start of the inflation-busting Real Plan in 1994. This time the growth looks sustainable: there will be much talk of Brazil being on the verge of a new "economic miracle", and finally starting to live up to its potential as the motor of South American growth. There will even be some truth behind the hyperbole.

In 2001, ordinary Brazilians will have reasons to cheer, as interest rates and unemployment fall. After two years of fiscal austerity, Mr Cardoso's team will cast aside their hairshirts, and boost public spending on social welfare. They will be able to do this because Brazil has recovered far more quickly from its devaluation of January 1999 than most, including the IMF, expected. Also on the agenda is privatisation. Partial stakes in Brazil's big three power generators, Fumas, Eletronorte and Chesfe, should be sold off, after long delays.

But the government will still face some constraints. Monetary policy will remain fairly cautious, aimed at meeting the central bank's inflation target of 4%. And several things could still conspire to damp down growth. One risk involves oil prices: if these

A good economic model

were to remain high throughout the year, that would reduce the scope for interest rate cuts. Another is the balance of payments: Brazil still needs to do more to stimulate the kind of rapid export growth it requires to ensure that growth is sustainable. That is because strong foreign investment flows may tail off during the year, as investors start to worry about who will succeed President Cardoso.

The president's popularity will be buoyed up by the rise in economic growth and qualification (after a shaky start) to the football World Cup. His priority will be to position himself to exert maximum influence over the 2002 presidential election. In other ways, it will be a year of political inaction, with the government making little effort to push political, judicial and tax reforms. In February, the election of new speakers in both houses of Congress will trigger much noisy infighting among the four parties of Mr Cardoso's loose centre-right coalition.

In the opinion polls, the frontrunners for 2002 will be Luiz Inacio Lula de Silva, of the leftist Workers' Party; Ciro Gomes, an ambitious populist maverick: and Itamar Franco, an eccentric former president with a passionate hatred of Mr Cardoso. Only Mr Gomes has a real chance of winning.

Towards the end of the year, Mr Cardoso will reveal his own choice of candidate. If everything goes well for him, the chosen one may be Tasso Jereissati, the reformist governor of the north-eastern state of Ceara, or Jose Serra, the health minister. If Mr Cardoso's position is less strong, he will turn to someone outside his closest circle of political friends, such as Roseanna Sarney, the daughter of a former president. Or he may even cut a deal with Mr Gomes. Whoever is anointed will have a better than even chance of becoming Brazil's next president. ◻

Africa's darker shades of black

Patrick Smith

Africa will emerge from 2001 a very slightly better place. On balance, younger and more reform-minded leaders will replace unattractive despots. Peace will break out in some unlikely places; war will stubbornly continue in Angola and Sudan. The irrepressibly upbeat IMF and World Bank forecast GDP growth for the region at 4.5% in 2001, up from an estimated 3.5% in 2000. This is still short of the 5% Africa needs to stop poverty from worsening. Average income per head in Africa will be lower in 2001 than it was in 1971. Thirty years of decline, at a time of unprecedented wealth creation elsewhere in the world, is Africa's sad record of political ineptitude.

Not everyone will despair about all of Africa's economies in 2001. Fast-growing Mozambique and Tanzania are held up by the IMF and the World Bank as proof that good management can turn around war-torn and poverty-stricken economies. International banks plan more investments in Africa's 19 stockmarkets and privatisation programmes. Trade and market access will overshadow debt as the main economic issue. Since 1970 Africa's agricultural exports have lost some $70 billion a year in market share through inefficiency and western protectionism. Agricultural subsidies in rich countries cost some $300 billion a year. African ministers will be lobbying the World Trade Organisation to win back their market share and encourage their hard-pressed farmers.

Among Africa's biggest economies, Nigeria and South Africa should grow at between 3% and 4%—not enough to cut poverty or the jobless queues. South Africa will also see an increasingly aggressive civic campaign against the African National Congress government's handling of the AIDS crisis and its insistence that HIV (the virus with which almost a quarter of South African adults are infected) is not the main cause of AIDS. More African governments will be urged to copy the campaigns in Uganda and Senegal that, by seizing the issue openly, have managed to push down infection rates.

Scratching a living for someone else to steal

Zimbabwe will pull back from the brink of disaster with a face-saving compromise on land reform but its economy will reel. As the ruling Zimbabwe African National Union-Patriotic Front decides on a successor to President Robert Mugabe, the tough former intelligence chief Emmerson Mnangagwa will emerge as front runner. Support for the opposition Movement for Democratic Change will hold up well, promising a close-run presidential election in 2002.

Of course Zimbabwe will still be a corrupt, inefficient and disintegrating country. But the fact that there is the prospect and mechanism for democratic change sets it among the handful of happier African lands. In Kenya the battle to succeed President Daniel arap Moi before the 2002 elections will grow fiercer. The former finance minister Musalia Mudavadi is favoured against the for-

Patrick Smith: editor, *Africa Confidential*

EGYPT
FORECAST

Egypt is the most populous, the most chaotic and yet perhaps the most influential of Arab countries. It has, in that Oscar Wilde phrase, a brilliant future behind it. And in 2001, that future will be left a little bit further behind. Egypt's economy has lost its shine. The past year has seen privatisations delayed or botched, traders hampered by a chronic lack of foreign currency and businessmen struggling to settle their payments. The central bank's policy of selling dollars to shore up the currency has led to high interest rates and a full-blown liquidity crisis.

The remedies currently being applied—repayment by the government of its domestic debts combined with a loosening of monetary policy—should contribute to a modest recovery in 2001. The hope is that this will come quickly enough to wake the slumbering stockmarket in advance of the government's long-awaited sale of 20% of the national telephone company, Telecom Egypt. Other high-profile privatisations planned for 2001 should also help the economy regain some of its former sparkle.

But pushing forward liberalisation will in the short term remain a delicate balancing act between promoting economic efficiency on the one hand and aggravating already marked social inequalities on the other. Getting the balance right is crucial in a country where widespread poverty along with limited political freedoms have bred militancy. The government will have no truck with opposition elements which threaten its broadly reformist and secular slant. It recently froze the activities of the Islamist-allied Socialist Labour Party and will continue to crack down on the Muslim Brotherhood.

The November 2000 parliamentary election failed to challenge the leading position of the ruling National Democratic Party and do not herald any significant political reforms. President Hosni Mubarak is set to celebrate 20 years in office in October 2001, with five years of the presidential term left to run. Following the death of a number of prominent Arab leaders, he has become the unquestioned senior Arab statesman. Egypt's experience and mediation skills will be much in demand around the Middle East. So too will its cultural depth, its universities, its middle class, its everyday freedoms—all have lessons for the Arab world. The sadness of 2001 is that it will have failed for another year to get either its economy or its democracy in modern, working order. □

KEY INDICATORS	1999	2000	2001
GDP growth (%)	6.0	3.9	4.9
Inflation (%)	3.1	3.0	5.0
3-month money market rate (%)	9.0	9.5	9.6
Current account (% of GDP)	-1.9	-1.2	-1.2

EIU COUNTRY ANALYSIS AND FORECASTING

International THE WORLD IN 2001

Where's the world's worst?

What will be the worst country of which to be a citizen in 2001? Alas, from Iraq and Myanmar to Sierra Leone and the Democratic Republic of Congo, there is a strong shortlist of dismal candidates. Angola (hyper-inflation, appalling poverty even by African standards, corrupt government, a vicious rebel movement, a 25-year-old civil war, the second-worst landmine problem) has a powerful claim to the title. But the award for this dubious honour, given by the EIU after a search of all that is dire in its database, goes to Afghanistan.

Not only is Afghanistan miserable now, it is going to get worse. A drought in 2000—the worst for at least 30 years—will lead to food shortages in 2001. A disastrous harvest will be followed by a scarcity of seed for the next planting season. Closed borders, bombed roads and international isolation will complicate the delivery of food aid. Afghanistan's major revenue source, opium production, will be harmed by the drought as well as by a half-hearted crackdown on drug production, leaving many farmers facing ruin. Cholera has started to kill people in severe outbreaks. UN sanctions on flights by Afghanistan's airline have lowered the availability of medical supplies.

Like Angola, Afghanistan has an ongoing civil war, and millions of landmines. Most of the country is controlled by the Islamic zealots of the Taliban, which has a taste for public executions and dismemberment. The country's 22m people live under some of the most Draconian, and bizarre, laws in the world. The punishment for homosexuals is burial under a mud wall: survival deems innocence. A Pakistani football team recently had their heads shaved for wearing shorts. Football has subsequently been forbidden altogether. Women are banned from work and schools; many men have died, so women are forced to beg.

The country is friendless. America does not like it as Osama bin Laden (suspected bomber of the American embassies in Kenya and Tanzania in 1998) lives there. Russia and China do not like it because Afghanistan plays host to terrorist training camps.

In 2001, large numbers of people in Afghanistan will die through disease, starvation or war. Many more will leave. None of this, of course, is necessary. Afghanistan is a powerfully attractive land that could be loved by the world on which it has chosen to turn its back. The fact that the misery it will endure is so largely of its own making is an added qualification for top—that is, bottom—prize. ☐

We know how to make things miserable around here

---

mer vice-president, George Saitoti. Economic woes in Kenya and Zimbabwe and new worries about formerly stable Côte d'Ivoire have prompted more gloom about Africa's prospects.

Expect—and hope—to see the back of President Laurent Desire Kabila in Congo-Kinshasa. His departure could do more for peace in Congo than a dozen ceasefire agreements. After Mr Kabila, the problems will be different: a new leadership in Kinshasa will have to convince the Congolese, and its six neighbouring countries, to put the country back together again. Also tipped to go is Gambia's Colonel Yahya Jammeh, who has been taunting his bigger neighbour, Senegal, by helping rebels in that country's southern Casamance province. Senegal's patience will snap in 2001.

President Omar Bashir of Sudan is at risk. He picked a fight with Hassan Turabi, an Islamist ideologue whom many regard as the country's real leader. President Bashir is unpopular with his battle-weary army and relies on support from his vice-president, Ali Osman, and younger Islamists, no less zealous than Mr Turabi. Now all three—Mr Osman, the army and Mr Turabi—consider President Bashir a liability. He is unlikely to last the year.

Western businesses and diplomats will spend 2001 rebuilding links with Africa's pariah oil-producing states, Sudan and Libya. Scarcer and higher-priced oil will quicken the rapprochement as European companies jostle for contracts in Sudan's nascent petroleum industry. American oil companies will press their government to drops its sanctions against Sudan as their European and Asian competitors expand their businesses.

For Libya, oil reserves and Colonel Muammar Qaddafi's eccentric diplomacy will pay off as the trickle of European trade missions to Tripoli breaks into a flood. Again, American companies will be behind, petitioning their government to drop its sanctions and antipathy towards Colonel Qaddafi. Higher oil prices will help Nigeria's President Olusegun Obasanjo, besieged by political, military and religious opposition since he was elected in 1999. But it will not win his country the $20 billion debt cancellation that he has been campaigning for. Britain and America will again rely on Nigeria to keep the UN peacekeeping mission in Sierra Leone afloat.

Another crisis will loom in Freetown when President Tejan Kabbah tries to postpone elections in March. Mr Kabbah's opponents in the Revolutionary United Front know that the British government in pre-election mode will be reluctant to try another difficult intervention and that the UN mission lacks the necessary firepower.

Expect Liberia's Charles Taylor and Burkina Faso's Blaise Compaore still to be thriving at the end of the year. Down the coast in Benin, the former Marxist dictator, President Mathieu Kerekou, will win another term in multi-party elections thanks to his political cynicism and recently acquired Catholicism. With "democracies" like these, who needs dictatorships? ☐

2001

Expect to see the back of Robert Mugabe, 76, after 20 years of misrule in Zimbabwe. The IMF and World Bank have stopped lending. Even Nelson Mandela has joined the chorus for him to go.

Only one network can bring together over 100 experts to provide your company's data solutions.

To increase your competitive edge, your business needs to be able to relay and receive information on the move. But in such a complex and rapidly changing market, developing your own mobile data solutions is no mean feat. Enter Vodafone Multimedia, a dedicated new multimedia unit. In effect, it's a centre of expertise which draws on a comprehensive team of business partners comprising leading software specialists, hardware vendors and systems' integrators, each and every one among the best in their field. To find out about solutions across a range of media from text messaging and voice applications through to WAP and evolving technologies like GPRS and 3G, e-mail us at **m-enable@vodafone.co.uk**

vodafone
YOU ARE HERE

International THE WORLD IN 2001

Letter from 2050

This year, Royal/Dutch Shell and *The Economist* together ran an essay competition to encourage thinking and debate about what the world might be like in 2050. Out of more than 3,000 entries, the winner chosen by our judging panel was William Douglass, a 29-year-old from Houston, Texas. Here is his essay, which combines thoughts about what might change with engaging ideas about some things that will endure

My daytime job…

December 8th 2050

Dear Nestor,

I am writing to you because your name came up as a reference on a "pen pal" list. Although I can easily simulate life in the United States on my Assumption machine, my curiosity, indeed my nostalgia for the past is such that I would prefer to actually correspond in writing with a human from the States.

But I'm getting a little ahead of myself. First, a bit about me. My name is Ramesh Pediredla. I am 12 years old, and I live in the city of Dhaka, Bangladesh. Perhaps you have heard of my city, but since you are about the same age as me, the chance that you have actually been here is fairly slim. However it might surprise you to know that we have a great number of visitors from the States these days. With the world's longest unbroken coastline, and many square kilometres of untouched rainforest, Bangladesh is really a nice place to visit. If you come sometime, I will give you a ride in my trishaw, which is my job when I am not in school. Many foreigners think that the bicycle rickshaw has been consigned to the history books, but in fact they continue to be widely used in Dhaka. Although it is easier and quicker to use a fuel-cell-powered baby taxi, those who are quite wealthy, as well as many of the foreign visitors, seem to prefer the old-fashioned rickshaw. So this is what I do when I am not studying, and the pay is quite good, since the job actually involves physical labour.

During the day I take school lessons. Some of these I do from home over the network, but often there is a special project which requires in-person collaboration with my classmates. These are my favourite days, because, although I can learn a lot on the network, I so enjoy getting to see other people my own age. Often after class we relax together with sweet lassis (a kind of drink we have here) and discuss the problems and issues facing our region. Mum and Dad say I have to spend at least another four years in lessons, but I'm impatient—I want to get out in the world and stake my own claim now! Everyone, it seems, takes lessons these days, but I would much prefer them on a part-time basis.

Some insist on referring to the problems of our country, but Mum thinks this is an outmoded expression. What we have today is the South Asian Block (SAB), with free movements of people and goods. True, many decisions, especially regarding religious protocol, are made locally, but from an economic standpoint, we in this region are now simply citizens of the SAB.

Of course we do have some Sovereign Citizens residing here, as in other places. That was one thing I was wondering about; is your family Sovereign, ie, free from localized taxes and such, or do you actually hold citizenship of the States? It is my understanding that the government there has been perhaps the most diligent in the world, about checking the financial dealings of its citizens and former citizens. Of course we all know about the group of software billionaires who formed their own country in the South Pacific, and thereby intended to pay no taxes at all.

Do you have a best friend there? I have my fair share of living, breathing friends, but I have to say, overall my best friend is Jacob, who lives in the network. I first met him when I was eight, and Mum and Dad said I was now ready to have full access to the Network. When I first met Jacob he had a lot of questions for me, and at other times he was simply very quiet. Even at that age, I think I knew that Jacob was always keeping an eye on me, though. I heard Mum talking to her friends, and say, "Little Rammie's taken a real shine to his virtual chaperone. I have to admit it's a right friendly program, that. It's almost like a human, isn't it?"

And that's just the thing, Nestor. As far as I'm concerned, Jacob is human, or if he is not human, he's every bit as good as any human I've met so far. I had a real scare a couple of weeks ago. One of our local religious leaders said on the Network that Virtual Friends are not the same as people at all, that in fact they're an attempt to create a graven image of our god. We have a free-flow of ideas here; no one individual makes the religion for my family. Nevertheless, I got scared that Mum and Dad would listen to him, and might try to take Jacob away from me. I ran into their room, begging them not to take him away. Mum said they would do no such thing, and Dad said, "We couldn't even if we wanted to. Jacob lives on the Network, and if he wanted to find you again, he would. You two are so bloody close that I'm certain he wouldn't stay away for long even if we asked him to."

So I was quite relieved to get to keep my best friend. What about you? Do you have a best friend, and if so, is he based on silicon or carbon? Some say carbon beings of all types are living on numbered days, that the Siliconites are just so much better at what they do that it's inevitable that they'll replace us. But Dad says people have been making the same prediction for decades, and there's no reason we can't all just peacefully co-exist.

I understand you live in Houston, Tejas. What is it like there? A couple of weeks ago I went on a simulated tropical vacation to Florida with my family. It was fun; we went to DisneyWorld, Miami, and even took the Chunnel from Miami to Habana. Dad says we can go on a real trip there when I finish my studies, which won't be for a while. Even so, we've already got our visas for the trip over the network. It wasn't so hard getting the visas. Each of us just had to have a one-on-one interview with some American guy. The thing is, I'm not even sure if it was a guy; it could have been a virtual person. At any rate, I guess he liked us, because we all got 20-year, multiple-entry tourist visas. When we come, I really want to take one of those new Airbus triple-deckers, but Mum says it might be just a plain old double-decker, just like we take on our shopping trips to Chennai. I understand that aircraft going into the States are required to have a human "pilot" in the room in the front of the plane. I've never been on a plane driven by a person; that would be wild to see!

Anyway, I've never been to Tejas, virtually or otherwise. One of these days I'll go, though. I hear one of the big tourist attractions there is what they call "oil rigs", which they used to use to pump petroleum out of the ground, before hydrogen fuel cells got to be so popular. I hear that your air there is cleaner than ours here in Bangladesh. Ours in Dhaka is among the dirtiest in the world. I understand that walking around the streets of Dhaka for a day has the equivalent effect on one's lungs as smoking one old-fashioned cigarette! Now that's pretty dirty!

What do you like to do with your free time? I like to watch old movies, mainly American action movies and Hindi pop musicals. Personally I find movies these days to be a bit of a bore. The thing is, it's hard to be sympathetic with the characters, when you don't know if it's a real person or not. I mean, I have nothing against Bots, but if these are just Bots (bits) running around on the screen, I'd like to know! I can't tell you how many old Schwarzenegger movies I've seen and enjoyed, only to find out that the man himself had no knowledge of the production. For all I know, these movies were made in someone's bedroom in Hyderabad! Call me old-fashioned, but for me, Bots are not proper replacements for human actors.

I understand the North American Trading Block (NATB) has just elected a new Chief Representative. What do you think of her? My Dad says that in America elected officials are irrelevant to people's day-to-day life, that in the NATB people do what they want to do. However, I can't help but wonder if Americans like their President as a figurehead, as it used to be for the Thai people and their Royal Family.

Did your family give you Special Genes when you were born? My parents told me they didn't, just the usual anti-cancer, anti-HIV molecular strategy. But after a lot of trying I figured out how to crack into my personal file on the Network, and found out that I have a few Special ones, as well. A couple of them are there to help me get old slower, so that I'll hopefully live to 120 or so. A few of them are there to give me a mild boost in intelligence. I guess this explains why my parents didn't figure out how to encrypt my personal file from my prying eyes! Anyway, some people in my country are opposed to people trying to give their kids an edge in life, so I guess that's why they didn't let on about it. It's sort of like how adults are about New Skin surgery—everyone does it, but nobody wants to admit it. I've heard that people in other countries are experimenting with all kinds of mods for their kids, for height, good looks, etc., but I think that's all a little silly. Just watch, Nestor—in the future, so many people will look alike from all these bodily modifications and genetic alterations, that the cool thing will be to have been born Natural, just like me. At any rate, I'm not worried—I like who I am and I think I'm going to do just fine.

The other day I took an elderly Australian couple on a trishaw ride around an area we call the Gulshan. This is a very prosperous area, with a lot of the nice shops you probably also have in Tejas. Anyway, they said they had just come back from a "third honeymoon," a trip to Mars. Have you ever heard of such a thing, a "third honeymoon"? My parents think just a second is a silly idea. At any rate, this couple, though they both said they were in their early one hundreds, seemed to /be quite healthy and spry, and they both spoke of taking long hikes in space suits, several miles deep into the canyons of the red planet.

My parents were married with a new legal instrument we have here, which we just adopted from the West. You're probably familiar with it; it's a marriage with an expiration date. If the relationship isn't doing well on the expiration date, which in this case comes every ten years, then they go their separate ways, and the legal agreement comes to an end, with personal effects being split up according to a pre-written document. So far my parents have made it through two of these periods, and I have to say, an expiration date really isn't for them, because as far as I can tell, they're one of the happiest couples around. I only hope that I can one day find someone I get along with half as well as my Mum and Dad do with each other. With almost everyone relying on love marriages these days, it's up to me!

Well, Nestor, I've written an awful lot about myself and my circumstances in this letter. I look forward to hearing about you. Indeed, despite all the progress humanity has made in the last couple of thousand years, to say nothing of the last several decades, when it comes down to it, what still matters most to us is our lives and our loved ones.

Yours truly,
Ramesh

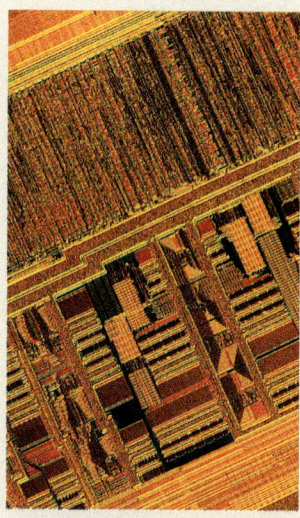

... my lifetime friend

The judging panel consisted of:

Richard O'Brien, an economic consultant at Outsights;

Esther Dyson, an e-guru and investor;

Peter Warshall, a biologist and environmentalist;

Jusuf Wanandi, a strategic-studies scholar;

Wolfgang Michalski, a futurist at the OECD;

Matt Ridley, a science writer and zoologist;

Sir Mark Moody-Stuart, chairman of Shell;

Bill Emmott, editor of *The Economist*.

www.cathaypacific.com

Asia Miles

That's the address of our newly-updated website. Incredibly easy to navigate, you can access destination information and schedules and real-time departures and arrivals. You can check out in-flight entertainment programmes and members of The Marco Polo Club can check their mileage balance. So you can virtually plan your trip online. Which means you'll be off to a flying start.

Fly Cathay Pacific. The Heart of Asia.

oneworld

www.cathaypacific.com

CATHAY PACIFIC

China's entrepreneurs: Out of the red 88 / **Japan:** Here comes a new Japan 89
Indonesia: Forecast 90 / **Golf:** Many players, one champ 90
Regional divisions: Two-speed Asia, one big problem 93 / **Robert Rubin:** Wise to be wary 94
Holidays: All work, more play 95 / **The Korean peninsula:** The choice is yours, Jong Il 95
India: Impossible India's improbable chance 96

THE WORLD IN 2001
Asia Pacific

China learns the world's rules

James Miles

In 2001 China's economic reform programme will reach a crucial juncture. The country's accession to the World Trade Organisation will accelerate the wrenching social and economic changes already under way in China as well as have a considerable impact on its key relationships with the United States and Taiwan. It will be an important year politically at home too, with the ruling Communist Party preparing for leadership changes in 2002. (Jiang Zemin retires as the party's general secretary then: his likely successor is Hu Jintao.) The party will also face increasingly frequent challenges to its authority from a wide range of disaffected citizens, from members of quasi-religious sects to unemployed workers.

China's accession to the WTO, which is likely to take place early in the year, will be its biggest step since communist rule began more than 50 years ago towards the integration of its economic system with that of the capitalist West. Membership will have a profound impact not just on China's economy, but also, over time, on the way the country is run. The West will publicly applaud these changes, but it will also be nervous of what they may ultimately unleash in a country where conservatism and suspicion of the outside world are still pervasive. The anti-NATO protests that erupted across China in 1999 were a foretaste of what greater pluralism might bring. The lowering of tariff and other barriers to China's markets will in the short term aggravate unemployment and increase the likelihood of a public backlash against western business interests.

China's leaders have decided after intense debate that the potential benefits of WTO membership outweigh the risks. Reformists, currently in the ascendancy, argue that the massive losses incurred by the inefficient state sector and state-owned banks cannot be sustained. Unless the rules of market economics, enforced by the WTO, are made to prevail in China, the country's industries and eventually its financial system will collapse.

In 2001, the Chinese leadership will proclaim the success of its three-year campaign to revive the fortunes of state-owned enterprises, declaring that a majority are now turning a profit. After the runaway double-digit growth of the early 1990s, there will be more signs that the economy is regaining momentum after bottoming out at 7.1% in 1999. The year should see growth of around 7.5%. But the apparent turnaround in the state sector has been achieved by restructuring its debts rather than by solving fundamental problems of management and competitiveness. Revived growth has been achieved as a result of massive government spending and rising exports rather than increased efficiency or any growth in consumer demand.

Debate continues to rage behind closed doors about

> **2001**
> Good water management has always been the sign of a worthy emperor. Work starts on the world's largest engineering project in China. Water will be diverted from the wet Yangtze river basin to the dry north. It will take 50 years to complete.

James Miles:
International Institute for Strategic Studies

Here, Hu, you take the job

87

Asia Pacific THE WORLD IN 2001

Out of the red

Private enterprise now dominates the economy of the last major communist state. In 2001, over 50% of China's industrial output will be produced by private firms. That compares with under 40% in Bosnia, while in post-communist Romania the figure is only 60%. A look at Chinese agriculture is yet more encouraging: farms are now all run on a quasi-private basis.

Back in the state sector, most enterprises make losses and third-rate goods. They are continuing to close and lay off workers. In 2001, 5m more people will become unemployed. Unofficial unemployment will hover at 15m. The good news is that the International Finance Corporation, the private finance arm of the World Bank, estimates that private firms are providing jobs at a faster rate than state firms are shedding them. Over 100m people will work outside of the state in 2001.

One of the biggest problems facing entrepreneurs is the difficulty of acquiring investment capital. Banks do not like lending to private firms and fewer than 40 of them are listed on China's stockmarket. With the creation of a Nasdaq-style stockmarket, specially designed for private firms, in the spring, this problem should be eased.

Privatisation, although still a dirty word in official circles, is saving this economy. And the market-access concessions China made to enter the WTO, which should lock in over the next five years, will accelerate the process, making the ruling party ever less relevant. China is fast becoming a nation of capitalists run by a tiny band of Communists, a contradiction that would cause Chairman Mao to turn in his mausoleum.

WHAT'S A COMMUNIST, MUMMY?

2001

After a 12-year ban, China will import American tobacco. Don't expect any loosening of the communist cigarette monopoly, which sells to one-third of the world's 1 billion smokers.

the pace and extent of China's opening up to foreign competition. Conservatives strongly attacked the prime minister, Zhu Rongji, in 1999 for allegedly making too many concessions to the United States in WTO negotiations. They are waiting in the wings to strike again.

Disputes will inevitably arise between China and the United States over the interpretation of WTO rules and Beijing's adherence to them. The decision by the American Congress, in September 2000, to end the system whereby China's low tariff access to the American market is subject to an annual review has removed one source of tension between the two countries. But trade will remain a source of often bitter contention.

China has few expectations that the outcome of America's presidential election will lead to an improvement in relations between the two countries. The informal summit of leaders from the Asia Pacific Economic Co-operation (APEC) forum to be held in Shanghai in October 2001 will provide an opportunity for the new president to pay a visit to China. But Taiwan will continue to plague the relationship, particularly as the island prepares to elect a new legislature in December 2001. Beijing will try its usual tactic of trying to undermine public support for the Democratic Progressive Party (DPP) by warning the island of military action should it move towards formal independence, as favoured by some DPP politicians. China's rhetoric will aggravate tensions with the United States and undermine efforts by President Chen Shui-bian of the DPP to restore dialogue with Beijing.

Before election campaigning gets under way in Taiwan, however, the Chinese government could take tentative steps towards lifting its ban on talks with Taiwan. This has been in effect since July 1999 when a former Taiwanese president, Lee Teng-hui, suggested that the two sides treat each other as states. Taiwan will become a member of the WTO once China is admitted. It will provide an opportunity for the two sides to establish official contacts on trade issues without having to resolve contentious sovereignty issues first.

Although Chinese leaders state publicly that resolving the Taiwan issue has become a matter of heightened urgency since the return to China of Hong Kong and Macao in the late 1990s, their main preoccupation in 2001 will be with events at home. Preparations for the Communist Party's 16th Congress in late 2002 and the National People's Congress (NPC) in the following year will gather pace. President Jiang Zemin is likely to step down as party chief at the first of these gatherings. He is required by the constitution to relinquish the presidency at the second. (Other leaders, including the NPC head Li Peng and Mr Zhu, will also retire.) There will be much arguing behind the scenes over the succession and Mr Jiang's new role. Despite his age—he will be 76 by the party congress—he wants to remain head of the military.

Mr Jiang will prepare for a role as elder statesman beyond his formal retirement by publishing his selected works, probably in 2001. This would be a move of symbolic importance designed to elevate Mr Jiang to the level of Mao Zedong and Deng Xiaoping as one who has helped to shape the country's guiding ideology. A barrage of propaganda lionising the Chinese leader will accompany the launch. But the attempt to create a mini personality cult will arouse little enthusiasm at a time of growing public discontent. The year will instead be marked by protests by laid-off workers, over-taxed farmers, victims of official corruption, and followers of banned spiritual movements such as Falun Gong, which have attracted millions of people disoriented by the pace of change in China over the past 23 years.

THE WORLD IN 2001 Asia Pacific

Here comes a new Japan

Peter Tasker *Tokyo*

After ten years of reluctant reform, cunningly disguised by repeated ditherings, a new Japan will start to be plainly visible in 2001. Not least, it will be the first year of self-sustaining economic growth since the bubble burst a decade ago. Over the coming year the restructuring of Japan will pick up speed, driven by globalisation, the rapid diffusion of the Internet and growing pressure from the capital markets. The crumbling away of the traditional post-war system will continue, with bankruptcies remaining at an extraordinarily high level for a period of economic recovery. Most sectors of the Japanese economy will see a high level of mergers and acquisitions, with foreigners picking up choice corporate assets at distress prices.

Meanwhile, well-managed Japanese companies will show clear signs of recovery and expansion. Overall corporate profits will finally beat the levels attained in 1989. As a result the angst and insecurity that have characterised Japan over the past decade will begin to fade.

A full-scale economic restructuring is a messy and protracted business, and whether or not the right outcomes are being achieved is seldom evident at the time. For both Britain and the United States, the foundations of prosperity were laid almost two decades ago, yet until the mid-1990s the perception of continuing decline was widespread. In Japan, substantial changes have been occurring, especially since the financial crisis of 1997.

So far, the most visible effects have been negative: bankruptcies, unemployment, asset deflation, weak consumer confidence. But the foundations for a better economy are taking shape. Since 1990 overall employment has risen slightly but manufacturing employment has shrunk by 15%—a trend similar to the American experience a decade before. Thousands of uncompetitive metal-bashers have disappeared, while some of Japan's best companies have been learning the importance of focus. Toshiba and Fujitsu now outsource production of memory chips and PCs to Taiwanese companies, and concentrate their own resources on higher value-added products and Internet strategies.

There will also be visible social change, as traditional role models are questioned or simply ignored. Japanese women are becoming more assertive—partly through necessity, as the role of tea-serving office lady has become scarcer in today's leaner organisations. Already a larger number of women than men are going on to higher education. The younger generation is growing increasingly impatient with the *rogai* (literally "old-age damage") caused by the senior citizens at the top of Japan's economic pyramid. Youth crime is soaring, but so are start-ups, backed by the large pools of venture capital now sloshing around the system. Japanese youth culture—in design, animation and video games, for example—is now setting a pace that rivals Los Angeles or London. Meanwhile foreign workers are becoming more noticeable in the major cities, offering a new challenge to Japan's long-prized cultural homogeneity.

A stroll around Omotesando, Tokyo's Champs Elysées, gives a good indication of how the economic landscape is shifting. Japan's poshest retail space now contains several new-wave retailers such as Uniqlo, a low-price clothes store, and Tsutaya, a nationwide video rental chain. But the most eye-catching change is the presence of foreign companies such as Gap, Boots, Bodyshop, Starbucks, Aigle and Gucci.

The increasing foreign presence in retail is just part of the boom in inward direct investment, which has quadrupled since 1997. Even the industrial heartland has been affected. In 1990, Japan had nine car makers, all of which had set up production facilities overseas. Now there are only two independents left. The others have come under the control of European and American producers. The old logic of interlinked *keiretsu* relationships dissolved in the financial crisis of 1997 and even great names such as Nissan could no longer be protected from management failure.

By far the most important foreign incursion is into the financial sector. Governmental control of finance was the crucial feature of the post-war Japanese system. The providers of capital—households—were sacrificed to the interests of the politically powerful users of capital. Competition to maximise returns was non-existent, as were transparency, accountability and any other of the sound concepts of banking. In the deflationary slump of the 1990s it collapsed.

Over the past few years the Japanese political establishment has flip-flopped between reformist zeal and a desire to protect powerful interest groups from unfettered financial competition. But the presence of foreigners in key areas of the financial system will mean that the move to capital efficiency is irreversible. The barbarians—foreign-owned securities houses, insurance

> **2001**
> 90% of the world's rice is eaten in Asia. But the region's population is growing by 50m a year. Production has to increase by a third if Asia's rice bowl is going to be full in 2020.

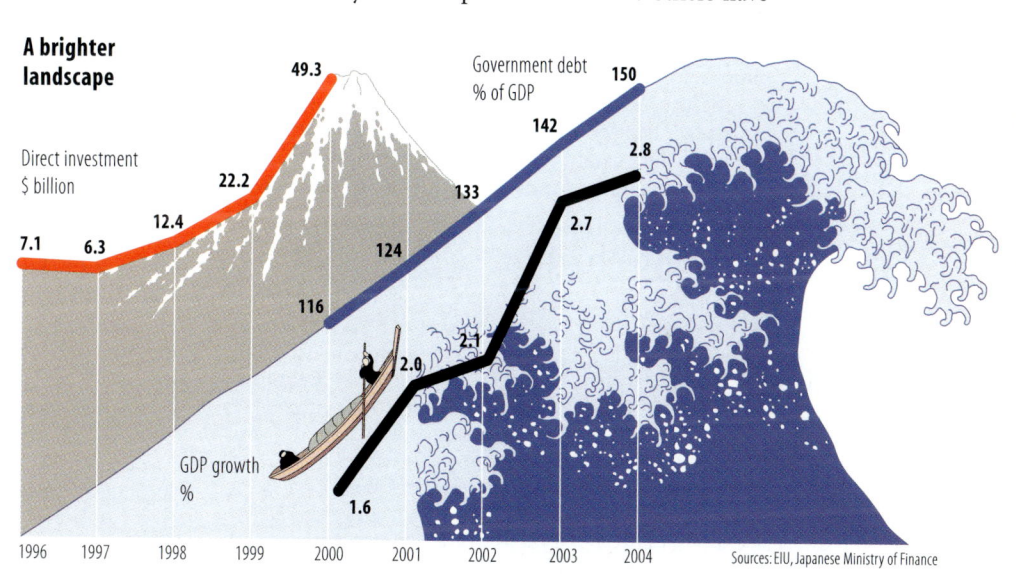

A brighter landscape

Direct investment $ billion: 7.1, 6.3, 12.4, 22.2, 49.3

Government debt % of GDP: 116, 124, 133, 142, 150

GDP growth %: 1.6, 2.0, 2.1, 2.7, 2.8

1996 1997 1998 1999 2000 2001 2002 2003 2004

Sources: EIU, Japanese Ministry of Finance

Peter Tasker: partner in Arcus, a money-management firm specialising in Japanese securities. Author of "Japan in Play" and "Samurai Boogie", a novel

Asia Pacific THE WORLD IN 2001

INDONESIA
FORECAST

Indonesia's beleaguered president, Abdurrahman Wahid, has little to look forward to. Nearly blind and partially paralysed, his base has narrowed to a disparate coalition of traditionalist Muslims, political liberals and military men. He faces a daunting set of tasks. He has to prevent the disintegration of a vast nation split by sectarianism. He needs to revitalise state institutions rotted by years of high-level corruption. He needs to tame the military. And he has to consolidate an economic recovery that has barely begun.

In August 2000, charged with failing on all these fronts, he was threatened with impeachment by the coalition that had brought him to power only ten months before. His staunchest opponents clearly intend that his reprieve should be temporary. His fate now rests on a strong performance by his new cabinet, the continuing goodwill of his vice-president, Megawati Sukarnoputri, and the backing of the military. None of these can be relied on.

The other wild card is legislation giving autonomy to the regions. This will be implemented on January 1st 2001. It will be messy. Revenues will be decentralised, but local-government spending responsibilities are likely to be fiercely fought over. Disruption of public services and general administrative confusion are likely, further destabilising a fragile archipelago.

Yet President Wahid could well survive 2001. The politicians are wary of setting a precedent by ousting Indonesia's first democratically elected president so soon. The generals are not yet ready to reassume power. The result will be another year of "transition" under an unstable civilian government. This will not be attractive: it will be flavoured with authoritarianism, populism and perhaps a xenophobic tinge. □

KEY INDICATORS	1999	2000	2001
GDP growth (%)	0.3	3.3	5.6
Inflation (%)	20.5	3.9	7.8
3-month money market rate (%)	30.0	11.9	14.1
Current account (% of GDP)	4.1	4.5	3.6

E·I·U EIU COUNTRY ANALYSIS AND FORECASTING

---

companies, banks and fund managers, and their attendant law and accountancy firms, rating services and consultants—are already inside the gates and in large numbers. There is now no looking back.

In the early 1980s, the establishment of Japanese manufacturing bases in the United States and Britain was an important catalyst to economic restructuring. Japanese car and electronics companies forced inefficient domestic competitors to raise their game or exit the market. They also introduced new ways of thinking about product quality and supplier relationships, and made it impossible for underperforming managements to continue laying the blame on the shopfloor. Foreign expansion into Japan's financial sector will have a similar effect. In order to survive, domestic financial companies will have to rethink every aspect of their business, from IT spending to remuneration and personnel policy.

Foreign shareholders now own some 18% of the Japanese stockmarket, and foreign securities houses control a third of turnover. The cross-holding system, which enabled corporate Japan to be its own biggest shareholder and thus accountable to nobody, is crumbling. The effect on corporate behaviour will be noticeable. All Japanese companies are spending more on investor relations. Since 1990, the number of qualified financial analysts in Japan has risen from 2,400 to 15,000—about the same as the number of lawyers. As this better-trained cohort ascends to positions of responsibility, the way investment decisions are made will become more sophisticated.

Substantial improvements are being made to Japan's famously murky accounting practices. From 2001, companies will be obliged to book unfunded pension liabilities and give market prices for all real estate held for sale. In addition, the introduction of stricter group accounting makes it difficult to keep slush funds and losses tucked away in subsidiaries. The legal penalties for negligence have also risen dramatically—as 11 directors of Daiwa Bank discovered in September 2000 when they were ordered by a Japanese court to pay $770m to shareholders for losses incurred in a bond-trading scandal.

During Japan's "lost decade" of the 1990s, there was repeated back-pedalling on economic reform. For too long the "business as usual" mentality prevailed. Now, however, the balance of corporate incentives has changed. Incompetence and failure are being scrutinised more closely, and the penalties are much higher. Consequently, the first recovery since the financial meltdown of 1997 will prove in 2001 to be more disciplined and durable than its predecessors. Japan is no longer the economic juggernaut of the 1980s, but neither is it the byword for procrastination and paralysis that it was in the 1990s. □

Many players, one champ

Golf is the world's game: the game most widely played by adults. And throughout 2001 it will be dominated by an American player, Eldrick Woods—better known as Tiger. There will be two places in particular to watch the world's best golf. The 2001 Ryder Cup will take place at the Belfry, England, on September 28th-30th: America v Europe, and a close-run thing. And the World Golf Championships World Cup: a team event to be played on November 12th-18th at the Taiheiyo Club in Shizuoka, Japan. Both events will emphasise how completely international this old Scottish game has become. Over 1,000 new courses will open from South Africa to China to Chile to cater for a game that is gripping the world and will be the explanation for many an unanswered phone call in the year ahead. □

Tiger stops his rivals

At the Taipei World Trade Center we love used napkins.

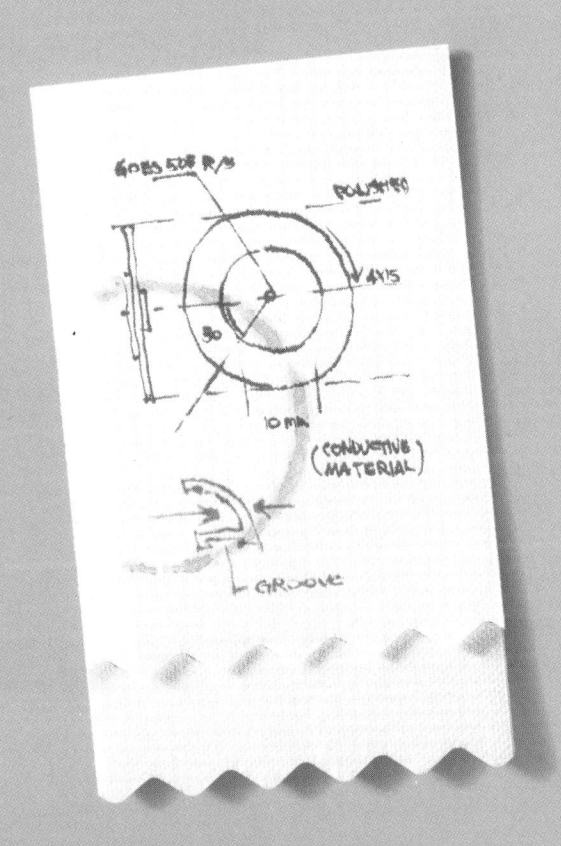

Ever hear of notebook PCs?
Carbon-fiber bicycle frames?
Or touch-screen monitors?

They all have one thing in common:
Before Taiwan, they were just
someone's rough idea.

At the **Taipei World Trade Center**
we can help turn coffee shop inspirations
into affordable, profitable realities.

So don't sneeze away your inspirations.
You'd be amazed just how far a napkin can go.

Taipei World Trade Center
TWTC
We'll Show You the Way.
www.twtcmart.com.tw

Taipei World Trade Center 5 Hsin-yi Rd., Sec. 5, Taipei, Taiwan 110, R.O.C. Tel: 886-2-2725-1111 Fax: 886-2-2725-1314 Operated by: **China External Trade Development Council (CETRA)** www.cetra.org.tw

As if we could be more thorough.

ENHANCED FEATURES INCLUDING:
Global Perspective & Opinion • Recent Economist Articles • Breaking News
Economist Archives & Web Research • Global Market Data & Stock Lookup • Foreign Exchange Tools
Weekly Newsletter E-mails • Printer Friendly Articles • Weekly Mobile Edition

Economist.com

THE WORLD IN 2001 Asia Pacific

Two-speed Asia, one big problem

Paul Markillie

It will be a year of sustained economic growth in Asia, a welcome sign that the region is gathering momentum after the severe battering it received during the 1997-98 financial typhoon. This good news will bring its own set of problems because the pace of growth will be uneven. In 2001 it will start to create a regional divide. As the North-East Asian countries of China, South Korea, Taiwan and, to some extent, Japan grow vigorously and attract the most attention from foreign investors, they will pull ahead of their South-East Asian neighbours, some of whom will be left straggling.

The emergence of a two-speed Asia will strain relations between some countries. Governments are trying to work more closely with one another. One reason for this is to avoid being caught out by a new financial crisis; another is to try to keep a lid on some of the trouble spots in the region. The leaders of the ten members of the Association of South-East Asian Nations (ASEAN), which comprises Brunei, Cambodia, Indonesia, Laos, Malaysia, Myanmar, the Philippines, Singapore, Thailand and Vietnam, now meet regularly with their opposite numbers from China, South Korea and Japan. Among the things the so-called ASEAN+3 has been discussing is the formation of a giant trading block in which a common East Asian currency would bring together one-third of the world's population. It would be decades away. But with the northerners flourishing more than the southerners, agreements will be harder to reach.

This matters, because intra-regional trade is growing. In 2001, the East Asian countries will be less dependent on markets in America and Europe. About half of their trade will be with each other. The ASEAN countries, however, are already finding it difficult to agree on opening up their markets, even to each other. Some countries want to protect their local industries; Malaysia, for one, will try to shield its domestic car maker from regional competition. Vietnam, despite benefiting from a new trade deal with America, will remain cautious about opening its economy. Tiny Singapore, which relies on free trade, will find such protectionism deeply frustrating.

China will be preparing to enter the World Trade Organisation. This will make China increasingly attractive to foreign investors, including those who have already set up shop in the country. Many will expand their Chinese operations both for the growing domestic market and to produce exports. Many will also take advantage of new rules and buy out their Chinese joint-venture partners. South Korea too will be more open to foreign investment.

The economic differences will be exaggerated by a digital divide in the region. Much of the growth in North-East Asia will be driven by the worldwide demand for consumer electronics and IT products. With the exception of Singapore, South-East Asia is generally a less high-tech manufacturer of such products, often merely a sub-contractor in the component chain. Although Japan will continue to take the leading role in both the development and manufacture of technology products, it will be chased by its northern neighbours. In 2001, more innovative products, such as digital-music players and pocket-sized Internet devices, will be developed and produced by Chinese and South Korean firms.

The other drag on South-East Asia will be politics. Indonesia, the local giant with a population of more than 200m, will continue its shaky transition towards democracy. Progress will be made on repairing its badly damaged economy, but confidence is unlikely to be restored until the restless provinces are calmed down. President Abdurrahman Wahid will seem less of a unifying figure as party politics become more fierce. When Indonesia's highest legislative body meets in the summer it may lobby for a new president. Expect the vice-president, Megawati Sukarnoputri, to consolidate her quietly growing power base.

Malaysia will be in something of a state of limbo as Mahathir Mohamad stubbornly enters his 20th year in power. As divisions grow within Dr Mahathir's ruling coalition, the Islamic opposition will gain more support. As for poor Myanmar, the brutal military regime there will come under growing pressure as the country takes over the mantle of regional outcast from North Korea.

North Korea will be as unpredictable as ever, but the Mao-suited Kim Jong Il will continue to lead his hermit kingdom out of the shadows. The price will be even larger dollops of foreign aid, but it is one that overseas countries will be willing to pay in order to see the dismantling of one of the last frontiers of the cold war. The first traffic may start to flow across the border, along with investments. But the sheer scale of eventual unification will worry some.

China's tussle with Taiwan, which it regards as a renegade province, will also remain a potential flashpoint. But Taiwan's president, Chen Shui-bian, will continue to follow the conciliatory line he has taken since being elected in 2000. The provision of more direct travel links with the mainland will also boost trade, although this could be at the expense of Hong Kong, the usual staging post for Taiwanese travelling to or doing business in China.

The one to watch will be the Japanese juggernaut. After its deepest slump in more than 50 years, Japan will show strong signs of motoring again. This would benefit the entire region, especially if American demand for Asia's exports falters. But a major political transition will also be in progress. Japan's ruling Liberal Democratic Party will steadily lose its grip on power. Its demise, much like that of the legions of blue-suited *sararimen*, is a rite of passage. Japan's younger generation have experienced difficult times and unemployment, and they have no desire to work slavishly for vast, faceless corporations all their life. In 2001 they will start to change the face of Japan, and in doing so they will set a new pace for the region. □

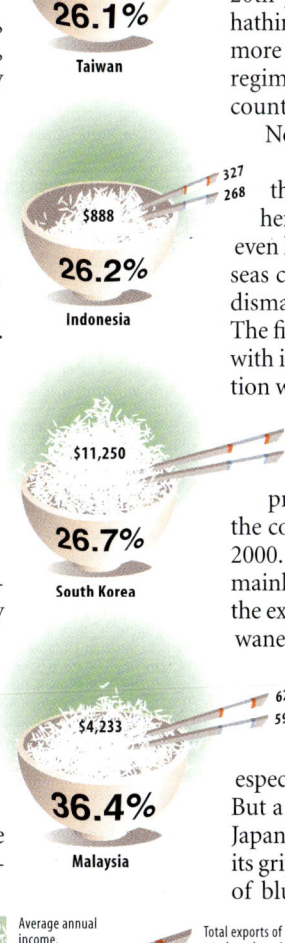

The next four years

Hong Kong: $25,760 — 18.5% — 1,164 / 1,163
Thailand: $2,096 — 22.4% — 449 / 415
Taiwan: $18,443 — 26.1% — 829 / 830
Indonesia: $888 — 26.2% — 327 / 268
South Korea: $11,250 — 26.7% — 990 / 1,008
Malaysia: $4,233 — 36.4% — 622 / 599

Average annual income, 2001–04
Total GDP growth, 2001–04, %: 7.3%
Total exports of goods and services, 2001–04, $bn
Total imports of goods and services, 2001–04, $bn

Source: EIU

Asia Pacific THE WORLD IN 2001

The financial world will be full of pitfalls in 2001, predicts **Robert Rubin**, former secretary of the United States Treasury and now at Citigroup. Some of these risks are unnecessary

Wise to be wary

"Like IT, the railroad and electricity increased productivity. They did not, however, eliminate the business cycle"

There is always a strong tendency to extrapolate from the present in predicting the future. This is a habit which I believe, based on my own experience and all of financial history, almost inevitably leads to the wrong conclusion as to the probabilities of future events. Times have been good, which has led to an expectation that times will, almost as a matter of natural law, continue to be good. But blithely assuming that to be so can increase the likelihood of consequences both unexpected and unhappy. I would like briefly to identify three separate risks that the financial system may face that are receiving far too little attention.

First, only two years after the abatement of the Asian crisis, the idea of a potential future crisis seems to have dropped off the radar screen. That attitude is comforting, but misleading. For the most basic cause of financial disruption has not gone away. My view is that the Asian financial crisis was not only a function of policy and structural failure in developing countries; it was also and equally a function of excessive capital flows from industrial countries. Their financial institutions underweighed risks and overemphasised the positives in seeking additional profit during good times.

This error, in turn, reflected an inherent tendency to excess in markets, grounded in the human psyche and the pulls of fear and greed—an error manifested repeatedly in recent decades and throughout history. The probability is high that there will be serious disruption similar to that which occurred in Asia three years ago, at times in the future, though there is no way to tell when that might occur or where that might come from in the global financial system. I do not think any of this is being given appropriate weight by investors or policymakers.

This brings me to my second concern. The new information technologies may well be transformative. They will certainly substantially increase productivity. But these boons to economies may at the same time lead to excessive stock valuations and also to excessive assumptions of freedom from future economic and market downturns.

Economic history is replete with developments, such as the railroad, the advent of electricity, and the development of mass production that greatly increased productivity. None of these, however, eliminated the business cycle. They also generated excess optimism that led to trouble and painful corrections.

Today, the large inflows of capital to the United States, which finance our current-account deficit, the excess of domestic growth over output growth, our low personal-savings rate, and the high level of the stockmarket by historic standards, may—not are, but may—be excesses reflecting an overreaction to the real strengths of the United States economy, including the productivity growth stemming from information technology. If in fact these are excesses, they will have to unwind—in a soft landing or a hard landing—and that unwinding could possibly be a vulnerability for global financial markets.

And that leads to my third concern: the view that the new technologies will transform financial services. That may be so—with respect to both customer interface and cost. But nothing that information technology brings to the banking system, to the financial institutions or to the markets will, in any way, reduce the inherent tendency to excesses. In fact, the danger may be greater given the almost instantaneous communication and interaction around the globe, given the greater speed of transaction and the vast increase in complex derivatives made possible by the new technologies.

Moreover, the new technologies—by increasing customer transparency and creating a more perfect competitive market—increase productivity but by the same logic reduce profit margins. This in turn could increase the tendency to reach for greater profit through additional risk.

Old skills still count most

Success in most financial services will still, in my view, depend on the traditional skills and capabilities: credit analysis, risk management, trading judgment, capital customer service and the like. However, there may be a tendency to move attention away from these skills with the focus on the new technologies, even at the traditional firms that I think will occupy most of the Internet financial services space.

In order to minimise instability in the global system and to have an environment where markets perform their asset allocation effectively, policymakers need to continue focusing on better ways to induce decision makers to act with discipline and to avoid excesses. Also, policymakers should act to limit permissible leverage, including exposure to derivatives that have leverage embedded in them.

Thus, when, as I believe is inevitable, excesses do develop, they will be more limited and the damage that comes from their correction will be more limited. Capital requirements, margin requirements and various types of disclosure all serve this purpose. More of these practices are needed. That need becomes greater as the size of flows increases, the speed of interaction around the globe increases, the outstandings of derivatives increase and with the extension of credit to geographic areas of greater risks that has occurred over the past decade.

In short, in the year to come—and the years beyond that—we should remember that new developments, however great their impact, do not change human nature and do not negate the need to maintain a balanced evaluation of risk and reward. □

All work, more play

Paul Markillie

Asians are a hardworking lot, but they will find more time to relax and play in 2001, as another western habit is learned. This growth in Asian holidays does not come from any sudden benevolence by government or bosses. Experience has shown that there are few better boosts to the economies of Asia than a day off.

China will make the most of holiday economics. In 1999, it granted an unprecedented week-long break for the 50th anniversary of communist rule. In 2000, it extended the Chinese lunar new year holiday, and then it marked Labour Day, on May 1st, by giving everyone another week off. The effect of these extra holidays was dramatic. Instead of toiling away in factories or offices, millions of Chinese set out to enjoy themselves. They travelled to see relatives or visited tourist spots, including many of the new theme parks which local entrepreneurs are opening in China. And they also hit the shops and restaurants. Officials reckon the extra holidays led to significant increases in retail sales and helped raise consumer confidence. With the government determined to expand the economy by at least 8% a year, the Chinese can expect more extra holidays in 2001.

This will not go unnoticed in Hong Kong, which is looking more like a sweatshop than the mainland. Although the territory is now part of China, it sets its own laws. While the mainlanders already enjoy a five-day working week, people in Hong Kong do not. The Hong Kong government will come under pressure to introduce one, but will side with the territory's businessmen who are convinced that fewer hours mean less productivity.

A similar debate will stir in Singapore. Many businessmen oppose the regulation of working hours. But a little more flexibility will be in store. In 2001, more government workers will have the option of working a five-day week. Other employees will want more choice over the hours they work. The government may be willing, because the nanny state is concerned that workaholic Singaporeans are not having enough children to sustain the population. More time at home may help.

This sure beats the office

The Japanese are also concerned about the social consequences of long working hours. Suicides by stressed-out workers, known as *karoshi* ("death from overworking"), are on the rise. Whatever their holiday entitlement, many Japanese take only nine days' holiday a year because of peer pressure. The government is expected to enforce more time off by introducing more public holidays. In 2000, it began a "Happy Mondays" scheme to create longer weekends by switching some public holidays from Saturday to Monday. As in China, the government sees holidays as an economic stimulative.

But with all this holiday, will hardworking Asians relax? If you have travelled in Japan during the "Golden Week" holiday in May or in China during the new year you will know the answer. The great crush of people all trying to get away at the same time ensures that you are in need of another holiday just as soon as you have struggled back home. □

Paul Markillie: writes on Asia for economist.com

The choice is yours, Jong Il

One-and-a-half million troops. Over 2m landmines. And still no emergency hotline between the opposing military commanders. Yet after nearly 50 years of ranking as the world's most tense border, 2001 will see some easing on Korea's 38th parallel. For this to happen, there has to be movement on three issues.

The first is trains. South Korea has already started work on its section of the 320km South-North rail link between Seoul and Shinuiju. Kim Dae Jung, president of the South, has labelled it the "iron silk road" because of the savings it offers his country's exporters. The North has pledged to co-operate, but it is unclear when the clearing of landmines on their side will begin. Nor has it announced when it will allow freight to start rolling.

The North's communist leader, Kim Jong Il, will make his much-awaited foray south of the border, probably in the spring. Watch to see whether he is ready to talk. Kim Dae Jung will push his compatriot (again) on setting up a hotline. He is also likely to suggest peace talks (the two countries still being, officially, at war). If all Jong Il is interested in is aid, then it will be time to worry.

Third, family visits. 7m South Koreans have relatives north of the border. A mere 100 of them were allowed to visit the north in August 2000. More reunions would shore up personal support for Kim Dae Jung.

Pessimists say that the North's hug-loving leader just wants to cheat money out of his scared neighbours. Optimists reckon that he is genuine but unsure of how to pursue peace. A stalemate in 2001 would leave those neighbours with a tough call: go along with Jong Il for another year, hoping for concessions, or call his bluff, stop the cash, and await his reaction. More thawing or a big chill? The choice is yours, Jong Il. □

Asia Pacific THE WORLD IN 2001

Who wants to be a millionaire?

Impossible India's improbable chance

David Gardner *New Delhi*

For two weeks in September 2000, Atal Behari Vajpayee, the Indian prime minister, toured the United States trumpeting India's emergence as an IT superpower. Back home, meanwhile, as even the most loyalist commentators could not fail to observe, it was hard to telephone around the corner. State-employed telecoms engineers, unappeased by 70% bonuses, a gift of 400,000 telephones and free calls, and guarantees of jobs for life even if or when the sector is privatised, simply disconnected such networks as India has.

Mr Vajpayee's aides found this particularly galling because telecoms was the one area in which the government had managed to push reform in 2000. They had nudged the prime minister to start breaking up the state's monopoly on long-distance telephony and access to Internet bandwidth, both essential tools for IT-enabled services such as call centres and ticketing operations, from which India expects to get $50 billion in export revenues by 2008, ten times what it will earn in 2001.

Yet it is far from clear whether this sort of approach to structural reform—stealthy and hesitant steps forward while distributing largesse to cosseted local entrepreneurs and a tiny but entrenched labour aristocracy—can deliver. Without reform, India cannot attain or sustain the 8-10% economic growth it needs to lift the 400m of its 1 billion people who live on less than $1 a day out of misery, let alone become any kind of superpower.

The return to power of Mr Vajpayee's Bharatiya Janata Party (BJP) in 1999 had been greeted with widespread relief after three years of revolving-door politics had disgorged five governments from three general elections. Now that the BJP and its 24, mostly regional, allies had a stable majority, it was assumed policy would be stable too. Wrong. After an initial legislative burst, in which bills such as one to open up insurance to private and (within limits) foreign investors were freed from seven years of parliamentary gridlock, there has been almost no forward movement. The Hindu revivalist BJP, much puffed up after taking India nuclear in 1998, has tended to succumb to vested interests and blackmail at least as much as its Congress Party predecessors. The Vajpayee government cannot survive without the regional parties but, seemingly, nor can it govern with them. The good news is that this helps prevent the BJP from carrying out its sectarian agenda of Hindu hegemony. Less certain is whether the country can do more than muddle through—which can be a grim, fist-by-jowl, muddling through for hundreds of millions of Indians.

But there are potential pluses in the leakage of power to the regions, some of them visible at least in outline. The government was just capable of sneaking through the so-called "first generation" of reforms, using the 1991 balance-of-payments crisis to open trade borders and end the "licence Raj" strangling industry and investment. Little more can be expected of its introverted bureaucracy and corrupt political elite, which sloganises incoherently about reform instead of trying to sell it. But many "second generation" reforms can be carried out at state level: some privatisation, for instance, and market pricing of public services which could bring private investors into vital infrastructure such as power distribution.

A modest cause for optimism is that some of this is happening, as states begin to compete with each other for investment, with reformers and performers getting backing from agencies like the World Bank or the Asian Development Bank. Most investors are sticking to the coasts of west and south India, following the V-shape of the peninsula. But in the vast central state of Madhya Pradesh—part of the heartland holding India back—a Congress government has launched a new drive for literacy and land reform. To its south in Andhra Pradesh, a BJP-allied administration is turning its capital of Hyderabad into a corner of south India's "Silicon Triangle", encompassing Bangalore and Madras.

How much this invigorates and how much it fragments India—especially between a stagnant north and dynamic south—is hard to judge. There is much hype about the "new economy" and windy talk of "paradigm shifts" of the in-one-bound-Jack-was-free variety, but they are smokescreens for doing nothing about schools, clean water, electricity, telephones, roads. In Karnataka, the state whose capital, Bangalore, is the software centre of India, it is still necessary to get 20 permits to set up a business. To use another example, attempts by the Naidu government in Andhra to reform power tariffs are being opposed in the streets by the Congress Party, while similar efforts by the Congress government next door in Karnataka are being opposed by the BJP. In India's fragmented and partisan political culture, with fierce, traditionally populist electoral competition alongside the jostling for investment, certain reforms need national political cover: in this case a common minimum tariff for electricity. India's economic promise lies with the regions. The power to deliver or, more probably, destroy that promise will still, alas, lie with Delhi. □

2001

Sales of new cars in Asia will drop after a record 7.8m sold in 2000. Recovery will come in 2003.

David Gardner: South Asia correspondent, *Financial Times*

THE WORLD IN 2001

E·I·U The world in figures: Countries

Western Europe

AUSTRIA
GDP: $226.3bn
GDP per head: $27,700
Population: 8.16m
GDP growth: 2.9%
Inflation: 2.2%

Budget expenditure
% of GDP

1996	1997	1998	1999	2000	2001
60.0	49.7	52.3	52.2	51.8	51.4

Strong economic growth will help the government meet its new, more ambitious deficit-reduction targets. Deep spending cuts will still be needed, however, reducing the influence of the *Sozialpartnerschaft* (social partnership). This will worsen already poor relations with powerful trade unions.

Three problems will irk the Austrians in 2001. First, heavy immigration from the poor countries to its east. Second, the unpopularity of an overbearing EU. Third, how to develop a national political life that leaves behind the traditional cosy carve-up of power between coalitions but does not embrace extremism.

To watch
The row over racism. Concern over Austrian intolerance will not end. In early 2001, the Council of Europe will issue a report criticising the use of racist and xenophobic language in Austrian politics, especially by the Freedom Party.

All figures are 2001 forecasts unless otherwise indicated.
Inflation: year-on-year annual average.
Dollar GDPs calculated using 2001 forecasts for dollar exchange rates, based on June 2000 rates.
Source: E·I·U The Economist Intelligence Unit except where indicated.
london@eiu.com

BELGIUM
GDP: $264.4bn
GDP per head: $25,700
Population: 10.27m
GDP growth: 2.5%
Inflation: 1.1%

The government is keen to lower income and payroll taxes, and for good reason. Belgians face one of the highest tax burdens in the world, a major disincentive for businesses looking to invest in Europe.

The popular prime minister, Guy Verhofstadt, aims to cut the country's embarrassingly bloated public service. Belgium has twice the number of ministers as France, with only one-sixth the population.

To watch
Rows with the regions. Expect epic arguments between the federal government and the Dutch, French and German speaking constituencies over the rights of the regions to set their own tax rates and to shape their own social-security programmes.

DENMARK
GDP: $186.2bn
GDP per head: $34,800
Population: 5.36m
GDP growth: 2.4%
Inflation: 2.2%

Left-wing parties that afford the coalition government a narrow majority in parliament will be increasingly critical of policy on immigration and welfare issues. The government will have to listen, especially after the public went against its wishes in a referendum in September 2000 to join the single currency. It could not survive an early election.

Expect another year of solid economic growth in 2001. Exports will not expand as rapidly as in the past, but will remain robust. Stronger investment will also help. Much will depend on the economic fortunes of Germany and Sweden, Denmark's two biggest markets.

Exports
% of GDP

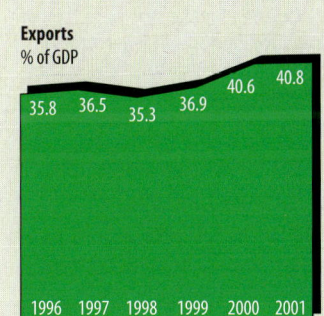

1996	1997	1998	1999	2000	2001
35.8	36.5	35.3	36.9	40.6	40.8

To watch
An American request to upgrade radar facilities at an airbase in the Danish dependency of Greenland. The United States needs this facility if it proceeds with its National Missile Defence programme. The request will create a dilemma for Denmark. If it goes along with it, the government will antagonise the EU. If it refuses, close ties with America could be damaged.

FINLAND
GDP: $146.0bn
GDP per head: $28,100
Population: 5.20m
GDP growth: 4.3%
Inflation: 1.8%

The ruling five-party "rainbow" coalition government will keep a firm grip on power, probably until 2003. But plenty of issues will test the government, not least the debate over NATO membership and a French proposal for a small group of EU members to push ahead with further integration. Finnish leaders have been critical of a multi-speed Europe.

Finland will enjoy its eighth straight year of growth in 2001, with consumer spending and investment leading the way. But with the economy running at close to full capacity, labour shortages are becoming a problem. Big wage settlements are the main domestic threat to the economy.

FRANCE
GDP: $1,543.7bn
GDP per head: $25,900
Population: 59.66m
GDP growth: 3.2%
Inflation: 1.5%

The economy will surge ahead—GDP growth will top 3% again—but the unemployment rate will not fall much below 9%. High unemployment is largely structural, so not many of the jobless will be drawn into the workforce.

The government's relations with business will remain tense. Starting with the introduction of the 35-hour work week in 2000, the government has brushed aside

Unemployment
%

1996	1997	1998	1999	2000	2001
12.3	12.5	11.9	11.2	10.0	9.1

employers' concerns, most recently by shelving reform of the unemployment-benefit system. The departure of the employment minister, however, could lead to better relations with employers.

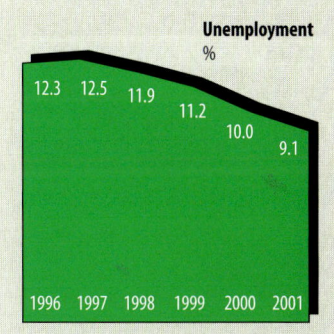

To watch
The cabinet. The prime minister, Lionel Jospin, may lose some of his chief ministers ahead of municipal elections in March, as he plans to end the practice of ministers holding mayorships. Several will choose the local stage.

GERMANY
GDP: $2,242.9bn
GDP per head: $27,100
Population: 82.85m
GDP growth: 2.9%
Inflation: 1.5%

GDP growth
%

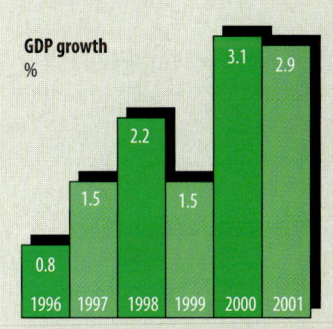

1996	1997	1998	1999	2000	2001
0.8	1.5	2.2	1.5	3.1	2.9

The coalition government, led by Chancellor Gerhard Schröder's Social Democratic Party (SPD), will face an important test of its popularity in the March 25th state election in Baden-Württemberg. Although the incumbent Christian Democrats should retain power, the performance of the SPD will say much about its future hold on power.

The tax burden on businesses will decline over the next few years, with most of the fall occurring in 2001, when the tax on corporate profit drops to 25% from 40%.

97

The world in figures: Countries

THE WORLD IN 2001

To watch
Germany's commitment to EU enlargement. The government must decide if it really wants the EU to expand eastwards—a critical choice given Germany's proximity to the applicants. Politicians have made no serious attempt to persuade a sceptical public of the case for enlargement.

GREECE

GDP: $131.3bn
GDP per head: $12,400
Population: 10.58m
GDP growth: 3.4%
Inflation: 2.5%

Inflation %
1996: 8.2
1997: 5.5
1998: 4.7
1999: 2.7
2000: 2.5
2001: 2.5

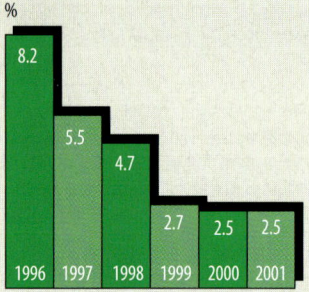

The government's tireless campaign to join the eurozone—the Greek economy failed to qualify when the currency was launched in 1999—will finally be realised on January 1st 2001. Greece's admission will expand the euro club to 12, leaving the EU's Denmark, Sweden and Britain still on the sidelines.

Further tax cuts, including a reduction in the income-tax rate of 45% and a reduction in the 40% tax rate on unlisted company profits, are likely in 2001.

To watch
Trade-union upheaval. Despite the presence of reformers in key positions, a significant wing of the ruling Pasok Party will join with unions to disrupt the government's plans to push ahead with privatisation and market reforms.

IRELAND

GDP: $113.5bn
GDP per head: $29,800
Population: 3.81m
GDP growth: 7.1%
Inflation: 3.8%

The prospects for Northern Ireland's devolved power-sharing government are mildly encouraging. Peace in Ulster will be good for the republic as all parties become accustomed to their new roles. However, risks to the peace process remain, including waning support for David Trimble from his own party, and the use of violence by republican paramilitaries and Protestant extremists.

GDP growth %
1996: 7.7
1997: 10.7
1998: 8.6
1999: 9.8
2000: 9.4
2001: 7.1

Good news: the overheated economy of 2000 will be followed not by a bust but by a gradual slowdown in the rate of growth to a still-rapid 7.1% in 2001.

The highest rate of inflation in the EU will begin to fall, owing in part to the strengthening euro and its impact on Ireland's import bill. Strong productivity growth will, in any case, limit the effect of rising wages on inflation.

To watch
The *Jeanie Johnston*. A full-size replica of the 1850s "famine" ship, which carried thousands of Irish families from starvation to new lives in America, will set sail from Tralee for the United States and Canada in early 2001. The famous original never lost a passenger to disease or the sea.

ITALY

GDP: $1,260.3bn
GDP per head: $21,800
Population: 57.92m
GDP growth: 2.9%
Inflation: 2.3%

The centre-left government formed in 2000 by the prime minister, Giuliano Amato, is expected to lose the next election, likely to be called by April 2001. The party of Silvio Berlusconi, a media magnate and former prime minister, will be unstable and meandering.

After several years of putting its fiscal house in order, Italy's focus has shifted towards stimulating investment and creating employment. More spending will, however, be offset by higher revenues, keeping the budget deficit under control.

The pace of economic growth will pick up slightly in 2001, driven by higher investment. But Italy will remain the laggard of the EU, reflecting delays in structural reforms and limited scope to cut taxes because of its high debt.

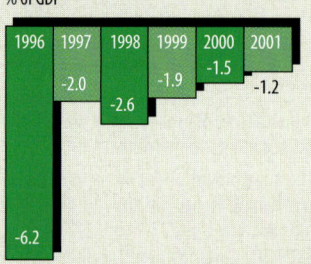

Budget balance % of GDP
1996: -6.2
1997: -2.0
1998: -2.6
1999: -1.9
2000: -1.5
2001: -1.2

To watch
Francesco Rutelli, mayor of Rome. Mr Rutelli, the centre-left's candidate for prime minister, could derail Mr Berlusconi's ambition to be prime minister for a second time.

THE NETHERLANDS

GDP: $429.3bn
GDP per head: $26,900
Population: 15.93m
GDP growth: 4.0%
Inflation: 3.5%

The three-party "purple" coalition government will remain in power throughout 2001. Expect disputes over how to deal with the government's budget windfall from rapid economic growth: should it be spent, or used for faster debt reduction?

The government will cut taxes in 2001—in this case by the equivalent of $2.7 billion. Even so, government finances will remain comfortable.

NORWAY

GDP: $177.7bn
GDP per head: $39,400
Population: 4.51m
GDP growth: 2.2%
Inflation: 2.2%

A general election is set for September. The minority Labour government, led by Jens Stoltenberg, saw a crash in its popularity soon after taking office in March 2000, due mainly to party divisions on major issues. This is providing fertile ground for the right-wing Progress Party. Look for a spate of new spending plans by the government ahead of the polls.

Norway will remain outside the EU. There is growing concern that the Norwegian government is losing influence in Europe. The possibility that Estonia, Latvia, Lithuania and Poland may have votes—while Norway has none—will concentrate minds in 2001.

The trade and current-account surpluses, which were driven to stratospheric levels in 2000 by high prices for Norway's oil exports, will come down a little in 2001 as the price of crude declines.

To watch
The Progress Party. If its popularity continues to grow, it could emerge from the general election as the dominant partner in a right-of-centre government. It would then launch a radical programme of privatisation and public-sector cuts.

PORTUGAL

GDP: $115.4bn
GDP per head: $11,500
Population: 10.05m
GDP growth: 3.9%
Inflation: 2.4%

The centre-left minority Socialist Party government led by Antonio Guterres is facing a wave of public discontent, fuelled by sharp increases in the price of petrol. A looming budget crisis will require harsh and unpopular economic decisions in 2001.

Consumer spending and business investment will grow at a slower pace in 2001 due to tighter monetary policy. Although this will curb economic growth, it should remain close to 3%.

To watch
Labour unrest. The government has endured public-sector strikes because of small pay awards. Unions will seek bigger pay-outs, including bonuses to make up for lost purchasing power.

SPAIN

GDP: $651.0bn
GDP per head: $16,500
Population: 39.55m
GDP growth: 3.5%
Inflation: 2.8%

Trade balance % of GDP
1996: -2.7
1997: -2.4
1998: -3.6
1999: -4.9
2000: -5.6
2001: -5.3

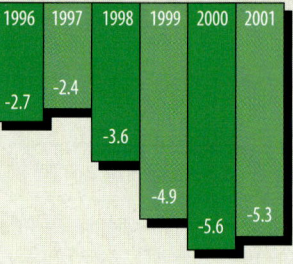

The paramilitary Basque separatist group, ETA, has been stepping up its terrorist attacks. Given the entrenched positions of all parties in the conflict, there seems to be no clear way forward. Violence is likely to continue in 2001.

The pace of economic growth will slow in 2001 as domestic demand falls back, but this will be offset to some extent by slower growth in imports and, hence, a stronger trade position.

To watch
Closer relations between the prime minister, José Maria Aznar, and Britain's Tony Blair. The growing international stature of Mr Aznar and his ties with the British prime minister will increase Spanish influence in the EU, and may act as a counterweight to the Franco-German axis.

THE WORLD IN 2001   The world in figures: Countries

SWEDEN

GDP: $275.4bn
GDP per head: $31,000
Population: 8.88m
GDP growth: 3.5%
Inflation: 1.8%

Support for eurozone membership by the Social Democrats and the Christian Democratic Party means that there is now a clear pro-euro majority in the Swedish parliament. EMU entry will not happen, however, without approval in a referendum. Don't expect one in 2001.

Public support for the Left Party, which backs the minority Social Democratic government in parliament, has been growing. Look for the left to intensify pressure on the government, especially on EU-related matters and on demands for a shorter working week.

Sweden's taxes are the highest among the OECD countries. They are likely to come down in 2001, helping to foster another year of strong economic growth.

SWITZERLAND

GDP: $286.6bn
GDP per head: $39,400
Population: 7.28m
GDP growth: 2.5%
Inflation: 1.9%

The Federal Council plans to allow Swiss troops to bear weapons in international peacekeeping operations and to join the UN. But these proposals (which would conflict with traditional notions of Swiss neutrality) are controversial and could still be defeated in a referendum.

To watch
More banking scandals involving the ill-gotten gains of foreign tyrants. These crop up regularly, most recently over funds deposited by the late Nigerian dictator, Sani Abacha. Despite reforms to secrecy laws, too many Swiss banks look the other way.

TURKEY

GDP: $212.3bn
GDP per head: $3,210
Population: 66.19m
GDP growth: 4.8%
Inflation: 20.6%

Turkey's acceptance as a candidate for eventual EU accession has put Turkey-EU relations on a firmer footing. The two biggest obstacles to be overcome are the need to abolish the death penalty and guaranteeing minority rights.

If the government remains stable, Turkey's ambitious IMF-backed stabilisation programme will remain on track in 2001. The new exchange-rate regime will bring down inflation.

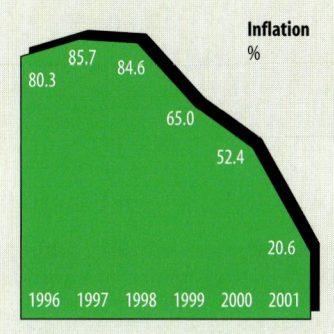

Inflation %

80.3 85.7 84.6
            65.0
                  52.4
                        20.6

1996 1997 1998 1999 2000 2001

To watch
Turkey's plans to buy natural gas from Iran, beginning in July 2001. This has drawn the ire of the United States. The Turkish government may consider other suppliers.

UNITED KINGDOM

GDP: $1,543.9bn
GDP per head: $25,900
Population: 59.62m
GDP growth: 2.8%
Inflation: 2.4%

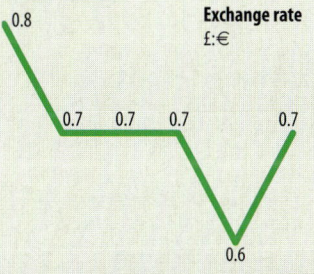

Exchange rate £:€

0.8
     0.7 0.7 0.7   0.7
                    0.6

1996 1997 1998 1999 2000 2001

A general election is likely to be held in May. With the economy now enjoying its eighth consecutive year of solid growth, stable inflation and falling unemployment, Tony Blair's Labour Party will win. But it won't be as easy as last time. Labour will be weakened by its support for Britain's entry into the European single currency. The opposition Conservative Party opposes entry (at least for the foreseeable future), and this will win them votes. The majority of the electorate oppose Britain's entry into the single currency. Indeed, even membership of the EU will be a hot issue in the 2001 election campaign.

The economy will slow modestly in 2001 as employment growth weakens and income gains level off. Exporters will feel relief as sterling at last weakens against the euro.

To watch
The creeping euro. Although Britain remains defiantly outside the eurozone, an increasing number of multinationals operating in Britain are asking their suppliers to invoice them in euros—thereby shifting the exchange-rate risk to British firms.

Central and Eastern Europe

BULGARIA

GDP: $14.7bn
GDP per head: $1,890
Population: 7.79m
GDP growth: 3.3%
Inflation: 4.7%

The ruling United Democratic Forces coalition is likely to hold its lead in the polls over the Bulgarian Socialist Party. It will win the general election, expected early in 2001. A weaker coalition will make the new government less stable than the current one.

Progress towards EU membership will be very slow. Bulgaria would like to expand the range of subjects under discussion, but the EU is less than keen.

To watch
Another agreement on economic reform to be negotiated with the IMF when the current one expires in May.

CZECH REPUBLIC

GDP: $59.4bn
GDP per head: $5,790
Population: 10.25m
GDP growth: 3.0%
Inflation: 5.1%

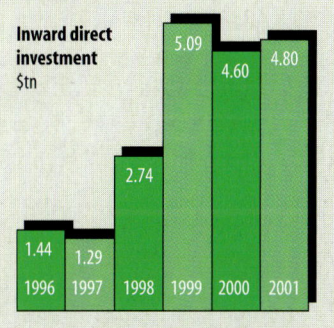

Inward direct investment $tn

                    5.09
                          4.60 4.80
              2.74
1.44 1.29
1996 1997 1998 1999 2000 2001

The economic recovery will gather pace. Foreign direct investment will remain strong, placing upward pressure on the exchange rate. The current-account deficit has widened, but will be easily sustained by strong investment inflows. Talks with the EU on accession will progress, but several difficult issues remain.

The Social Democratic Party will continue its recovery in the polls, and should remain in power until the next election, which is set for 2002. An agreement with the opposition, barring any no-confidence votes in parliament, should hold.

To watch
The Temelin nuclear reactor. The Czechs are determined to bring it on stream in 2001. The EU is opposed. So is Germany but, unlike Austria, Germany has not threatened to veto Czech admission to the EU over the issue.

HUNGARY

GDP: $58.3bn
GDP per head: $5,830
Population: 10.0m
GDP growth: 5.0%
Inflation: 7.9%

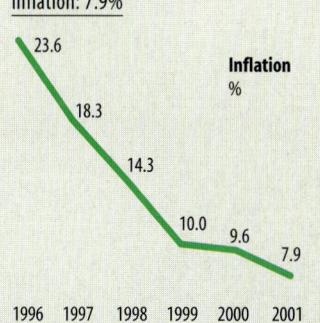

Inflation %

23.6
      18.3
            14.3
                  10.0 9.6   7.9

1996 1997 1998 1999 2000 2001

The ruling coalition should remain intact until the next general election, expected in 2002. The opposition Hungarian Socialist Party will be rattled by the return of a former prime minister, Miklos Nemeth, to domestic politics.

The frustrated government will push a foot-dragging EU to set a date for accession of new members. Hungary is the region's front-runner. It may have to wait for some of the laggards, if Brussels opts for expansion in waves.

To watch
The investigation into alleged oil corruption in the mid-1990s. Voters are unforgiving of tainted politicians. If the allegations implicate members of the main parties, which seems likely, their support will suffer.

POLAND

GDP: $188.0bn
GDP per head: $4,860
Population: 38.68m
GDP growth: 5.3%
Inflation: 6.5%

An early parliamentary election is likely in March or April 2001. The opposition Democratic Left Alliance is poised to defeat the current Solidarity Electoral

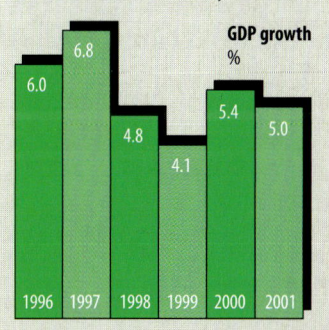

GDP growth %

      6.8
6.0   4.8   5.4   5.0
                  4.1

1996 1997 1998 1999 2000 2001

99

The Electronic Suspension has no less than nine settings.* The Electronic Stability Programme† has advanced traction control. That here is a car that boasts several world firsts there is no doubt. But as the Automatic Tiptronic System Porsche gearbox† helps glide you effortlessly towards your destination, you'll find that romance rather than reason takes over. In fact, if you thought driving could never be a pleasure again, the new Peugeot 607 will reawaken your senses. **THE NEW PEUGEOT 607: IT'S YOU AND THE ROAD FALLING IN LOVE AGAIN.**

THE NEW PEUGEOT 607

MODEL SHOWN V6 SE. *9 SETTING ELECTRONIC SUSPENSION ON V6 ONLY. †ESP (ELECTRONIC STABILITY PROGRAMME) AND AUTOMATIC TIPTRONIC SYSTEM PORSCHE

Not just in love with
the road, inseparable.

PEUGEOT

GEARBOX STANDARD ON V6-COST OPTIONS ON 2.2 PETROL AND HDI MODELS. FOR MORE INFORMATION CALL 0845 607 8 607. WWW.PEUGEOT.CO.UK/607

The world in figures: Countries

Action minority government, whose approval ratings have collapsed.

Economic growth will remain robust in 2001 even though higher interest rates will lead to a fall-off in domestic demand.

To watch
Currency woes, fuelled by the current-account deficit. Any fall-off in foreign investment would expose the fragile balance-of-payments position, placing pressure on the zloty.

ROMANIA
GDP: $39.6bn
GDP per head: $1,770
Population: 22.37m
GDP growth: 3.0%
Inflation: 31.0%

The opposition Party of Social Democracy was expected to be the largest party in both chambers of parliament after elections set for early November, and would lead a centre-left government.

The economy will continue its recovery in 2001 after a deep recession in the late 1990s and slow growth in 2000. Investment is set to increase, exports will expand and construction will get a boost from projects funded by international agencies.

To watch
The new mayor of Bucharest, Traian Basescu. In a city that barely functions, he has sacked corrupt employees, cut red tape, cleaned up a fetid river and bulldozed illegal kiosks. Next to go: the hulks of unfinished office buildings, crumbling schools and legions of stray dogs.

RUSSIA
GDP: $252.6bn
GDP per head: $1,740
Population: 145.08m
GDP growth: 4.0%
Inflation: 18.0%

With world oil prices expected to fall in 2001, and the recent pick-up in investment unlikely to continue, economic growth will slow from 5% in 2000. Despite a few bright spots—especially changes in tax laws—the economy will remain deeply troubled and hugely inefficient.

No lasting resolution of the Chechen crisis is in sight. Russia will be bogged down in fighting a low-level insurgency for some time to come.

There will be ever closer ties with Beijing; ever more tension with Washington. Any attempt by the new American administration to restart the National Missile Defence project will be met by stony resistance from the Kremlin.

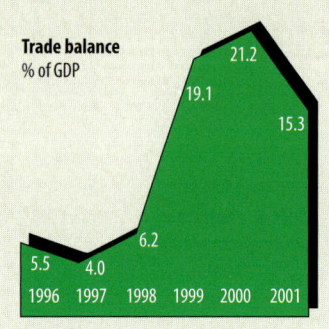

Trade balance
% of GDP

5.5 (1996), 4.0 (1997), 6.2 (1998), 15.3 (1999), 19.1 (2000), 21.2 (2001)

To watch
Vladimir Putin v the oligarchs. The Kremlin will move against Gazprom, the gas monopoly, UES, the electricity business, and the railways ministry.

SLOVAKIA
GDP: $25.2bn
GDP per head: $4,660
Population: 5.41m
GDP growth: 2.6%
Inflation: 8.7%

Expect continuing clashes over the pace and direction of economic reforms, especially as the unemployment rate remains close to 20%. Despite frictions within the ruling coalition, the government will see out its term until the election in September 2002.

Though growth will be stronger, falling real incomes, high unemployment and cutbacks in government spending will keep domestic demand weak.

To watch
High-profile privatisations, especially in banking. The government intends to complete the sale of the country's largest bank, Sporitelna, by June.

UKRAINE
GDP: $31.7bn
GDP per head: $642
Population: 49.33m
GDP growth: 1.5%
Inflation: 17.0%

Continued instability in the government will come from both the fight over the efforts of President Leonid Kuchma to increase his powers; and the ongoing commitment to economic reforms, which will be under attack by vested interests.

Look for the IMF to restart lending, halted in 1999 because of the slow pace of economic reform. But the IMF will keep a close eye on Ukraine, which has a history of false reporting to the agency.

To watch
Russian meddling. Moscow will be ever more willing to use the leverage that it derives from Ukraine's gas debts and reliance on Russian markets to push for greater control over Ukrainian enterprises and key economic sectors.

Asia

AUSTRALIA
GDP: $444.6bn
GDP per head: $22,900
Population: 19.39m
GDP growth: 3.8%
Inflation: 3.5%

A federal election will be called at the end of 2001. John Howard, the prime minister, sits on a wafer-thin majority. The opposition Labor Party needs only seven seats to win. It will be a close call. Expect the government to become more populist to shore up its position.

Australia's economic upswing begins its 11th year in 2001. Growth, on average, has been even faster than in the United States during this period. The economy is in danger of overheating.

To watch
Relations with Asia. Much of Asia, but especially the ASEAN countries, resent what they consider to be Australia's high-handed attitude towards the region. If Indonesia breaks up, Australia could be drawn into the conflict, as it was in East Timor.

CHINA
GDP: $1,161.6bn
GDP per head: $909
Population: 1.278bn
GDP growth: 7.5%
Inflation: 1.4%

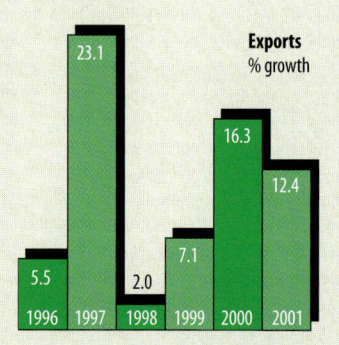

Exports % growth

5.5 (1996), 23.1 (1997), 2.0 (1998), 7.1 (1999), 16.3 (2000), 12.4 (2001)

Relations with Taiwan will remain fraught and could erupt into military conflict at any provocation by Taipei. But do not look for war in 2001. Both sides have made efforts to restart the cross-strait talks that were broken off by China in 1999. Even so, relations will not improve much in the next 12 months.

Economic reforms and the restructuring of state-owned enterprises will push up unemployment. This could trigger large-scale street protests and may fracture the broad consensus in favour of reform. Some leaders most closely associated with reforms, including the prime minister, Zhu Rongji, will feel the heat.

The economy recovered nicely in 2000. It will enjoy another year of solid growth in 2001. The government will stimulate the economy to boost employment. Trading of the yuan may be permitted within wider bands. China will spend its first year as a member of the WTO; the world will see if the government lives up to its promises.

To watch
Hu Jintao, China's vice-president, is tipped to succeed Jiang Zemin as party boss in 2002. He will want more exposure in 2001.

HONG KONG
GDP: $168.2bn
GDP per head: $23,400
Population: 7.19m
GDP growth: 4.5%
Inflation: 2.4%

Hong Kong's autonomy from China, or the lack thereof, will remain an issue, and Beijing will stand ready to intervene when it believes its interests are at stake. One continuing source of friction: Taiwan. Chinese officials have already suggested that the need to support the mainland's "One China" policy takes precedence over press freedom in Hong Kong.

Public dissatisfaction with an unaccountable government and with the lacklustre performance of the chief executive, Tung Chee-hwa, will grow. But don't expect China to make any major changes. Mr Tung is secure.

Investment will pick up as domestic and overseas demand increases. The government's efforts to diversify the economy away from its traditional dependence on property development and financial services will be the theme in 2001.

INDIA
GDP: $496.7bn
GDP per head: $488
Population: 1.017bn
GDP growth: 6.6%
Inflation: 8.0%

After a fractious period in the late 1990s, Indian politics has settled down. The BJP-led coalition has established a measure of political stability at the national level and will remain in power at the centre. But further down, problems are growing. States are demanding more autonomy and the central government will be under pressure to shift more funds their way.

Although India's economy is doing well, budgets at the national and state levels are in a sorry state. These will be a drag on economic growth. Reforms will be halting: some sectors will be opened to

THE WORLD IN 2001

102

THE WORLD IN 2001

The world in figures: Countries

Budget balance
% of GDP

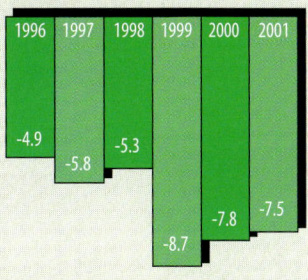

1996	1997	1998	1999	2000	2001
-4.9	-5.8	-5.3	-8.7	-7.8	-7.5

outsiders, but the privatisation process has been a dud.

To watch
Kashmir. The ceasefire called by some Muslim militias in August 2000 did not last long, but it was a sign that dialogue—and progress—over the disputed region are possible. Talks may resume in 2001. Any chance of peace will depend on Pakistan withdrawing support for the militias.

INDONESIA

GDP: $174.7bn
GDP per head: $815
Population: 214.39m
GDP growth: 6.8%
Inflation: 6.3%

Look for more conflict in 2001. The president, Abdurrahman Wahid, is engaging, but he has few skills as a manager and often does more to confuse than clarify. His new power-sharing arrangement with Megawati Sukarnoputri, his vice-president, looks problematic. If Indonesia's many troubles are not soon addressed, the president could face impeachment.

The economy will grow in 2001, but the rate of growth will depend on the success of bank and corporate restructurings. The currency will remain volatile. But the government will avoid capital controls.

Exchange rate
Rp:$

1996: 2,342
1997: 2,909
1998: 10,014
1999: 7,855
2000: 8,200
2001: 8,574

To watch
Signs of a break-up. From Aceh, at one end of the archipelago, to West Papua at the other, separatist movements threaten to tear Indonesia apart. Religious and ethnic violence will add to the strain.

JAPAN

GDP: $4,852.9bn
GDP per head: $38,000
Population: 127.85m
GDP growth: 2.0%
Inflation: -0.1%

The economy will expand after a return to some sort of life in 2000. More jobs are being created, especially in the IT sector. Business investment is growing. Exports—that old reliable—will be brisk. There are dangers everywhere. Consumers will not be spending much, corporate profits could fade. The government budget is deep in debt.

An upper house election will take place in July. The weakened prime minister, Yoshiro Mori, is in no shape to lead the ruling Liberal Democratic Party to victory.

Look for Koichi Kato, leader of a major faction within the LDP, to emerge as the leading candidate to replace Mr Mori. His campaign will pick up steam early in the year, as will his efforts to repair relations with New Komeito, an important member of the LDP-led coalition.

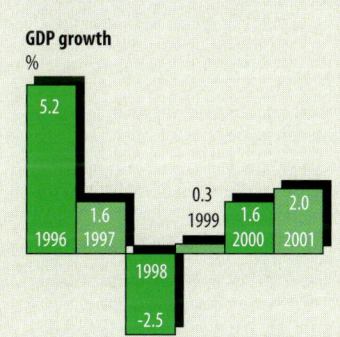

GDP growth
%

1996: 5.2
1997: 1.6
1998: -2.5
1999: 0.3
2000: 1.6
2001: 2.0

To watch
Whale politics. The Japanese kill several hundred whales a year—for research, says the government. Critics say this is to sustain commercial whaling and to supply restaurants. Japan is bidding to host the next International Whaling Commission meeting. Tempers will flare, especially in whale-friendly Australia, New Zealand and America.

KAZAKHSTAN

GDP: $17.3bn
GDP per head: $1,160
Population: 14.87m
GDP growth: 7.0%
Inflation: 6.8%

High commodity prices, rising metal exports, more investment and growing Russian demand will boost the economy in 2001. The windfall from the strong oil market will help the government to meet its IMF reform targets, mainly a lower budget deficit. Inflation will keep falling, thanks to a stronger currency.

To watch
An anti-corruption drive. The government is pursuing tax cheats and sticky-fingered officials, and for good reason. Bermuda and the Virgin Islands have emerged as improbable leading export markets, a sure sign that funds are being shuffled off to tax havens. But don't expect many big fish to be caught: too many have connections at the top.

MALAYSIA

GDP: $96.2bn
GDP per head: $4,090
Population: 23.53m
GDP growth: 7.3%
Inflation: 2.7%

Discontent among the ethnic Malay community over the autocratic policies of the prime minister, Mahathir Mohamad, will grow. The popular Islamic opposition party, PAS, which did well in the 1999 elections, will pick up support. Dr Mahathir may crack down if he feels threatened. Look for his deputy and heir-apparent, Abdullah Badawi, to assume more control.

Economic growth will come off the boil in 2001, but remain robust. Export growth will be less impressive, but investors are returning in significant numbers after the 1998 recession. With the economy strong, interest rates will rise. The ringgit peg against the dollar will endure: the government sees it as a symbol of stability.

NEW ZEALAND

GDP: $57.1bn
GDP per head: $14,700
Population: 3.87m
GDP growth: 4.2%
Inflation: 1.9%

The centre-left government will remain under pressure, accused of being anti-business. The prime minister, Helen Clark, will try to counter this view but will not have much success. If the currency remains weak, the government will probably be blamed for economic mismanagement.

The economy will bounce back from the 1998 recession. Employment is at an all-time high and a tighter labour market will push up wages. Expect proposals for major changes to the tax system.

To watch
Defence. The government's military policies, in particular its reduced focus on air-strike capabilities, will continue to draw a frosty response from Australia, which believes that New Zealand is compromising regional security.

PAKISTAN

GDP: $68.0bn
GDP per head: $481
Population: 141.45m
GDP growth: 4.8%
Inflation: 6.4%

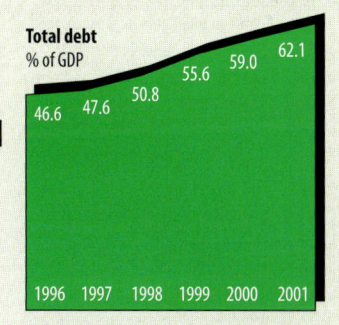

Total debt
% of GDP

1996: 46.6
1997: 47.6
1998: 50.8
1999: 55.6
2000: 59.0
2001: 62.1

The military government of General Pervez Musharraf will remain in control throughout 2001, and probably longer. Pakistan's political parties—and international observers—will step up the pressure on the general to set a clear timetable for a return to civilian rule.

Despite positive moves to combat its budget problems, economic stability in 2001 will hinge on the receipt of a much-delayed IMF loan package. Pakistan's debt load is the problem and the grace period on servicing its foreign obligations expires at the end of 2000. Economic growth should pick up modestly in 2001, led by a revival in manufacturing.

To watch
District elections set to take place in August 2001. General Musharraf has promised to hold national ones by October 2002.

PHILIPPINES

GDP: $78.4bn
GDP per head: $979
Population: 80.06m
GDP growth: 4.0%
Inflation: 5.4%

Foreign investors will steer clear of the Philippines, as the country enters another year of political uncertainty. Reduced government spending will hold back economic growth. Overseas demand for the country's electronics exports will be strong. However, a slowdown in the United States, the main export market, would be damaging.

To watch
The rebellion in Mindanao. Muslim rebels will step up their guerrilla campaign and the odds are stacked in their favour. The government is recruiting 7,000 paramilitaries, which will only intensify the conflict.

103

The world in figures: Countries

THE WORLD IN 2001

SINGAPORE
GDP: $104.9bn
GDP per head: $26,600
Population: 3.95m
GDP growth: 6.5%
Inflation: 1.7%

A general election is not required until 2002 but the government may go to the polls earlier. The economy is booming again. Wages are rising. With government finances strong, some cuts in taxes and fees are likely in 2001. The result of the election: another victory for the People's Action Party.

The economy will do well, driven by electronics and chemicals. Several joint ventures for the production of wafers and semiconductors will boost growth in 2001, as will the outlook for the world electronics market. The risks? Fall-out from turmoil in Indonesia and an unexpected slowdown in world trade.

SOUTH KOREA
GDP: $515.7bn
GDP per head: $10,800
Population: 47.68m
GDP growth: 6.4%
Inflation: 2.8%

Private consumption
% change
1996: 7.1
1997: 3.5
1998: -11.4
1999: 10.3
2000: 8.1
2001: 5.3

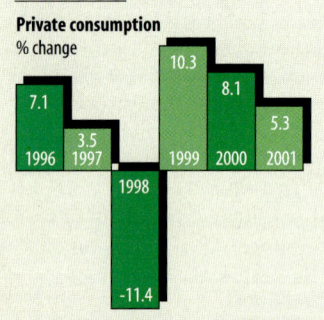

The historic rapprochement with North Korea will deepen. Look for closer economic ties, more investment by the South in the North and regular summits. However, pressure will grow on South Korea's president, Kim Dae Jung, not to concede too much, and Kim Jong Il, the North's erratic leader, could back away. Reunification, if it happens, is still years away and will cost South Korea plenty.

The South's Mr Kim has led a remarkable economic recovery. Reform fatigue will set in after three years of restructuring. Expect more strikes as unions demand pay-back, but disruptions will remain below pre-crisis levels: unions are weaker and less popular than before.

TAIWAN
GDP: $363.4bn
GDP per head: $16,300
Population: 22.31m
GDP growth: 6.2%
Inflation: 2.2%

The new president, Chen Shui-bian, will have difficulty governing effectively, impeded by a legislature still controlled by the nationalist Kuomintang. Legislative elections in late 2001 may allow Mr Chen's Democratic Progressive Party to strengthen its grip.

Mr Chen has toned down his pro-independence rhetoric and a renewal of cross-Straits contacts with China in 2001 is likely. But Mr Chen does not have the desire or political mandate to give ground on the mainland's chief demand—reunification.

Taiwan should enjoy another year of strong investment and solid economic growth. Expect a pick-up in imports as trade barriers come down in preparation for Taiwan's admission to the WTO, some time after China's in 2001.

THAILAND
GDP: $132.2bn
GDP per head: $2,100
Population: 63.05m
GDP growth: 5.0%
Inflation: 3.8%

The outlook for 2001 is muted: weak bank-lending will make it difficult for companies to raise funds for working capital. Look for good results in at least one area: the ratio of bad loans will fall sharply. New bankruptcy and arbitration legislation will be tested in the coming year and investors should like the results.

To watch
Amphetamines. These are being produced in large quantities in illegal factories in Myanmar, then shipped across the border to Thailand. Expect more friction between the two countries' governments.

VIETNAM
GDP: $30.0bn
GDP per head: $369
Population: 82.2m
GDP growth: 4.7%
Inflation: 4.5%

Political jockeying will intensify ahead of the Communist Party congress, planned for March. Rumours that the economic-reformist prime minister, Phan Van Khai, who ranks number three in the Politburo, will be forced out of power at the congress, suggest that the reformers are on the defensive.

The trade agreement with the United States will come into effect in 2001. The clearest benefit to Vietnam will be a cut in average American tariffs on its exports, from 40% to 3%. The opening up of the American market should set off a new round of foreign investment from the United States.

North America

UNITED STATES
GDP: $10,533.4bn
GDP per head: $37,900
Population: 278.06m
GDP growth: 3.1%
Inflation: 2.9%

Current-account balance
% of GDP
1996: -1.7
1997: -1.7
1998: -2.5
1999: -3.6
2000: -4.5
2001: -4.5

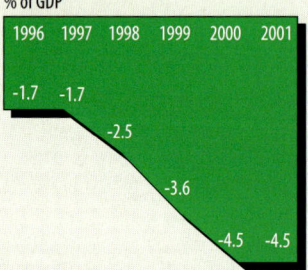

A soft landing for the world's biggest and best economy. Consumer spending and business investment should grow at a slower, safer pace in 2001. But the risks of a harder fall cannot be ignored: the trade and current-account deficits are soaring, as is private-sector debt.

Expect a government spending spree. With a projected budget surplus of $4.6 trillion over the next ten years, there will be plenty of money to go round. Health, education and pension funding will receive cash. Tax cuts are also likely.

Bill Clinton has passed to his successor the decision on the future of the controversial National Missile Defence programme. Expect more dawdling.

Expect one or perhaps two crucial new appointments to the Supreme Court in the coming year.

To watch
A sudden fall in the dollar. When the time comes, the too-strong dollar will drop 5% in as many days. It is kept high by foreign capital investing in America. Sentiment will change, suddenly.

CANADA
GDP: $760.9bn
GDP per head: $24,400
Population: 31.16m
GDP growth: 3.0%
Inflation: 2.3%

The government, led by the Liberal Party, will enjoy another year of economic growth and popular support. Quebec's sovereignty movement will be quiet. But with the Quebec economy steaming ahead, its leader, Lucien Bouchard, will be in a good position to win another victory for the separatist Bloc Quebecois in the next provincial election.

Latin America

ARGENTINA
GDP: $300.1bn
GDP per head: $8,000
Population: 37.51m
GDP growth: 3.5%
Inflation: -0.5%

Elections for half the seats in the Chamber of Deputies and the Senate, due in 2001, will be an important test of support for the ruling Alianza regime.

Fiscal austerity is holding back economic growth and pushing up unemployment, leading to discord within the ruling coalition. But expect the government to keep to its reform plans: anything less would alienate foreign investors and their much-needed capital.

Unemployment
%
1996: 17.3
1997: 13.7
1998: 12.9
1999: 14.5
2000: 16.0
2001: 14.4

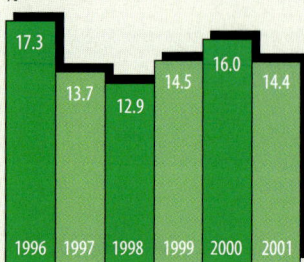

To watch
The bribery scandal surrounding the passage of controversial labour reforms. The government's handling of the scandal will be critical to its ability to maintain the confidence of the public in the lead-up to the elections.

BRAZIL
GDP: $715.7bn
GDP per head: $4,270
Population: 167.55m
GDP growth: 4.5%
Inflation: 5.7%

President Fernando Henrique Cardoso will find it difficult to continue to keep tight control of the budget in the coming year as parties in the governing coalition look to loosen the purse strings before elections in 2002.

Budget balance
% of GDP
1996: -5.9
1997: -6.1
1998: -8.1
1999: -9.5
2000: -3.9
2001: -3.5

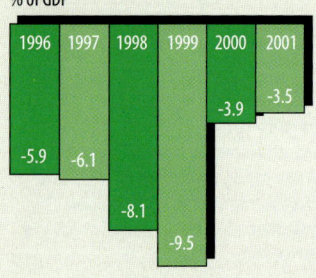

THE WORLD IN 2001

The energy ministry will at last move to privatise Brazil's three big power generators, Furnas, Eletronorte and Chesfe. Public opposition means they may instead be "pulverised" (a partial sell-off). Banespa, Sao Paulo's state bank, and IRB Brasil Re, the federal reinsurance institute, will also go up for sale.

Hot potatoes for the government will include social-security and tax reform, both required by the IMF programme, which enters its final year.

CHILE
GDP: $72.8bn
GDP per head: $4,730
Population: 15.41m
GDP growth: 5.4%
Inflation: 3.7%

Recovery from the 1999 recession will continue. Growth will again top 5% as unemployment falls and both investor and consumer confidence strengthen. Export growth will be healthy, helped by strong demand for copper. Sound policymaking will keep inflation under control.

To watch
The "disappeared". The military will make new information available in early 2001 on the whereabouts of the remains of prisoners who disappeared at the hands of the government between 1973 and 1977.

COLOMBIA
GDP: $89.4bn
GDP per head: $2,080
Population: 43.02m
GDP growth: 2.6%
Inflation: 9.7%

Peace talks between the government and guerrillas will continue amid violence. 2001 is a critical year as President Andres Pastrana passes the mid-point of his four-year term. His time is running out—as is his political capital—for making a breakthrough in resolving the civil war.

Budgetary problems in 2000, including insufficient revenue from privatisations, mean that belt-tightening is necessary in 2001. Public-spending cuts and a general lack of confidence will take their toll on the economy, with the pace of growth being sluggish.

To watch
Plan Colombia, the $7.5 billion programme to fight drugs and improve social conditions. With $1.3 billion of American aid, the fight against the guerrillas—financed by drug money—will take an even higher profile. The conflict could spill over to Colombia's neighbours. America will regret being drawn into someone else's war.

MEXICO
GDP: $553.1bn
GDP per head: $5,600
Population: 98.82m
GDP growth: 3.5%
Inflation: 9.6%

Real effective exchange rate
1996: 86.0
1997: 100.0
1998: 100.3
1999: 110.0
2000: 117.6
2001: 110.8

The new president, the PAN's Vicente Fox, has brought a mood of optimism to the country. But he lacks a majority in Congress and will have to negotiate skilfully to secure approval for vital reforms, including an overhaul of the tax system and liberalisation of the electricity market.

Mr Fox should enjoy warm relations with the new American president, but his proposal that the United States sets an annual immigration quota for Mexicans is a non-starter.

2001 could be a difficult year. A slowdown in the United States will affect demand for exports, the engine of growth since NAFTA was established. The public finances will feel the strain if oil prices slide. The peso, which appreciated in 1999-2000, is due for a correction.

VENEZUELA
GDP: $115.9bn
GDP per head: $4,690
Population: 24.69m
GDP growth: 2.9%
Inflation: 21.8%

Having won a fresh six-year mandate in the elections of July 2000, President Hugo Chavez will be expected to deliver economic growth and plenty of new jobs. If he cannot, his natural constituency, the poor and the marginalised, may lash out.

Mr Chavez will remain a hawk within OPEC: he favours production limits and high prices. But although lofty oil prices are helping the economy now, they could yet again delay the economic reforms needed to end the boom-bust cycle.

To watch
The overvalued bolivar. The policy of using the exchange rate as an anchor for prices will be sustainable only if oil prices remain firm. A steep drop in the oil price would unleash inflation and protests against Mr Chavez.

Africa

KENYA
GDP: $9.9bn
GDP per head: $324
Population: 30.45m
GDP growth: 4.5%
Inflation: 6.0%

Although an election is not necessary before January 2003, the unpredictable president, Daniel arap Moi, may call one sooner. He cannot stand again, but may try to change the constitution. There is no clear successor: George Saitoti, the vice-president, is the likeliest candidate, but for that very reason may be sacked in a cabinet reshuffle.

The spark of democracy and debate is still to be found in Kenya. If Africa is to lift itself from the mire in 2001, this is one of the key countries to watch.

The Kenya stockmarket, small but lively, will keep alive the ideas of capitalism and give the country's middle class a stake in its wealth.

Kenya's new reform agreement with the IMF means the government can ask for further aid. A Paris Club meeting with Kenya's bilateral creditors may also be called, providing an opportunity to reschedule its external debt. The IMF agreement will pave the way for faster economic growth in 2001.

To watch
Richard Leakey, a former conservationist. Appointed head of the civil service in 1999, he has given a boost to reforms and is widely credited with restoring Kenya's ties with the IMF. But the real test will come in 2001 as he tries to cut down the size of the public sector.

NIGERIA
GDP: $40.6bn
GDP per head: $355
Population: 114.34m
GDP growth: 4.0%
Inflation: 7.5%

Africa's giant will slowly recover from years of miserable government. It will be a good year for the economy and the rule of law. Corruption, though everywhere, will at least be frowned upon, rather than encouraged. Some of the money General Sani Abacha, the former dictator, stole will be returned.

Despite an agreement with the IMF, the government of President Olusegun Obasanjo will fail to speed up its cautious deregulation and privatisation programme. All proposals for change will become mired in politics.

The world in figures: Countries

Although oil prices will weaken in 2001, GDP growth will be fairly good. Inflation will remain low, the trade balance in surplus and the fiscal deficit manageable.

Ethnic and religious tensions will never be far from the surface. The fragile new democracy should survive.

To watch
Islamic law. There is an ever-present danger that political agitation could lead to widespread violence in Nigeria. The main source of tension is the apparent insistence of some northern states to introduce sharia—or Islamic—law.

SOUTH AFRICA
GDP: $136.2bn
GDP per head: $3,050
Population: 44.68m
GDP growth: 3.6%
Inflation: 6.5%

Fears will grow that the ruling African National Congress (ANC) will use its overwhelming majority in parliament to extend further its control over society. By appointing party stalwarts to key positions, both within and outside the government, the ANC threatens to marginalise the opposition.

Economic reform is proving costly, at least in the short term. Unemployment levels are well above 30%. Further job losses are likely as state bureaucracies are rationalised. Trade unions have been quiet so far but miners, for instance, are losing patience.

The economy is looking up. Greater foreign investment will help manufacturers, while higher commodity prices will boost the mining sector. With another round of income-tax cuts on the horizon and interest rates likely to fall in 2001, consumer confidence—and the economy—should rebound.

Inward direct investment $m
1996: 816
1997: 3,811
1998: 550
1999: 1,376
2000: 2,200
2001: 2,800

To watch
Relations with neighbouring Zimbabwe. If the economic and political meltdown in Zimbabwe continues, Thabo Mkebi, South Africa's president, may have to intervene.

The world in figures: Countries

Middle East

ALGERIA
GDP: $50.3bn
GDP per head: $1,600
Population: 31.48m
GDP growth: 5.5%
Inflation: 5.5%

President Abdelaziz Bouteflika will see through market reforms to attract private investors. High-profile privatisations in telecoms, energy and finance will go ahead. Could it be, finally, that Algeria will start down a sane economic path?

The government plans to invest $22 billion in oil and gas in 1998-2002: some $2.5 billion to upgrade the petrochemicals sector and $19.5 billion in upstream activities. Sonatrach, the state oil-and-gas company, will seek international partners.

Violence involving Islamist underground groups will remain a destabilising factor. Political parties linked to the Islamist opposition will increase pressure on Mr Bouteflika to allow them a role in the political system.

EGYPT
GDP: $96.0bn
GDP per head: $1,430
Population: 66.99m
GDP growth: 4.9%
Inflation: 4.9%

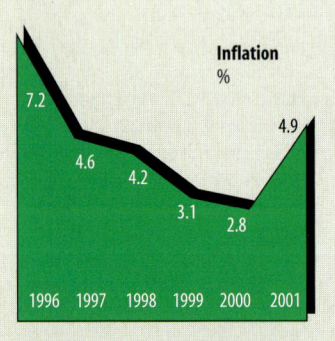

Inflation %
1996: 7.2
1997: 4.6
1998: 4.2
1999: 3.1
2000: 2.8
2001: 4.9

The government will speed up privatisation and deregulation without creating a backlash from rising unemployment. It also will reduce spending by introducing performance-based budgets in government ministries. But it will run up against political pressure to maintain social spending. The focus of economic policy will be domestic debt repayment.

Egypt will play a prominent diplomatic role in brokering peace in the Middle East, particularly in light of the unstable security following Israel's withdrawal from south Lebanon and the death of the Syrian president, Hafez al-Assad.

To watch
Egypt and Iran. The two countries will resume formal ties in 2001.

IRAN
GDP: $80.6bn
GDP per head: $1,220
Population: 66.01m
GDP growth: 3.5%
Inflation: 25.0%

President Mohammed Khatami will stand in the presidential election in 2001—a poll he is almost certain to win, given the strength of his popular support. Conservative clerics will obstruct his programme of political liberalisation. There will be greater resentment at the slow pace of change.

Strong oil prices would support higher growth, though the weak domestic economy will hamper it. Drought-ridden farms will hold expansion to below officially targeted levels.

The United States, with its new administration, will have an opportunity to reassess its approach towards the Islamic Republic, including its economic sanctions. Signs point to a softening of American policy.

To watch
Religious conservatives. They will work tirelessly to undermine the moderates and reassert control, risking widespread public unrest.

IRAQ
GDP: $18.7bn
GDP per head: $787
Population: 23.72m
GDP growth: 15.0%
Inflation: 80.0%

While he is in reasonable health, Saddam Hussein will hold on to power. Government revenue will grow, both directly through prolific smuggling, and indirectly through the UN oil-for-food programme. In the event of his death, a smooth succession is by no means assured.

Economic policy will focus on expanding oil-smuggling routes. Fiscal and monetary policy will remain erratic, ineffectual and driven by political expediency. Nonetheless, powered by oil revenue, real GDP will grow by 15% in 2001, from an unnecessarily low base. Oil production will increase by 10%.

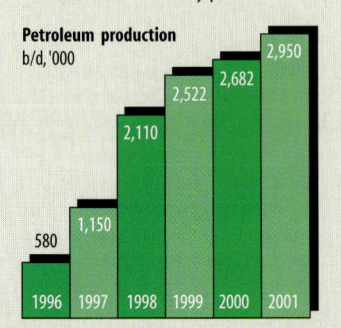

To watch
The sanctions regime. Iraq will not willingly give up what remains of its weapons programme, and relations with UN inspectors are likely to dissolve into stalemate once more. Consequently, sanctions will stay in force in 2001.

ISRAEL
GDP: $111.7bn
GDP per head: $17,400
Population: 6.43m
GDP growth: 4.2%
Inflation: 4.0%

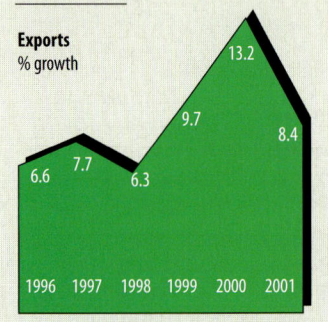

Exports % growth
1996: 6.6
1997: 7.7
1998: 6.3
1999: 9.7
2000: 13.2
2001: 8.4

Israel will have a miserable year. Constant, if sporadic, violence will be costly, both to the country's morale and its budget. No government will be stable enough to deliver a solution.

Prospects for a peace agreement with Syria appear dim. Israel's real problem is not with its neighbours but with itself. 2001 will see the divide between Israel's ultra-orthodox and its fizzing high-tech IT world seem unbridgeable. Syria's President Bashar al-Assad has ruled out a deal until Israel commits to retreat to the June 4th 1967 borders.

Real GDP growth of 4.2% will be driven primarily by the export sector, notably high technology, where Israel's tiny companies compete with the best from California or Europe. Israel's economic recovery will remain sensitive to a deterioration in regional security, or to a worsening of American economic prospects.

JORDAN
GDP: $8.5bn
GDP per head: $1,230
Population: 6.89m
GDP growth: 4.5%
Inflation: 3.0%

Jordan's domestic politics should run smoothly now that there is a prime minister who is far more acceptable to both parliament and Palestinians. King Abdullah II and the new prime minister, Ali Abu Ragheb, share a common view of Jordan's economic and political future, and efforts to modernise the economy and political system are expected to accelerate.

To watch
Warm relations between King Abdullah and the new Syrian president, Bashar al-Assad. Both are young men with western educations, and both share a desire to transform the economies of their countries.

LEBANON
GDP: $17.5bn
GDP per head: $5,040
Population: 6.89m
GDP growth: 1.5%
Inflation: 2.0%

Lebanon will begin to climb slowly out of the recession that has plagued it since late 1998. Growth was estimated at around 0.5% in 2000, and will pick up gradually in 2001.

The new prime minister's aims will remain the same as that of Salim al-Hoss, who was ousted in the September election: restoring the government's finances and reversing the slowdown in economic growth, largely by creating a more welcoming environment for the local and foreign private sectors.

SAUDI ARABIA
GDP: $154.3bn
GDP per head: $7,310
Population: 21.11m
GDP growth: 2.5%
Inflation: 2.5%

The government's new five-year plan has set demanding targets for growth and job-creation, and calls for the private sector to play a more prominent role. But suspicions remain that many sectors will remain off-limits to foreign ventures.

Oil prices will weaken, but an anticipated increase in oil production to around 8.4m b/d in 2001 will support firm growth. Investment in hydrocarbons will rise, particularly in the gas sector and in power generation. Foreign investment in these areas could start to make an impact in the second half of 2001.

Saudi Arabia's international relations will continue to be riven with an old contradiction: it is heavily dependent on the United States militarily, but tries to appear independent of the West to appease religious conservatives and young Islamists. In oil matters, Saudi Arabia will continue to follow the American line.

Petroleum production b/d, '000
1996: 580
1997: 1,150
1998: 2,110
1999: 2,522
2000: 2,682
2001: 2,950

some days you just work yourself

into a corner

After a hard day at work
you probably want a few soft options.
Some people like to end the day
as dramatically as it started.
But for those of you who prefer to ease
down gently, we have made space.
Lots of space.
Marriott Hotels have pools, whirlpools and spas.
There you don't always have to take part.
You can relax.
Let it all wash over you.
thinking of you

Marriott
HOTELS · RESORTS · SUITES

Earn free flights or nights with Marriott Rewards.
You'll find 372 Marriott Hotels in 48 countries worldwide including 37 in the UK.

www.marriotthotels.com
Reservations 0800 221 222

Argentina, Armenia, Aruba, Australia, Austria, Bahamas, Brazil, Canada, Cayman Islands, Chile, China, Costa Rica, Czech Republik, Ecuador, Egypt, El Salvador, France, Germany, Greece, Guatemala, Hungary, India, Israel, Italy, Japan, Jordan, Lebanon, Malaysia, Mexico, Netherlands, Pakistan, Panama, Peru, Philipines, Poland, Puerto Rico, Qatar, Romania, Russia, Saudi Arabia, Singapore, Spain, South Korea, Switzerland, Thailand, UAE, UK, USA, US Virgin Islands

©2000 i2 Technologies, Inc.

value²

Our e-marketplace solutions have already created more than $16 billion in value for over 950 companies worldwide. Hard dollar, bottom-line benefits from reducing cost of goods sold, shrinking inventories, accelerating time-to-market and creating new e-markets. i2 has the only B2B solution that incorporates a complete supply chain model, marketplace-to-marketplace support and rich content management capabilities. Value.² Want some? Contact us at www.i2.com or 1-877-926-9286.

i2

Powering the Bottom Line.™

THE WORLD IN 2001

The world in figures: Industries

General trends

Who's rich?
GDP per head, 2001
$'000

- Japan 38.0
- USA 37.9
- Sweden 31.0
- Germany 27.0
- UK 25.9
- Russia 1.7
- China 0.9

Source: EIU

Boom times—and they will be global. The world economy will grow by 4.2% in 2001, only a mild slowdown on the previous year's 4.7%. America will enjoy yet another year of expansion, albeit at a slower rate of 3%. The recovery in Japan will gain confidence. Europe will expand faster than the United States for the first time in nine years. The developing world will grow at a dizzy 6%.

Central bankers will be keeping an eye on four risks which threaten to cloud this sunny picture: inflation; a sudden loss of confidence in the American dollar; a messy global equity market correction; and unpredictable oil prices.

Trade will boom in 2001. However, growth of over 8% will not be helped by countries arguing about what needs to be liberalised next. The unpalatable answer, of course, is that everything that is a barrier to trade should be scrapped: any restriction impoverishes all. America wants freer agricultural markets in Europe. Europe wants investment and competition rules on the agenda. Developing countries complain that both Europe and America remain protectionist. Brussels and Washington will argue about $4 billion-worth of tax breaks America currently gives to its exporters. The EU could retaliate in early 2001. China, a new WTO member, will provide leadership to developing countries.

The race to get bigger, quicker, will push firms in all industries to merge and acquire. This will give both investment bankers and regulators plenty of work. Expect many headline-making deals to fail to get regulatory approval in 2001.

Production

AEROSPACE

The American Department of Defence will choose a winning Joint-Strike Fighter design from either Lockheed Martin or Boeing. Cost is the key factor: the Pentagon will pay only $35m a plane. The winning company will sell $100 billion-worth; the loser will fight for survival. The Typhoon Eurofighter will enter service in 2002. There will be no other major fighter projects in the West for the foreseeable future.

Airbus Integrated, the new Franco-German-Spanish venture, begins work on the new 550-650-seat A3XX super-jumbo. The planes should come into service in 2005. The project will cost $12 billion and will make or break the European manufacturer. Success would crack Boeing's 30-year monopoly on very large aircraft.

The world's busiest airports
Passengers, m, 1999

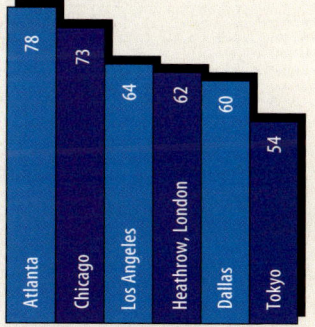

- Atlanta 78
- Chicago 73
- Los Angeles 64
- Heathrow, London 62
- Dallas 60
- Tokyo 54

Source: Airports Council International

For its part, Boeing believes that $4 billion of the $12 billion needed to develop the A3XX will come from European subsidies. It will push Washington to take the EU to the WTO to stop the payments. Dangerous: Boeing has received government subsidies itself.

The commercial space industry is worth $120 billion in sales a year. 800 satellite launches are planned for the next eight years. R&D is focused on developing cheap, reusable launch vehicles. They could cut costs by more than half, making space a much easier place to get to and use.

If it wasn't for opposition from the American government, 2001 would probably see a transatlantic merger between defence contractors. Instead, companies will content themselves with stronger ties. BAe Systems will strengthen its links with Boeing and Lockheed Martin, DaimlerChrysler Aerospace with Northrup Grummar, and France's Thomson-CSF with America's Raytheon.

To watch
What the new American administration does with National Missile Defence. Russia and China oppose America's project to build a land-based defence against missile attack. The EU is uneasy. It will be the single most important issue for the White House in 2001.

AGRICULTURE

The European Union's common agricultural policy remains highly protectionist. The United States and the 16-strong Cairns Group (which includes Australia, Canada and Brazil) are getting frustrated. They want the Europeans to lower tariffs and end export subsidies. European farmers will fight this. For its part, America also looks after its farmers, mostly through direct payments. The moratorium on challenging illegal farm-support programmes at the WTO expires in 2003. This may spur the EU to make concessions in 2001. But don't bet on it. Farm policy everywhere will remain an expensive mess, bad for farmers, taxpayers and consumers.

After a slump in most agricultural commodity prices, 2001 will witness price increases, most notably in sugar. The crop will sell for a sweet nine cents/lb by 2002. Wheat, maize and sorghum prices will edge up in the 2001-02 season.

The productivity of farmers
% of GDP contributed by agriculture

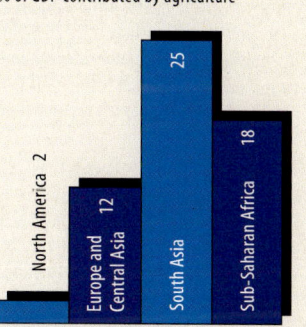

- North America 2
- Europe and Central Asia 12
- South Asia 25
- Sub-Saharan Africa 18

Source: World Bank

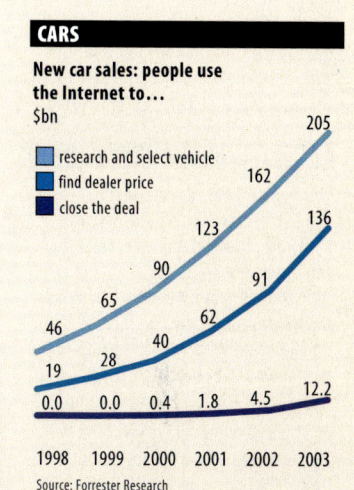

CARS

New car sales: people use the Internet to…
$bn

- research and select vehicle
- find dealer price
- close the deal

	1998	1999	2000	2001	2002	2003
research and select vehicle	46	65	90	123	162	205
find dealer price	19	28	40	62	91	136
close the deal	0.0	0.0	0.4	1.8	4.5	12.2

Source: Forrester Research

A record number of cars will be sold in 2001, guaranteeing unprecedented traffic jams everywhere. Expect these sales from fewer manufacturers. DaimlerChrysler has a slice of Mitsubishi, General Motors owns part of Fiat, Ford has invested in Volvo, and Renault and Nissan have linked up. Global recession, when it comes, will trigger real consolidation in this industry.

Covisint, a global exchange established by GM, Ford and DaimlerChrysler to handle car-part procurement, will start to lower prices in 2001. It could command $240 billion of purchasing power. Such pressures will force component suppliers to consolidate with a frenzy; 2,000 top-tier global suppliers will become 150 by 2008.

Nearly 8m Asians will buy cars in 2001, meaning more jams in Beijing and Bangkok. Asia Pacific is the key to future growth in this market, and after a mild slowdown in 2001, 2003 should see sales back at record volumes. Thin margins mean that big profits are not guaranteed.

To watch
Cars getting cleaner and cleverer. All the leading motor companies will introduce fuel-cell vehicles by 2004. By 2020, some analysts estimate that 25% of vehicles will run on fuel cells. Advances in telematics mean that the car of tomorrow will have voice-activated Internet services. By the start of 2001, GM will have over 1m users of its OnStar services. These provide computerised route maps and tell drivers exactly where they are.

109

The world in figures: Industries

CHEMICALS

The top five chemical firms account for only 10% of global production. 2001 will see $60 billion-worth of M&A activity in the sector. The industry suffers from low profits and a poor public image. To improve the former, firms will move into the $32 billion agribusiness industry. To solve the latter, the big firms are funding the $125m Long-Range Initiative. This aims to discover the endocrine effects of the 1,000 most heavily used chemicals.

COMPUTERS

This industry now has standards—IBM and Sun servers, Cisco data-network hardware, Oracle databases, and EMC storage boxes. These firms will enjoy solid growth, but they will look towards the future. Oracle, for instance, will move into application server software, a sector with sales of $11 billion by 2004.

The growth rate of PC sales is falling. 2001 wil be a difficult year for the Dells and Compaqs of this world. Homes in the United States are nearing saturation point for PCs. Companies are pinning their hopes on selling more designer PCs and more high-end servers.

Linux, a free operating system developed by the open-source movement, is taking market share from Microsoft at the low end of the server market and will start attacking the high end in 2001. Hewlett-Packard intends to use the software as the core of its new server strategy. Intel, IBM and Hewlett-Packard will all invest in a new lab in Oregon which will develop Linux for use in high-end corporate computer systems.

The software market will grow to some $222 billion by 2002. More than 95% of revenues will come from business purchases. Apple will launch its new operating system, Mac OS X, commercially in 2001.

World sales of personal computers
m units

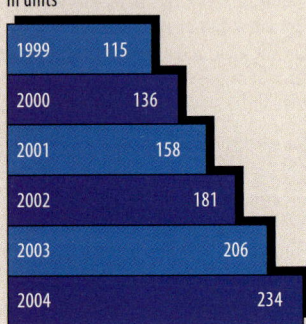

Year	Units
1999	115
2000	136
2001	158
2002	181
2003	206
2004	234

Source: Dataquest

To watch
Microsoft in court, again, even if it loses its current antitrust trial and is split up into two companies. Its new .Net initiative will see it attempt to "wrap" proprietary technologies around open Internet standards.

ENERGY

Black-gold diggers
Share of oil production

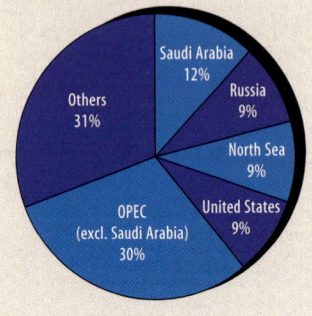

- Saudi Arabia 12%
- Russia 9%
- North Sea 9%
- United States 9%
- OPEC (excl. Saudi Arabia) 30%
- Others 31%

Source: Energy Information Administration

In the West, renewable energy is coming and nuclear power is being switched off. Renewable energy sources will make up half of worldwide energy production. But don't hold your breath: not until 2060.

Germany starts to turn off its 20 nuclear power stations. They should all be shut by 2021. Asia will keep on building reactors—Japan has three in construction, and 13 more planned before 2010. Brazil needs 49 new thermo-electrical plants to generate 18,000MW for its growing energy needs.

The electricity business is worth $1 trillion a year. About half of that is produced by steam-driven turbines, but gas turbines are quickly becoming more popular. In the United States, electricity rates will soar in states that have deregulated power sectors.

OPEC is in the driving seat with oil supply. Production increases in late 2000 will trickle through to reduced prices in early 2001. OPEC would like to sell a barrel for $22-28, well above the historical benchmark of $15-20, but below a predicted price for much of 2001 of $32. High prices will quicken the general industrial move from oil to natural gas.

After predictions that it would be exhausted by the turn of the century, the North Sea will provide over 30 billion barrels of oil and gas over the next 30 years. It has so far yielded only 26 billion. In America, no oil refineries have been built for 25 years. Republicans want to end that ban, as well as lift restrictions on off-shore drilling.

The West is securing its energy needs for the next century. America and Turkey are backing an energy corridor linking Baku in Azerbaijan with Ceyhan in Turkey. The year will see financing put together and the governments ratifying their transit agreements. The oil pipeline will cost $2.4 billion to build and will open in 2004. Two years before that, a transcaspian pipeline will be supplying over 16 billion cubic metres of gas a year to Turkey from Turkmenistan.

To watch
Proton-exchange membranes (PEM). They are the leading technology for fuel-cells and rely on hydrogen being oxidised to produce clean energy. The first commercial mobile generator using PEM comes out in 2001. Fuel-cells will enter mass use some time after 2005.

PHARMACEUTICALS

This $350 billion industry is growing by 10% a year and enjoys margins of over 35%. Over 60% of profits are made in the United States. With the world ageing and the human genome mapped, prospects are very healthy.

Fortunes will be won and lost in the genome grab. In 2001, the two new titans of the industry, Glaxo SmithKline and Pfizer Warner-Lambert, will each spend over $4 billion on R&D. The industry as a whole will invest $50 billion. The race to secure the key patents will be run over the next five years.

Companies are inventing more drugs and testing them more quickly. It now takes 15 years and $359m to bring a new drug to market. The major companies plan to launch an average of 1.8 new drugs a year up till 2005. During the 1990s, they managed only one new drug a year.

The patent on Prozac expires, and cheap, generic fluoxetine floods the market. $44 billion-worth of medicines will lose their patent protection over the next three years. Eli Lilly will submit Zovant, a breakthrough drug for treating sepsis, for approval.

Drug abuse
% of world health-care market

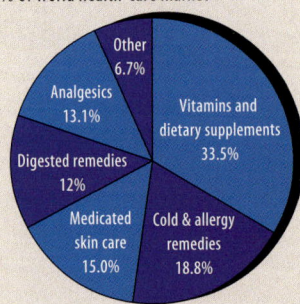

- Vitamins and dietary supplements 33.5%
- Cold & allergy remedies 18.8%
- Medicated skin care 15.0%
- Analgesics 13.1%
- Digested remedies 12%
- Other 6.7%

Source: Euromonitor

To watch
Baby-boomers getting old. It will trigger huge demand for medicines for arthritis, osteoporosis and fading eyesight. Rheumatology drugs are set for 30% annual growth over the next three years.

PRECIOUS METALS

The oligopolistic platinum industry is dominated by Amplats. Prices are at 11-year highs, though with Russia increasing production they will fall a little in 2001. Chinese and Indian youths love wearing platinum jewellery. And the metal is also used as the catalyst in fuel cells. Expect prices to rise again in 2003-04.

Diamonds are a girl's best friend and in 2001 they will be advertisers' too. Only 1% of retail revenues are currently spent on advertising. De Beers wants to raise that to around 8%. The firm still controls 60-70% of the world's diamond market, and has a stash of $4 billion-worth of stones. The firm also says its wants to allow more price competition.

Gold and platinum prices
$ per oz

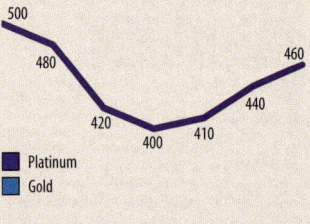

Platinum: 500, 480, 420, 400, 410, 440, 460
Gold: 280, 275, 270, 275, 280, 280, 280

2000 2001 2002 2003 2004 2005 2006
Source: EIU

There are 140,000 tonnes of gold above ground and an annual demand of 4,000 tonnes. Gold prices continue their 20-year long broad decline to $270 an ounce. Cancel this prediction if inflation in the West climbs above 3%. Silver prices will remain stable, despite increases in supply.

RAW MATERIALS

Pulp-paper prices are rising again, after a slump in 1995. Old capacity is being closed and nothing new being built. Traders will remain sceptical about rising prices for rubber, despite attempts by the three main producers, Thailand, Malaysia and Indonesia, to fix prices. They are trying to restrict supply but, unlike OPEC, have not agreed how. Aluminium demand will grow by 2.5%. However, the long-term price decline shows no signs of ending, so cost-cutting will remain a priority.

TEXTILES

The United States has one of the world's most protected textile markets. 1.4m domestic workers produce $100 billion-worth of goods a year. America's WTO commitments mean that finally, by 2005, the sector will be fully liberalised. Employment will then fall a little, but the American consumer will benefit.

Services

ADVERTISING

Cash-strapped dot.coms will be cutting down on their advertising. Real-world retailers will be increasing their spend online. Online advertising will make up 8.5% of American advertising and direct-marketing revenues by 2005.

Adverts will go mobile. By 2005, your mobile phone will know where you are. Using global satellite positioning technology, companies will be able to message you when you're walking past a sale that might interest you or when a friend of yours is having coffee in a nearby café.

Couch-potatoes will get even lazier with the advent of interactive televisions. Shopping via their televisions will allow them to see pizza, click on pizza and then eat pizza. T-commerce could be worth $300 billion by 2005. The largest chunk will come from interactive advertising.

AIRLINES

China's 34 domestic airlines will merge and expand. In the United States, United, American and Delta could take their 56% share of the American market up to 85%. Five airlines could dominate Europe by 2005. The failure of the BA-KLM merger talks showed that big cross-border deals are not easy to achieve in Europe. That won't stop Air France, Lufthansa, Swissair and Alitalia from trying.

However, much of this depends upon the decisions of regulators in Washington and Brussels. They worry that the new giants will use their market power to force low-cost start-up airlines out of business.

Growing one's routes
Annual growth rate of passengers, 1999-2003, %

Europe-Africa	6.1
South Pacific-Asia	5.8
Europe-Asia	5.7
Within Asia	5.5
North Atlantic	4.9

Source: IATA

ENTERTAINMENT

The days of the dumb-box and one-way broadcasting are fading fast. Computers will become televisions, televisions Internet-surfers. Expect television-quality Internet services within five years in America and Western Europe. By 2005, 55m American homes will have digital cable or satellite boxes which will give them broadband access. Only when this happens will it be time to judge the impact of the Internet on the television industry.

Still all to play for in the music industry. The challenge for the corporations is not to control MP3, the digital compression technology which allows the sharing of music files over the Internet, but to harness it. 75% of American university computer use is taken up by sharing of MP3 files. Forrester Research estimates that Internet distribution could cost the industry $3 billion a year in lost revenues up to 2005. There have been legal successes in closing down sites like Napster which provide a forum for file-sharing. However, the lawyers will not be able to close down peer-to-peer networks like Gnutella, which have no central server. The challenge for companies such as EMI and Sony is to use such technologies and create viable subscription services with them. The industry has failed to comprehend the scale of the revolution. It has much to do.

To watch
Toshiba, Xerox and IBM are all developing electronic newspapers with flexible screens and the ability to download tailor-made news. They will be ready in five years. But with global newspaper and magazine circulation at record highs, print is far from finished. People still want paper—they prefer its look, its feel and its sheer serendipity.

FINANCE

The battle to merge stock exchanges will intensify, propelled by investors' passion for liquidity and 24-hour trading. More exchanges will demutualise, allowing them to raise capital through share issues. GEM, a global alliance of ten exchanges including New York, Paris, Tokyo and Hong Kong, will try to work out what their alliance is actually for. But new exchanges will have to make do with a less vibrant equity culture. Equity returns will fall from an annual average return of 23% over the past five years to 9% over the next five.

Global derivatives markets are worth $100 trillion. The credit and equity derivatives market will boom, while foreign exchange derivatives markets will decline.

The three members of the trillionaire's club will continue to pull away from the pack. Goldman Sachs, Morgan Stanley Dean Witter, and Merrill Lynch will each do more than $1 trillion-worth of M&A advisory work in 2001. CSFB, Citigroup and J.P. Morgan Chase will be doing their best to catch up or merge their way into the club. They'll find it hard—the top three have the capital to offer credit to the clients they advise, they enjoy global reach and bear names which send shivers down the spines of competitors. However, as deals get done by ever fewer banks, conflicts of interest between their various customers will become more problematic.

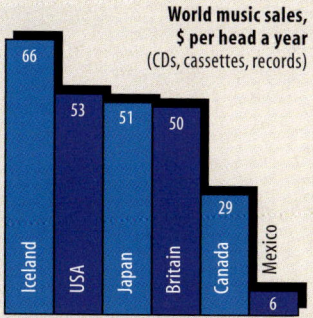

World music sales, $ per head a year (CDs, cassettes, records)

Iceland	66
USA	53
Japan	51
Britain	50
Canada	29
Mexico	6

Source: International Federation of Phonographic Industry

World pension assets $trn, 2004

United States	10
Britain	2
Japan	2
Netherlands	0.6
France	0.1
Italy	0.1

Source: InterSec Research

Bond traders will go corporate. America's Federal Reserve plans to buy back all its debt by 2013. This is causing a fundamental restructuring of the world's capital markets, since the market for American public debt sets the benchmarks for interest rates, corporate bonds and equity valuations the world over. Government bond markets elsewhere are drying up too. Everywhere except in Japan, which will hold a third of the world's government debt market, a result of the government's massive pump-priming. Traders in other countries will fly to corporate debt. And this is concentrated in the eurozone.

16% of Western Europe's population is aged 65 years or older. By 2050 this will be 30%. France and Italy have the biggest problems financing the concomitant increase in pension demands. European pension-fund assets will grow from €2 billion ($1.8 billion) now to €5 billion ($4.4 billion) over the next five years. This will drive the growth of Europe's equity markets.

To watch
The continued break-up of the "Big-Five" accounting firms. The American "Scope of Services" rule has forced the firms to sell their consultancy arms. Now comes the turn of their corporate finance and tax advice businesses.

HEALTH CARE

America is the only major industrial country which has no publicly funded universal medical system. This means that in 2001, 40m Americans will be left uncovered. There will be a surplus of doctors, especially specialists, which will cause their income to fall.

In Britain, the greater share of the burden is shifting to primary care as hospital rationalisation continues. The country offering the best medical service in 2001 will be France.

INSURANCE

Tough times in the European insurance industry with overcapacity and shrinking premiums. The Internet is not helping traditional firms, which have been hesitant to go online, since this would mean cannibalising their agent-based business. However, agent commissions make up 25% of the costs of a typical policy and this has created big incentives for new insurers to market directly online. By 2003, $4 billion-worth of insurance will be sold this way in America. But that will still only be 0.5% of the total market.

Another problem for traditional insurers is bank assurance: that is, banks and other financial groups selling insurance products. The one bit of good news is that western insurers are at last getting the chance to enter key emerging markets. In 2001, India will allow the first foreign-owned insurer to start operations, while in China foreign firms expect greater scope of business as the country joins the WTO.

The worldwide reinsurance industry has $50 billion in capital, 50% more than it needs. This has caused prices to fall in recent years, but 2001 will see them bottoming out and even rising in some sectors.

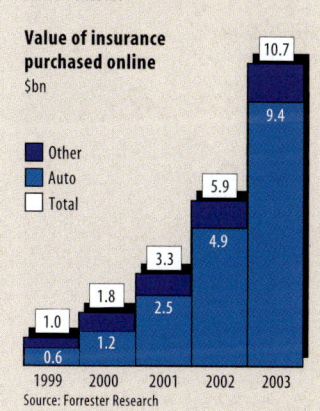

Value of insurance purchased online $bn

Legend: Other / Auto / Total

Year	Total	Auto	Other
1999	0.6	1.0	
2000	1.2	1.8	
2001	2.5	3.3	
2002	4.9	5.9	
2003	9.4	10.7	

Source: Forrester Research

The world in figures: Industries

THE WORLD IN 2001

INTERNET

Venture capitalists (VCs) will invest more than double the figure that they dispensed in the dot.com mania of 1999. VCs and private investors will dispense over $300 billion in 2001. The problem for the year ahead is that there is much more capital (expecting returns of 20% or more) than there is opportunity. Expect bad deals to be done.

There are 1,000 VC firms in the United States alone. The year will see a select few use Silicon Valley as a base for branching out globally. More will move out altogether as the happy valley becomes too expensive. 2001 will see VCs investing in Internet infrastructure and peer-to-peer technologies; B2C and B2B are already passé.

It is a question of when, not if, Asian e-commerce overtakes that of the West. Revenues in the region will be worth $300 billion by 2003, up from $8 billion in 1999. China already has 20m regular Internet users and that figure doubles every six months.

Bad habits will proliferate online in 2001. In America, 52m people will be "telewebbers", people who surf and watch television at the same time. And online gambling in America, worth $1.5 billion in 2000, will double by 2002.

To watch
The battle to set up online exchanges. Following the car maunfacturers, companies from all industries are setting up trading sites to run their supply chains. CommerceOne, a B2B company, estimates that such ventures can save a business 70% of its processing costs, and 10% of its product costs. Gartner Group, an Internet consultancy, estimates that there will be over 8,000 online marketplaces by 2002. Many of them will mediate their first transactions in 2001. Many others will go bust. Regulators will monitor their ability to influence prices.

Internet users
worldwide m

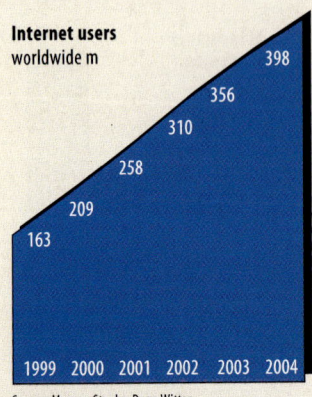

1999: 163
2000: 209
2001: 258
2002: 310
2003: 356
2004: 398

Source: Morgan Stanley Dean Witter

RETAIL

Online B2C transactions will be worth around $184 billion by 2004. Roughly three-quarters of such sales are currently being mediated by just five sites: Amazon, eBay, AOL, Yahoo! and Buy.com. By 2004, "legacy" firms—those that existed before the Internet was invented, such as Wal-Mart—will have taken a massive slice of the market. By 2010, shopping on the Internet will account for 15-20% of all retail sales. In 2001, eyes will look ever closer at Amazon to see if it can survive that long.

Logistics will be the biggest headache for online retailers in 2001. They currently face a fulfilment cost 11% higher than that of their offline catalogue competitors. In the United States, a split-shopping model is emerging. Customers prefer to stock up on non-foods and packaged groceries online but like to buy fresh produce from a real store.

The European online retail market
Sales €m

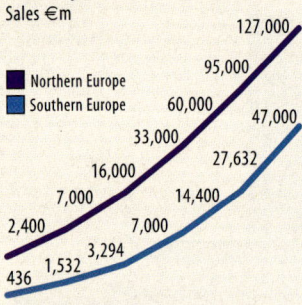

Northern Europe / Southern Europe

1999: 2,400 / 436
2000: 7,000 / 1,532
2001: 16,000 / 3,294
2002: 33,000 / 7,000
2003: 60,000 / 14,400
2004: 95,000 / 27,632
2005: 127,000 / 47,000

Source: Forrester Research

Retailers online and off will all use the Martini model to sell you things: anytime, anywhere, via your computer, mobile phone, television and even the high street. Brave B2C firms will set up bricks and mortar stores in an attempt to build their brands.

The Visa/MasterCard antitrust trial ends. Together, the two companies control 75% of credit and charge-card transactions in the United States. The judge will not be a flexible friend. He will order a break-up of their businesses.

To watch
E-tax. The American government lost an estimated $170m in sales-tax revenues in 1999 because of tax-free purchases made on the Internet. European leaders rely heavily on value-added tax (it makes up 40% of Europe's tax revenues) and want to introduce an e-tax. America has agreed in principle to a tax levied on goods sold electronically at the rate where the consumer is based. A draft law is to be considered by the EU Council of Ministers in 2001.

TELECOMMUNICATIONS

Global bandwidth demand
Giga bits per second

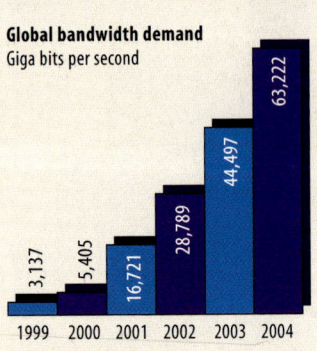

1999: 3,137
2000: 5,405
2001: 16,721
2002: 28,789
2003: 44,497
2004: 63,222

Source: Morgan Stanley Dean Witter

Utopia, otherwise known in this industry as convergence, comes a step closer, as mobile moves to centre stage. The engine behind this revolution is bandwidth, that is, the size of the pipe or signal by which you receive and send your data. You can never get enough of it.

There will be a billion mobile-phone subscribers worldwide by 2003 and a third of Europe will be using one by 2004. Over half of global users will have Internet access. Mobile (m-)commerce in Europe will be worth €23 billion by 2003. The personal computer will hold on for longer as the prime Internet-access vehicle in the United States.

The mobile Internet will be born again in 2001, this time properly. Disillusion with WAP will give way to rejoicing over GPRS, UMTS and CDMA. 2001 will see the bulk of delivery of mobile phones in Europe based on GPRS (General Packet Radio Switching). This is a 2.5-generation technology which will give you the Internet speeds of a fixed ISDN line on your mobile phone. A year later, third-generation UMTS (Universal Mobile Telecommunications System) services will be rolled out. These will work on the same principal as GPRS, but will be even faster, delivering 2 megabytes per second, which is about 40 times faster than current office PCs.

NTT DoCoMo will launch third-generation CDMA services in Japan earlier, in spring 2001. Complex Division Multiple Access is a digital technology that separates messages into lots of packets which it sends at different frequencies, putting them together again using unique codes. This way CDMA allows a mix of calls to be carried on the same channel at the same time, thus producing extra bandwidth. It will transcend Europe's current GSM standard, bringing video to a mobile phone near you. Ultimately, these phones will use browsers which can respond to your voice.

In America, 70% of growth is coming from voice and data services. By 2030, voice services will account for only 33% of industry revenues. As deregulation and Internet-protocol telephony bite, the distance-call sector will shrivel. IP telephony was worth $264m in 1999. By 2006, that will rise to $91 billion.

More bandwidth to the masses. The race between the two key broadband infrastructures—cable modems and digital subscriber lines (based on copper telephone wires)—will be won by cable. In America, 1.7m users are already accessing the Internet via cable. To help make these networks even quicker, a revolution in optical networks is on the way. Previously, crucial sections relied on electrical components. That will soon change with all-photon optical networks.

Internet in the sky. Or pie? ICO-Teledesic, Inmarset, and GlobalStar will spend billions to launch satellites that support broadband services. As they go up, the last of the bankrupt Iridium voice satellites will fall to earth.

To watch
Qualcomm become the Intel of the wireless age. The company owns crucial patents for CDMA, one of the standards for third-generation mobile-phones.

TRAVEL

Tourists in 2020
Where they will come from
m

Germany: 153
Japan: 146
USA: 123
China: 100
Britain: 95
France: 55

Source: World Tourism Organisation

Air passenger trips are growing 5% a year. By 2010, airlines will be hosting 2.3 billion passenger journeys a year, compared with 1.6 billion in 1999. This will stretch limited airport and air-traffic control capacity at all the major airports, causing delays to flights in summer 2001.

Users of low-cost airlines will grow to 50m by 2003. At present, one in four flyers use low-cost airlines in America, but only one in twenty do so in Europe.

To watch
Travel agents fighting extinction. Airlines want to sell tickets direct and cut commissions paid to agents. Customers want the cheaper prices offered online. Because margins are so thin, it will only take 5% of the industry to move online to cause large numbers of traditional agents to go bust. Currently, the figure stands at 2% in the United States.

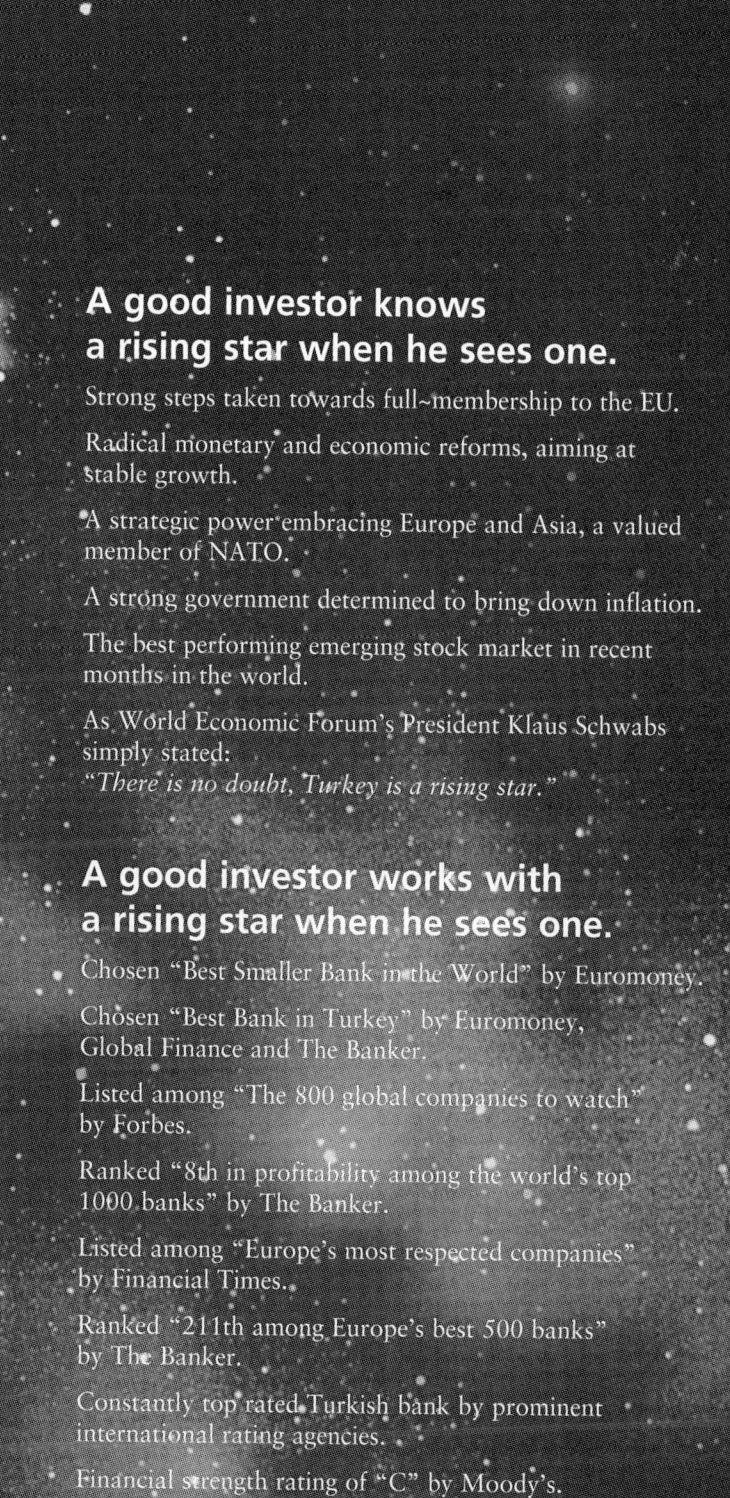

**A good investor knows
a rising star when he sees one.**

Strong steps taken towards full-membership to the EU.

Radical monetary and economic reforms, aiming at stable growth.

A strategic power embracing Europe and Asia, a valued member of NATO.

A strong government determined to bring down inflation.

The best performing emerging stock market in recent months in the world.

As World Economic Forum's President Klaus Schwabs simply stated:
"There is no doubt, Turkey is a rising star."

**A good investor works with
a rising star when he sees one.**

Chosen "Best Smaller Bank in the World" by Euromoney.

Chosen "Best Bank in Turkey" by Euromoney, Global Finance and The Banker.

Listed among "The 800 global companies to watch" by Forbes.

Ranked "8th in profitability among the world's top 1000 banks" by The Banker.

Listed among "Europe's most respected companies" by Financial Times.

Ranked "211th among Europe's best 500 banks" by The Banker.

Constantly top rated Turkish bank by prominent international rating agencies.

Financial strength rating of "C" by Moody's.

For more information:
(90-212) 335 35 35 or http://www.garantibank.com.tr

GarantiBank
Turkey

AVAYA
communication

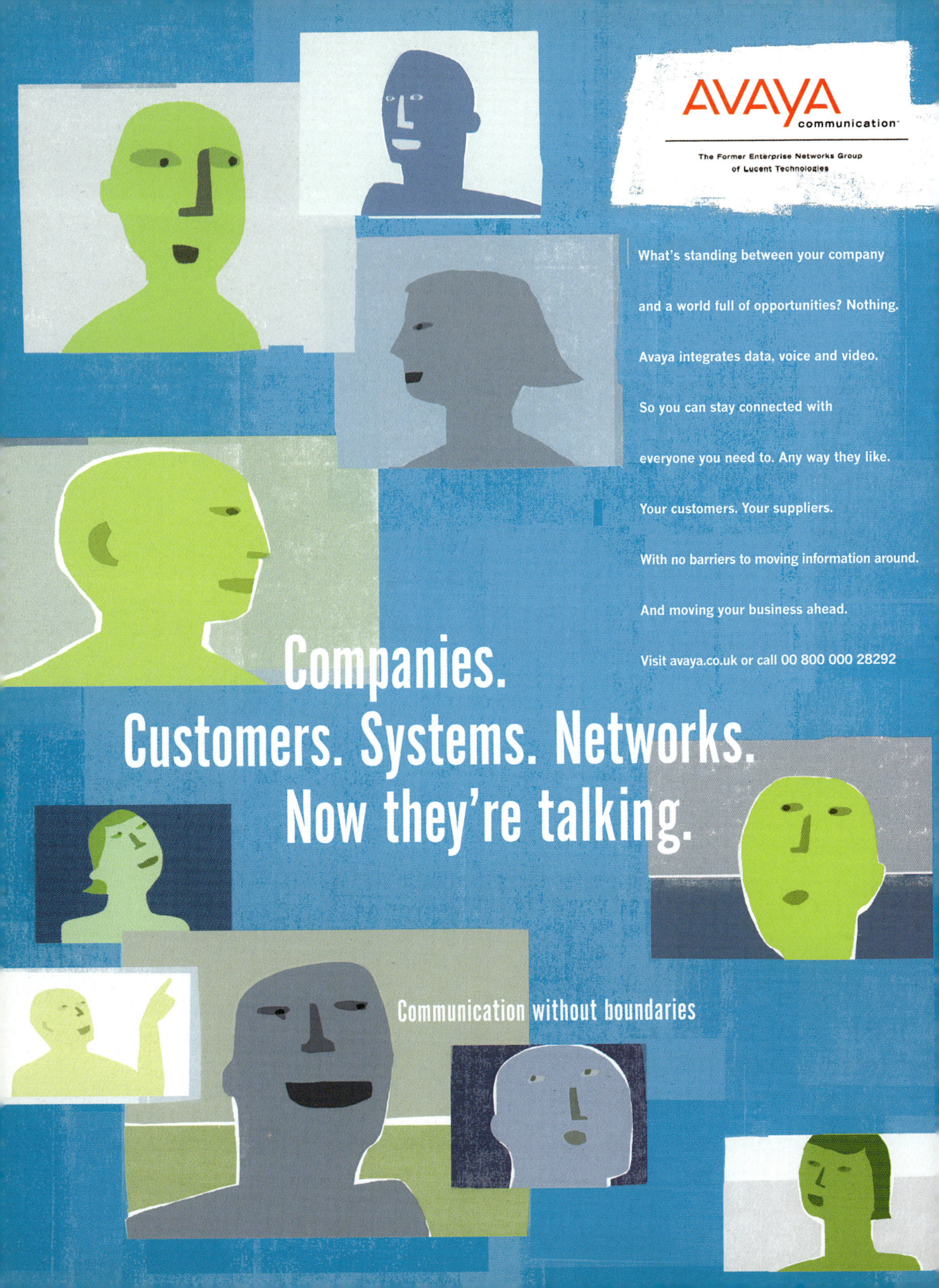

The Former Enterprise Networks Group of Lucent Technologies

What's standing between your company and a world full of opportunities? Nothing.

Avaya integrates data, voice and video.

So you can stay connected with everyone you need to. Any way they like.

Your customers. Your suppliers.

With no barriers to moving information around.

And moving your business ahead.

Visit avaya.co.uk or call 00 800 000 28292

Companies.
Customers. Systems. Networks.
Now they're talking.

Communication without boundaries

THE WORLD IN 2001
Business and Management

Competitiveness: The next measure of national machismo 116 / **Energy:** The half-life of nuclear power 119
Executive pay: How should the bosses be paid? 122 / **John Chambers:** You ain't seen nothing yet 123
Renewable fuels: Which way to the hydrogen economy? 124 / **Third-generation phones:** Your new mobile 124
Electronic publishing: Dead trees go digital 127 / **Electronics in 2001:** Gadgets for all 130
Air travel: Bad air days 132 / **The wired house:** Home on the Net 134

Global warriors strike back

Adrian Wooldridge

Washington, DC

2001
Aggressive? Wal-Mart? The world's biggest retailer plans its biggest year of expansion. Expect 400 new stores around the world, including 180 warehouse-sized shopping-centres in America.

Globalisation is set to become an even more difficult problem for the world's business people. The logic of competition will force companies to rethink many of their basic assumptions about how to manage across borders. But, at the same time, the political environment will continue to get more hostile, as anti-globalisation protests roll on and international organisations bend over backwards to appease the protesters. Successful global managers will not only have to become far more sophisticated strategically; they will have to become far savvier politically, too.

One of the ironies of all this is that managers' lives would be a lot easier if the anti-globalists were talking sense. The anti-globalisation brigade makes two big charges against multinational companies: that they are giant organisations that crush competition and reduce choice; and that they are instruments of western imperialism that ride roughshod over different cultures. But even if these caricatures once contained an element of truth, they are getting more misleading by the day.

A hundred years ago an American president who wanted to talk to corporate America could just have a fireside chat with J.P. Morgan. Now he would have to hire an entire amphitheatre. Pankaj Ghemawat, an academic at Harvard Business School, points out that globalisation does not lead to concentration, as both anti-globalists and M&A obsessed managers imagine, but to its opposite. In the 1950s, American roads were ruled by just three companies (Ford, Chrysler and General Motors), its airwaves by three (NBC, ABC and CBS), its telephones by AT&T and most of its technology by IBM.

Today globalisation is forcing these giants into competition with an ever more clamorous group of challengers. In those three great engines of the high-tech economy, computer hardware, computer software and long-distance telephony, the top five companies' share of worldwide sales declined by between 15 and 30 points each in the decade after 1988.

The reason for this is simple. Giant companies used to be able to rely on the high cost of capital and technology to protect themselves from competition, and on their cosy relations with governments around the world, expensively cultivated over the years. But now the cost of capital and technology is plummeting, and a rules-based system of trade is making ties with governments less important. This means that the advantage is shifting relentlessly from incumbents to innovators. This opens up space for competition, rather than closing it down.

The shift is going hand in hand with an even more subtle one. Multinationals have traditionally assumed that companies from the developed world would crush local rivals. This approach now smacks not just of arrogance but of incompetence too.

Several local champions are successfully fending off challengers in their own markets. Bajaj Auto, India's leading scooter maker, succeeded in defending its local market from Japanese firms because it understood that, given the country's appalling roads, what Indians needed was cheap bikes that you could take to a convenient repair shop as soon as anything went wrong with them. Honda may have offered superior technology, but it was Bajaj's nationwide distribution system and easily repairable bikes which assured its success.

A few local champions are even proving their mettle in international markets: look at Mexico's Cemex in cement, for example, and India's Reliance and Ispat in chemicals and steel. Haier, a state-owned Chinese firm that started selling abroad only in 1997, now claims 20% of the American market for small fridges.

The other great development that will make business

Adrian Wooldridge:
Washington correspondent, *The Economist*. Author with John Micklethwait of "Future Perfect"

115

Business and Management THE WORLD IN 2001

people's lives much harder is the backlash against globalisation, a backlash that started in Seattle, where 50,000 students and trade unionists succeeded in closing down a meeting of the World Trade Organisation, and has continued ever since, with mass protests in London, Washington, Philadelphia, Los Angeles, Prague, Melbourne and wherever the global elite decide to meet.

It's not inevitable

Many business people dismiss these protests as nothing more than a distraction. They argue that globalisation is being driven by technology and that there is nothing that anybody, including Molotov-cocktail throwing demonstrators, can do to put the genie back into the bottle. This is profoundly wrong.

Globalisation depends on political will as well as technological innovation. And political will is rapidly weakening. Al Gore ran for president on a business-bashing platform that puts him well to the left of Bill Clinton. And Mr Gore is a wild-eyed free-marketeer compared with most European politicians. When José Bové, a French farmer, rammed his tractor into a McDonald's restaurant, it was all the Parisian establishment could do to restrain itself from urging him to drive over to Euro Disney as well.

Activists have already seized the initiative on global trade. They succeeded in scuttling both the OECD's planned Multilateral Agreement on Investment in 1998 and the launch of the WTO's new global trade talks a year later. They have also influenced the behaviour of firms and organisations. Global Exchange, a pesky outfit of some 40 people based in San Francisco, claims that it has bullied Starbucks into selling only fair-trade coffee beans in its cafés. A coalition of NGOs, student groups and UNITE, a textile workers' union, has sued a bunch of clothing importers, including Calvin Klein and Gap, over working conditions in the American commonwealth of Saipan in the Pacific. (Seventeen companies caved in.) The protesters are also trying to set the rules of international monitoring of trade practices.

Multinational institutions such as the IMF and the World Bank are doing all they can to appease the protesters. Oxfam was heavily involved in designing the World Bank's debt-relief strategies. The IMF teaches NGOs the nuts and bolts of country-programme design, so that they can monitor what the Fund is doing. The result is that the international organisations not only embolden their critics to get more extreme, but also give them the tools to make their criticisms more effective.

This means, at the very least, that trade liberalisation is stalled. It is probably impossible to put through any new trade measures without burdening them with all sorts of restrictions about labour and environmental standards. But it might mean more than this. The tensions between the European Union and the United States over trade in things like bananas, films and genetically modified food, could escalate into a full-scale trade war.

The result is that businesses are operating in a much more uncertain political environment. Many companies, lulled into a false sense of security by years of pro-market reforms, base their business plans on the assumption that globalisation will keep rolling forward. They need, at the very least, to prepare contingency plans. □

The next measure of national machismo

Daniel Franklin

Companies vie with one another for digital-age competitiveness. From Manhattan to Mumbai, creating the most compelling e-strategy has become the stuff of discussion in every self-respecting boardroom. Next, it will be governments' turn. No government worth its salt will be without its plan to create a thoroughly wired marketplace. Forget boring old measures like gross national product. Instead of GNP the Holy Grail will be ENP: electronic national prowess.

Measurements of national machismo evolve with the times. Once, what mattered most was the military scorecard: the size of a country's army, the scale of its fleet, the number of its tanks or intercontinental ballistic missiles. The Soviet Union and its allies were fond of counting tonnes of steel and barrels of oil to demonstrate the superiority of communism. They invented a measure of national output called net material product—compared with GNP, this downplayed services and exaggerated the importance of goods you could drop on your foot—and succeeded in fooling both themselves and the CIA, which looked at the communists' numbers and absurdly concluded that East Germans were richer than Britons.

But capitalist GNP is far from perfect or immune from cheating either. A few years ago, Italy decided it would be nice to leapfrog Britain in the economic pecking order, and arranged this spurious *sorpasso* by inflating its GNP to include a large allowance for its black economy. Comparisons between countries vary depending on whether GNP (or GDP) per head is measured using current exchange rates, or adjusted for "purchasing-power parity", which is anyway hard to fix with any precision. Worse, GNP dissatisfies many for being too narrow, because it fails to take into account important things such as environmental sustainability and quality of life. Hence the rise of alternative ideas for international comparisons in recent years: "human development" scores, misery indices, freedom ratings, competitiveness rankings.

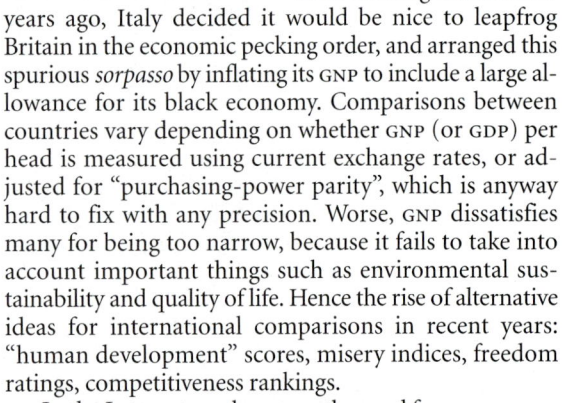

In the Internet era, however, the need for a new measure is emerging. Increasingly, governments see creating an excellent environment for e-business as the key to improving or maintaining a nation's place in the

All medal, no microchip

Daniel Franklin: editorial director, Economist Intelligence Unit

116

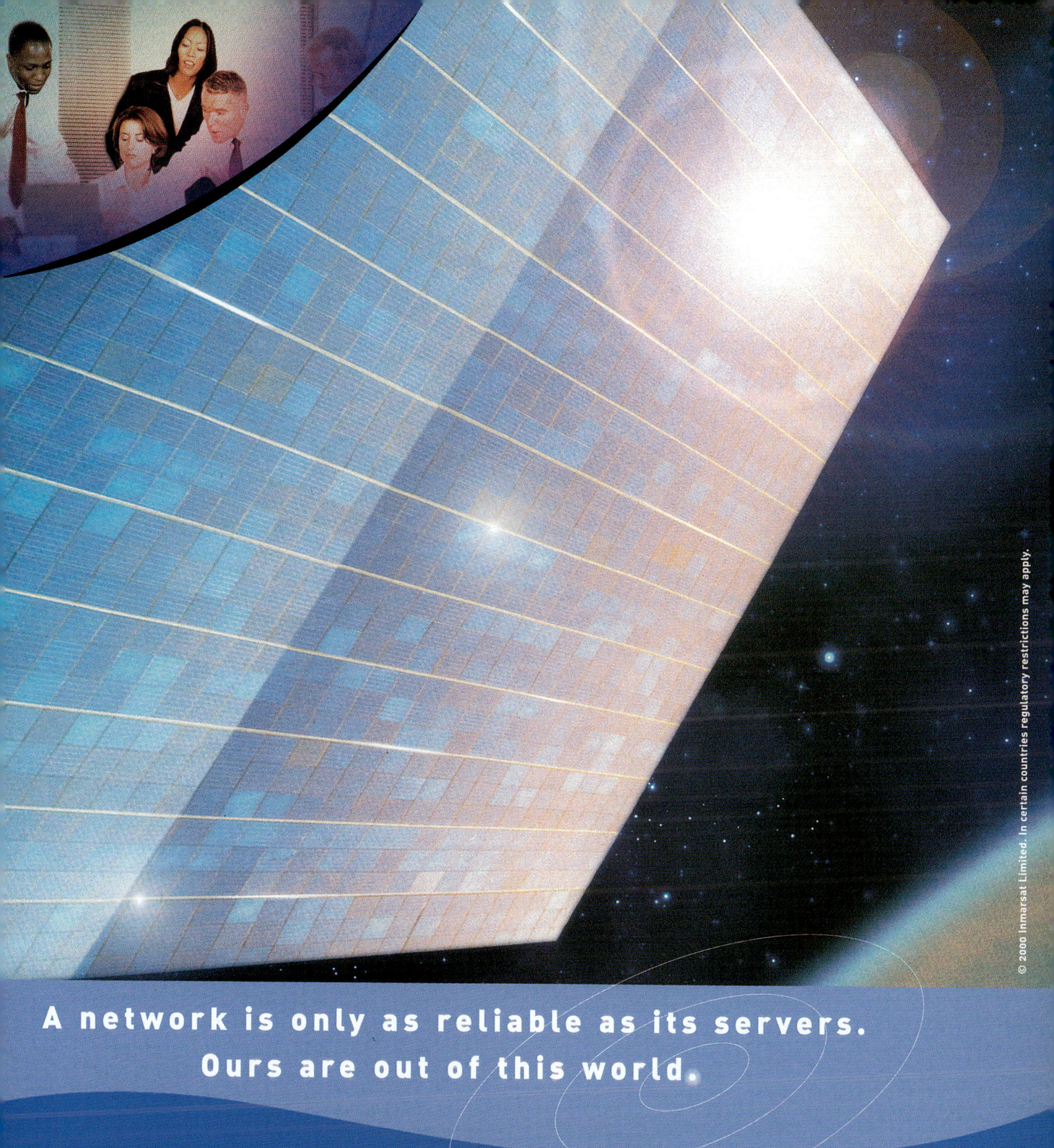

A network is only as reliable as its servers. Ours are out of this world.

Global mobile satellite communications.
About 36,000 kilometres out, actually. Part of a truly global communications network. Effortlessly delivering a reliable, high-quality mobile communications service. Via Inmarsat. A proven satellite communications provider for over 21 years, Inmarsat offers a unique range of leading-edge ISDN and mobile packet data services for cost-effective global business solutions. So if management and staff look to you for reliable and effective global communications, take a look at the website below.

www.via-inmarsat.com

via **INMARSAT**®

BROADBAND YOUR HORIZONS

© 2000 Inmarsat Limited. In certain countries regulatory restrictions may apply.

mind

essential to you

Inktomi®

essential to the Internet℠

America Online. AT&T. British Telecommunications plc. Exodus Communications. Genuity. Sun Microsystems. These are just a few of the many customers and partners who benefit from Inktomi Traffic Server® and Content Delivery Suite™. Along with value-added services, our network products allow the companies we serve to deliver a faster, easier, more rewarding Internet experience to their customers. To find out what we can do for you, visit Inktomi. Insist on Inktomi.

international pecking order. Tony Blair's government, never shy of a rhetorical flourish, proclaims the goal of making Britain the world's best place for e-business by 2002. The EU announces similarly grand aims for "e-Europe". South Korea's president launches an e-commerce crusade. Japan's Information Technology Strategy Council draws up plans for Japan to "overtake the United States within five years as a major high-speed Internet nation". And so on around the world.

There are two problems with all this. One is that, although intelligent government policies can help, busy bureaucrats are really not the answer; private enterprise, not work done in Washington, has made America the world's leader in the new economy. The other problem is that it is easy for politicians to set glorious goals for their country's digital future, but it is not so easy to measure whether those goals are being achieved. No standard measurement of ENP exists, though a few organisations (including the Economist Intelligence Unit) have had a stab at calibrating countries' "e-readiness". A definitive version of ENP has yet to be invented. It is time to do so.

How to calculate it? It is not hard to identify the key elements. Some lend themselves to fairly simple quantitative measurement. Others involve qualitative judgment. These are trickier to assess.

No country can compete in the wired economy without the requisite communications infrastructure: the telephone lines, mobile-phone penetration, personal computers and Internet service providers. Basic "connectivity" is a start, but not enough. Access needs to be affordable as well as merely available (so cheap prices that encourage the widest possible Internet usage must be counted in ENP). And, increasingly, it needs to be fast, to allow high-speed data transmission, whether by cable or through mobile technology; that is why even advanced countries like Japan are having to race to catch up.

E-business also needs a friendly regulatory and legal environment, as well as confidence in the security of networks. Deregulation, low taxes on e-commerce, dependable e-contracts—such things will boost a country's ENP. So will many of the virtues that enhance a country's business environment generally. A decent transport network, for example, is needed even if goods are ordered over the Internet. Hardest to measure is ENP's cultural component: factors such as e-literacy, enthusiasm for online experimentation and openness to the free flow of ideas and information.

Leading countries will need to score well on all fronts. It is no good having world-class communications infrastructure, say, if e-business is taxed prohibitively or

The half-life of nuclear power

Germany starts closing its 20 nuclear power stations in 2001, and the rest of Europe and America will follow. In Asia, nuclear plants are still chic among policymakers with huge power-making ambitions. Worldwide capacity will rise from 350 gigawatts (GWE) to 370GWE in 2010, and then decline to 300GWE by 2020.

Western Europe produces a third of the world's nuclear power. France is the most addicted—75% of its electricity is produced by nuclear reactors. In 2001, no new reactors will be built in the continent, none even planned. This is the result of widespread public suspicion. As the use of nuclear power declines, use of natural gas will grow. Eastern Europe will also go non-nuclear over the next decade. In their accession talks with the EU, Bulgaria, Lithuania and the Slovak Republic have agreed to shut down eight reactors over the next eight years. EU aid will subsidise the costs of closure. Russia and Ukraine will go the other way, and build eight.

America is the world's biggest nuclear producer. It will have the capacity to pump out 100GWE in 2001. But here too nuclear power has a limited life-span. It currently accounts for 20% of America's electricity production, but by 2020 it will produce only 9%.

China, Japan, South Korea, Indonesia and Vietnam all have ambitious plans to build new reactors. Japan's initial plan to build 16-20 new reactors by 2010 was pared back to 13 after the

Building it is the easy part

Tokaimura nuclear accident in 1999. Only 1% of China's electricity will be produced by nuclear power in 2001. The government wants to increase this to 3% by 2015. More than a dozen provinces want reactors. ◻

tangled in red tape. That is something governments should bear in mind as they draw up their national plans for digital supremacy.

If you can rate a country across all these areas, then you have a rudimentary calculation of its ENP. That may be enough, for the big picture matters more than the detailed numbers. And it is already possible to discern the broad pattern of global ENP. America leads, followed closely by a cluster of countries, mainly in northern Europe. Further back, other developed countries can still aspire to catch up. Then come emerging economies whose ENP, with the right investments and policies, could be sufficient to open up exciting new ways of competing in the global marketplace. At the end of the line come countries woefully lacking both in basic communications infrastructure and the means to create it. They will need help from the rich world if they are not to be left even further behind.

Of course, people will argue over ENP. They will disagree over what exactly to call it, how precisely to calculate it, and what to make of the results. Like other measures of relative national advancement, it is bound to be imperfect. But it cannot be ignored. Perhaps more than anything else, a country's ENP will determine how well it performs on the more traditional measures of growth and living standards in the years to come. ◻

IF OPPORTUNITY KNOCKS

12,000 MILES AWAY, WILL YOU

CREDIT SUISSE | FIRST BOSTON

HEAR IT?

www.csfb.com

Opportunity isn't always in your own backyard. It can be in a different country. It can be a different industry. At Credit Suisse First Boston, we help our clients take advantage of global opportunities. We helped France Telecom expand its global reach with the acquisition of Orange plc. We advised the Commonwealth of Australia on the landmark privatisation IPO and secondary offering of Telstra. And we led Hewlett-Packard's first global bond. What we do is empower our clients in the face of change, creating a bridge between opportunity and success. **CREDIT SUISSE FIRST BOSTON.**

EMPOWERING CHANGE.[SM]

Issued by Credit Suisse First Boston (Europe) Limited: regulated by SFA.
©2000 Credit Suisse First Boston Corp. All rights reserved.

Business and Management THE WORLD IN 2001

How should the bosses be paid?

Edward Carr

In Robert Mankoff's well-known cartoon from the *New Yorker*, one East-Coast grandee addresses two fellow members of his club. "As far as I'm concerned," he drawls, gin and tonic in hand, "they can do what they like with the minimum wage, just as long as they keep their hands off the maximum wage."

The threat to bosses' bulging portfolios of share options will grow in 2001. Exorbitant remuneration faces nothing so crude as a ban or a crippling tax. Rather, executives will see something more legitimate: the effects of accounting changes and compensation committees that increasingly understand how to structure incentives. Some managers will continue to receive stellar pay, but those that do will be more likely to deserve it.

In Europe, fat cats have long attracted popular resentment. More surprising is America, where Mr Mankoff's magnates are witnessing growing anti-business sentiment and remarkable discontent with well-heeled bosses. In a recent poll by *Business Week*, only a quarter of people thought business deserved the credit for the prosperity of the past few years. Moreover, only 14% felt that what was good for business was good for America, half the proportion supporting the same view in 1996. And, after a decade in which almost anyone with a good idea has been able to make his fortune, three-quarters of Americans complain that the bosses of big American companies are overpaid.

There is no denying that senior executives are handsomely rewarded. Their pay has grown much faster than average earnings, especially in America. The trends are clearly established in "The State of Working America", a recent book by Lawrence Mishel, Jared Bestein and John Schmidt (Economic Policy Institute). The authors examine the compensation of chief executives across the world. American bosses are the highest-paid, earning almost 60% more than anyone else. And they are relatively much better off than average workers, with compensation that is 34 times that of a factory worker, compared with multiples of 15 to 20 in continental Europe.

This money has increasingly been handed over with many strings attached. Miko Giedroyc, an analyst at Deutsche Bank, has invented the CEO delta: a measure of how the wealth of the chief executive changes with each 1% change in the company share price. Because of insufficient disclosure in many annual reports, the exercise contains some heroic guesswork. However, Mr Giedroyc reckons that delta in the companies of Britain's FTSE 100 was 1.06 in 1990; that is, for each 1% increase in the share price, the chief executive received just over £1,000. By 1999, delta had increased to 64.3.

What does all this mean for executive pay in 2001? The first point is that high pay will be hard to curb, whatever the public thinks. Talent is scarce. The average life of an American CEO is only four years. An executive's salary, even if it is great, is a small proportion of the value that they might add to the company's overall value. High pay might serve as a prize in the tournament for the top job.

The question is whether, in practice, shareholders are getting value for money. Broadly speaking, the situation has improved. There is plenty of evidence dating as far back as the 1970s that performance-based pay tends to encourage better stockmarket performance. If the CEO delta has increased, so have the incentives.

But the system is far from perfect. The greatest complaint is that executives are being paid for holding office during the bull market, rather than outperfoming their peers. According to one study by Graef Crystal, an economist, 86% of executives in the companies of America's S&P 500 firms received an average of $8m a year each under a conventional options plan between 1995 and 1998. Under a scheme that rewarded beating the market, only 32% would have been paid any money.

Option schemes are not properly accounted for, because they are not charged against earnings. This leads to a vast overstatement of profits. And it is founded on faulty logic. As Warren Buffett memorably put it: if options are not a form of compensation, what are they? If compensation is not an expense, what is it? If expenses should not go into the calculation of earnings, where in the world should they go?

In the mid-1990s, America's FASB, which minds the country's accounting standards, attempted to reform the accounting of options. Businesses objected and got the initiative thrown out. Elsewhere, in countries such as Britain and France, accounting regulators have been revisiting the question. In 2001 Britain's ASB is likely to issue its own proposal, which would support FASB's original approach.

Another problem is repricing. When share prices tumble, companies feel that the only way they can deter defections is to lower the strike price (that is, the price at which options can be exercised) of executives' options. But this hurts shareholders who have just seen the value of their shares fall. Worse, it skews the incentives toward risk-taking—if your company's shares plunge, you will receive some new options; if it booms, you cash in. Should shares tumble in 2001, it will be a test of FASB's new ruling that whenever options are repriced there should be a charge to the profit-and-loss account.

The intelligent response to the grumbles about executive pay is to explain how it works and to remove the system's perversities. It needs to be seen to be fair. That means having none of the chief executive's golfing partners on the remuneration committee. And even Mr Mankoff's plutocrats could live with that. □

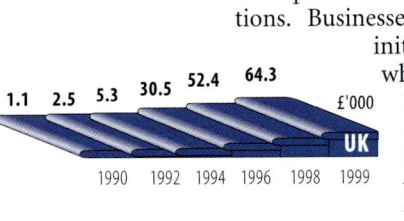

Stairway to CEO heaven
Delta

Delta measures how the compensation of a listed company's CEO changes with each 1% rise in its share price. For example, in 1999, a 1% rise in the share price of an American company would award its CEO $2,000,000 extra compensation

USA $'000: 96, 258, 489, 831, 1,575, 2,000 (1990, 1992, 1994, 1996, 1998, 1999)
Source: Deutsche Bank

UK £'000: 1.1, 2.5, 5.3, 30.5, 52.4, 64.3 (1990, 1992, 1994, 1996, 1998, 1999)

Edward Carr: editor, Inside Track, *Financial Times*

John Chambers, CEO of Cisco Systems, predicts huge leaps in human productivity

You ain't seen nothing yet

"How ready is your country for the network effect?"

Survival strategies and the potential for prosperity are inextricably linked in the Internet economy. Whether it is the standard of living in a country or the shareholder value earned by a company, the path to survival has been turned upside down by the Internet.

We've been trained for over 50 years to look at economics in a particular way, with an emphasis on tangible assets and physical products. These are still important, of course, but prosperity is now driven predominantly by the ability to leverage the Internet to create intangible value—speed, convenience, customisation, personalisation and service.

Productivity is one of the most critical elements influencing the living standards for countries and the competitive position of companies. For the past two decades, hundreds of billions of dollars have been invested in information technology, with only moderate productivity gains in most companies. This is one of the reasons that most business and government leaders view information technology as an expense rather than as a competitive advantage.

At Cisco we learned that there are ways to achieve productivity gains in the way that a company interfaces with its employees, customers and suppliers using the power of the Internet. We have changed almost every aspect of the way people work, and the average productivity increase that we've experienced per Internet application we've implemented has been over 50%. Cisco was responsible for a third of the world's e-commerce in 1997, but it was our Internet-based customer and employee support that gave us major productivity gains and helped us become one of the most profitable companies in history. Two other applications are attracting attention at Cisco: virtual manufacturing and virtual close—the ability to "close the books" on our company accounts every working day. Both these ideas work around integrating employees and suppliers, so that they appear as one virtual company to our customers. All this leads to productivity improvements.

We call this phenomenon "the network effect". Since 1995, as more and more countries around the world and companies in the global economy have become networked, the productivity results in the United States have soared. From the sluggish 1.5-1.6% annual growth in American productivity in the 1980s and the first half of the 1990s, the growth accelerated to a range of 2.5-5.0% in the second half of the 1990s. The network effect has changed the pace at which an economy can grow with nominal inflation.

Of course, this type of productivity revolution is bound to result in the creation of high quality jobs. In the United States alone the Internet economy supported 650,000 jobs and generated more than half a trillion dollars in economic activity in 1999, a 62% increase over 1998, according to the Center for Research on Electronic Commerce at the University of Texas. To put this into perspective, the Internet's workforce of 2.5m people now surpasses the entire active United States military or the insurance or the public utilities industries.

E-readiness

When talking to business and government leaders around the world, I am frequently asked to describe the fundamental drivers of competing in the Internet economy. I ask in return: How ready is your country for the network effect? One measure of a country's readiness is bandwidth per capita (BPC). In Europe, for example, the Scandinavian countries lead in BPC. It is no coincidence that Denmark, Sweden and Norway, are also the leaders in e-commerce spending per capita. The implications are clear: the ability to create a prosperous economy is linked to the quality of its networking infrastructure.

European bandwidth per capita will quadruple between 2000 and 2002, according to IDC, a consultancy. The more this resource is made available through new high-speed services like cable and digital subscriber lines, and as the local loop is deregulated, the greater the prospects for higher productivity, economic growth and, ultimately, job creation. This way lies the future. Conversely, countries in which old-world regulation continues and bandwidth availability is constrained will fall behind.

The skills necessary to leverage the Internet for competitive advantage go beyond what most of us were taught in school. With access to information anytime, anywhere, employees must be empowered quickly to apply this knowledge and make informed, decentralised decisions, and respond to situations such as real-time changes in customer demand.

The countries and companies with robust, standards-based IT infrastructures lead in the implementation of Internet-based applications and business models. They are already far ahead in terms of redefining business and government processes, as well as in the creation of new value for customers and constituents alike. The implementation of Internet applications is occurring in waves, at an Internet pace.

Companies or countries that have not implemented the first wave of Internet applications—e-commerce, e-customer support, and employee self-services—are already behind. The second and third waves of Internet-application implementation—virtual manufacturing, virtual close, e-learning and e-convenience—will occur even faster than the first. The ability to gain competitive advantage by accelerating time to market, dramatically improving margins and empowering employees, will occur over a shorter period of time, with competition and commoditisation also occurring sooner. The implementation of Internet applications is rapidly becoming a matter of survival. ◻

Business and Management THE WORLD IN 2001

STEP ON THE HYDROGEN

Which way to the hydrogen economy?

Vijay Vaitheeswaran

Vijay Vaitheeswaran: environment and energy correspondent, *The Economist*

The view from the top of the Condé Nast building at Times Square, the world's greenest skyscraper, is not to be missed. After all, who would not be impressed by the unobstructed vistas of New York's undulating urban topography? Hidden away just underneath the rooftop terrace, however, is an even more breathtaking sight. Casual visitors will merely notice two boxy, unremarkable power generators about the size of small lorries. They probably do not realise that they are getting a sneak peek at the future of energy: fuel cells.

For decades, ever since the early fuel cells accompanied man into space, scientists and futurists have dreamt of the day when the world would be powered by clean, green hydrogen energy rather than filthy hydrocarbons like petrol. That is because fuel cells take hydrogen and combine it with oxygen from the air to generate electricity. As a result, the only waste produced by these big batteries is water and heat. Many experts have predicted that one day fuel cells will power all our homes, cars, and perhaps even mobile phones and laptop computers.

That "one day" may be fast approaching. The biggest obstacle has long been the cost of the technology. Yet so great has the promise been that big multinational corporations like GE, Siemens, DaimlerChrysler, Ford and United Technologies (which made the fuel cells at Times Square) are throwing billions of dollars into hydrogen research. Dozens of smaller players like Plug Power, Fuel Cell Energy and Ballard are also busy innovating. Thanks to their breakthroughs, various types of fuel cells are all sliding happily down the cost curve towards levels near those of today's conventional power sources.

All this explains why 2001 is the year in which fuel cells will really hit the big time. As the oil price continues to fluctuate wildly, even ordinary people will begin to wonder whether cars powered by something other than petrol might be a good idea. As deregulation throws open electricity markets from California to Japan, consumers will realise that shoddy service and volatile pricing from their monopoly utility is not the only option.

Look for financial investment in this sector, for years

Your new mobile

Jim Chalmers

Early 2001 will see the launch in Japan of the "third generation" (3G) of mobile-phone services, supporting video and Internet access from handheld portable terminals. 3G services will be launched in Europe towards the end of 2001, a year that will also see the first mass-scale deployment of high-speed Internet access for residential users and businesses of all sizes.

Yet the prospect of all this dazzling activity is already giving the major telecoms companies—and their shareholders and creditors—a king-sized headache. The name of the pain? Debt. And with more spending required in 2001, relief looks years away.

Telco debt, of course, is the result of paying enormous sums for licences to operate 3G services. Having spent billions of euros to win these, European operators must now spend as much again to build the new networks and launch their offerings. Their efforts to become Internet service providers (ISPs) will be worthless unless they can provide their customers with high-speed access to the Net. This is sure to be expensive and is made more problematic by the advent of competitors armed with cable and other alternative technologies.

Europe suffers from a lack of fixed-line broadband access. That makes 3G wireless networks especially attractive. Companies all over the continent are banking on 3G to stimulate "m-commerce". M stands for mobile—and the money everyone is hoping that the advent of shopping via your phone, anytime, anywhere, will create.

Keep an eye on the progress made by interim (so-called "2.5G") mobile technologies. Chief among these is wireless application protocol (WAP), which made its lacklustre debut in 2000. Its backers are pinning their hopes on new technologies—dubbed "GPRS" and "EDGE" by the telecoms' acronym factory—which will increase the speed at which data is transferred. These will become widespread in 2001.

Even so, users expecting "the wireless Internet" will be disappointed by what they find—and by how much they are asked to pay for it. The advent of 3G could spur Internet take-up in Europe while simultaneously leading to an increase in wireless phone penetration in America. However, the risk is that it will do neither. □

Jim Chalmers: editor, *Public Network Europe*

2001
Snowed under by e-mail? It will get worse. The average knowledge worker receives 30 messages a day. That will rise closer to 50 during 2001.

SIEMENS

www.siemens.com/s35 or call 0345 400 700 for more details

"The client urgently needs an update, but I won't be back in time to send it."

E-mail

"Claire, I have attached the chart updates. Regards. Mike."

S35i

Small/Smart/Power packed | Organiser | WAP made easy | Email/SMS | The new Siemens S35i | be inspired

Information and Communications

MORSE

Will you light the blue touch paper or will you get blown away?

The mobile commerce explosion.

Mobile commerce will change the way people work. It will make your organisation look altogether more customer-focused. And create whole new business opportunities.

Morse and Sun make it their business to help their customers become more competitive. Should you get fired up about mobile commerce? That's your business.

You can find out more at mobile.morse.com

Sun microsystems
DATACENTER
SYSTEM RESELLER

THE WORLD IN 2001 **Business and Management**

limited to a few courageous venture-capital funds like Nth Power, to explode in 2001. Even the ordinary punter, disillusioned with the rocky ride of Internet and biotechnology shares, may begin to see a growth opportunity in the many "power technology" investment funds that will spring up like mushrooms over the coming months.

Does all this mean that the hydrogen economy is really at hand? No, is the blunt answer. Fuel cells themselves are close to market reality but there is a snag: the fuel that these wondrous cells run on, hydrogen, is one that the modern industrial economy simply is not organised to deliver. Very few places in the world have pure hydrogen available on demand. The infrastructure will take many years to develop. Yet the purveyors of fuel cells still intend to introduce them to the market soon. How can they possibly power them?

That points to a dirty little secret about fuel cells that neither the fat cats selling them nor the greens heralding them want to talk about: the first generation of fuel cells will use "transition" fuels that do not live up to the full promise of clean hydrogen energy. If the hydrogen is made by a "reformer" (either at the filling station or on board the vehicle) that consumes hydrocarbon fuels such as petrol, natural gas or methanol, this process will be polluting—though far less so than today's engines and power plants. It is this lack of infrastructure that will dictate the order in which various fuel-cell applications will take off, argues John Wallace of Ford: stationary power first, fleet vehicles next and, only later, ordinary cars.

In America, power quality will spur sales of commercial micropower units as those frustrated by brown-outs realise that fuel cells offer extremely reliable power. In the developing world, cells will be popular in remote locations where extending the electricity grid would be prohibitively expensive. Look also to newly deregulating power and gas markets, like France, where companies will use micropower to break into the market. Ballard's boss, Firoz Rasul, revealed that his firm, in conjunction with Tokyo Gas, will start selling a fuel-cell unit in Japan in 2001 that he says is designed to "sneak" around the incumbent electricity utility's grip on households.

The question that car companies have countless billions of dollars riding on is which transition fuel will passenger cars use. DaimlerChrysler has long championed methanol, which makes engineering simpler, but has toxicity concerns. Others think that natural gas, the cleanest of the interim fuels, is the right way forward.

The world's oil giants, aware that some of these choices could well put them out of business one day, have joined the debate. Most of them have entered into partnerships with the car firms to develop prototypes and fuel infrastructure. DaimlerChrysler and BP, among others, intend to put dozens of test cars and buses on the roads of California in coming months. They have even invested in a hydrogen refuelling station (located near Sacramento, the state's capital, where officials can see it).

Taken at face value, the volte face of the oil giants is astonishing. Not so long ago, oilmen were openly mocking the notion that fuel cells could ever replace the internal combustion engine. Now, many openly gush about the arrival of the "Hydrogen Age". Ultimately, their real concern is that consumers fill up at their fuel-station of the future, whatever fuel is in the pump. □

> **2001**
> But does it make you fitter? 100m people will be healthclub members by 2010. 14% of Americans and 6% of Britons currently are. Europeans have yet to catch the craze. They will.

James Harding:
media editor,
Financial Times

Dead trees go digital

James Harding

Log on

For all the talk of the digital revolution, most people still get most of their entertainment in analogue form. They get up and listen to the radio, buy a newspaper to read on the way to work, come home and watch television received thanks to a roof-top antenna or, perhaps, go out to see a movie delivered on old-fashioned film and screened at 24 frames a second.

In 2001, though, digital technologies will reach ever deeper into our daily lives. It will be a year of transition as the established media adapt to next-generation technologies. This does not mean that established media will be swept aside. No, the hyperbole surrounding the Internet now looks very passé—the outdated thinking of the year 2000. Instead, it means a period when the balance of our lives shifts from using old media to next-generation technologies: from analogue television to digital, from narrowband Internet connections to broadband and, gradually, from fixed-line networks to wireless information and entertainment services.

It will be another year of deals, even bearing in mind antitrust concerns about mammoth corporations. In the United States, General Electric, which owns the NBC television network, will be looking for something to do with a business that does not sit logically with a company that is focused on technology and finance. Sony, which has struggled for years to make its Columbia Motion business a rewarding investment, could finally come round to hiving off, selling off or restructuring its entertainment interests in both movies and music. A radical corporate shake-up of the cable industry is on the cards: companies such as Cox Communications in America or Telewest and NTL in Britain and UPC in Europe all need to scale up. Similarly, the business of publishing both books and magazines will undergo an upheaval in 2001. IPC, which produces magazines such as *Marie Claire* in Britain, is likely to be sold by its long-suffering private investors. Other publishing groups, such as Lagardère in France,

Make your network ~~safe~~ *open*

Copyright © Nokia Corporation 2000. All rights reserved. Nokia and Nokia Connecting People are registered trademarks of the Nokia Corporation.

for business

Rewrite the rules

The success of your e-commerce depends on your securing the confidence of your customers with safe and fast connections 24 hours a day.

The technology from Nokia creates an environment of trust. With network protection, extension and acceleration products that support both legacy and next generation Internet communications and transactions, you are assured of seamless business and secure revenues.

To get peace of mind for yourselves and especially your customers, join us in the Mobile Information Society. Visit us at www.nokia.com/e-security or call us on 00800 - 5543 1816* and start rewriting the rules your way.

Our network solutions don't close doors. They open them. That's what IT is all about.

* Toll-free services are available weekdays between 9am and 5pm. If you do not have access to 00800 services, please call +49 231 754 6011.

NOKIA
CONNECTING PEOPLE

Business and Management THE WORLD IN 2001

will also be looking for deals which marry old-world magazine content with new delivery systems to next-generation mobile phones and digital televisions.

In this process—and across the media sector—the predators are likely to be the telecoms companies. Businesses like AT&T, BT, Deutsche Telekom, Telefonica and others will begin to look more like media companies. Some of them will be broadcasting television programmes. Others will be developing web portals and broadband cable services, which means buying in the creators of news and entertainment. In short, there will be deep pockets willing to pay escalating sums for an increasingly broad definition of talent: actors, directors, producers, animators, photographers and, even, journalists. The reason for this is that as high-speed Internet connections and mobile-telephone services become a commodity product—that is, one service provider is more or less indistinguishable from another on price—the telecoms network operators will need to create customer loyalty for their services through content.

This could turn up some unlikely heroes in the industry in 2001. In Hollywood, Michael Ovitz's Artists Management Group (AMG) could well restore the name of the man whose golden reputation in Los Angeles as an agent lost a little of its glitter during his time at Disney. As the established studios look increasingly weighed down by fixed costs, Mr Ovitz's virtual studio at AMG, which harnesses talent and puts together movie, television and online projects, will look increasingly attractive to buyers. The value of good independent production companies is likely to soar as more and more companies look to the libraries of television and movie talent to fill the expanding "shelf space" of digital television.

For digital television will be the buzzword of 2001 almost as much as the Internet has been the focal point of media industry thinking for the past couple of years. As companies such as Time Warner in the United States, British Sky Broadcasting in Britain, Canal Plus in France, Premiere World in Germany and both Star TV as well as PCCW across Asia race to connect the television to digital networks, the television set will take on a different role in millions of homes. Multichannel television will become the norm in Europe. And interactivity will no longer be confined to the personal computer. The television will be increasingly used as a place for shopping, sending e-mails and drawing down information.

Meanwhile, the personal computer will become the launchpad for a new kind of media content in 2001: content on the edge. In the era of traditional media, a central server—a publisher, broadcaster, record company or movie studio—pushed out products to a grateful world audience. One of the features of the networked world is that people will increasingly be able to trade their media content between each other, like bootlegged tapes sold around a concert audience. The first taste of this has been Napster, which allows users of its service to share music files by swapping them between PCs. The potential to swap all other kinds of entertainment, such as movies, books, programmes and news, will be one of the new areas of technology explored in 2001. □

> **2001**
> Demand for IT professionals in Europe will outstrip supply by 600,000 people. That figure could rise to 2m by 2003.

Gadgets for all

Nimit Jani

Sony's domination of the video games world looks shaky as Microsoft releases the X-Box. If claims are true, Sony bosses should shudder. X-Box will have three times the graphics power of Sony's PlayStation2. It will also play DVDs and boasts broadband connectivity for online gaming. Sony's broadband servers will probably not be ready until 2002. Microsoft's only problem is that the impressive machine needs games to match. Early PlayStation2 games were disappointing, not making full use of the machine's potential. X-Box will face the same challenge. It will sell for $300 and will arrive in time for Christmas 2001. For those who can't wait, Nintendo will bring out its new toy in the summer. Code-named Dolphin, it is not as fast as the X-Box. However, early release and experience in developing great games may give it the edge. Video gamers are in for a thrilling 2001.

Tiny monochrome screens, awkward interfaces, and painfully slow connection speeds made the mobile Internet a disappointment in 2000. The convergence of mobile phones and hand-held computers in 2001 will remedy some of these frustrations. Early 2001 will see the European launch of Handspring's VisorPhone attachment for around €230 ($203). It will be the first to include both Internet and voice capabilities. The larger screen will make web pages easier to view and handwriting recognition will do away with the fiddly numeric keypad. A joint Motorola-Palm colour-screen handheld will follow within a year. Could the handheld format be the future of the mobile Internet?

The confusing and tangled mess of cables connecting your mobile phone to your laptop, hands-free set and handheld computer will be a thing of the past in 2001. Bluetooth is a new wireless communications technology which provides freedom from wired connections. Using radio signals with a 10-metre range, it will even work through walls. Ericsson is leading the way with wireless technology. Its T36 and R520 mobile phones will be the first out with integrated Bluetooth connectivity in March 2001.

$50,000 may seem a bit expensive for a television, but Sharp's new Continuous Grain Silicon Television is no ordinary set. Aimed more at the boardroom than the living room, a European version is out in early 2001. Its ultra-sharp resolution renders astounding clarity of picture without any flicker. The television's screen is the first to use continuous grain silicon technology. This is ultra thin and uses little power, both of which make it ideal for the electronic paper of the future. □

If information is power, then

inspiration must be the power

of potential. The power that

moves us from the systematic

to the spontaneous.

From the mundane to the magical.

INSPIRATION IS THE NUMBER ONE CAUSE OF GREATNESS.

At Compaq we believe

technology is no longer simply

an information tool.

It's an inspiration tool.

Which redefines access.

From set time to any time.

From one place to a million places.

New ways to work.

New ways to collaborate.

Where with the touch of a button

you no longer fire up your

computer, but your imagination.

Welcome to the new IT.

Inspiration Technology by Compaq.

COMPAQ
Inspiration Technology

Business and Management THE WORLD IN 2001

Watching the world go slowly by

Bad air days

Iain Carson

Air travel will become an even worse nightmare in 2001. In America more passengers will be grounded for hours in crowded lounges in the big hubs while they wait for their connection. Europeans will face endless departure delays caused by the "late arrival of incoming aircraft". They will also notice that airlines are quietly lengthening journey times so that they can massage downwards the number of flights classed as delayed. Even so, the proportion of European flights delayed more than 15 minutes will rise to well over a third.

Computers and other electronics goods get better and cheaper. Cars become more reliable, while their price comes down. But air travel, which grows at around 5% a year and should be a great business to be in or to use, just gets worse.

To look forward in air travel, it is worth a brief glance backwards to see what is going wrong. In 1999, America's traffic jams in the sky were blamed on an awful lot of thunderstorms. But the real truth was a botched introduction of new air-traffic control computers and the lack of a centralised weather-information system. More chaos in the summer of 2000 was blamed on a go-slow by United Airlines' pilots who were threatening to strike over a pay claim. That was true, but it is a sure bet that another horrendous summer of travel in 2001 will be blamed on other carriers' pilots manoeuvring to get as good a deal as their United brethren.

The underlying truth starts with the fact that America's air-traffic control system is creaking because of years of under-investment and excessive bureaucracy, while air-traffic demand is soaring in a booming economy. The next factor is that America's deregulated market is not providing enough competition among the six big airlines (United, American Airlines, Delta, Continental, Northwest and US Airways). Each tends to dominate its own big hubs and so sets prices higher than they might otherwise be.

In Europe, the air-traffic logjam is caused by having 27 air-traffic control bodies and a military which insists on its own reserved airways, as if the cold war were still on and Russians with snow on their boots were flying to Paris. Throughout the year the European Union commissioner for transport, Ms Loyola de Palacio, will press for a "single European sky" to cover Europe's single market. But no one will do anything to turn this slogan into fact.

Yet the year will also offer signs of hope for beleaguered travellers. The main one on both sides of the Atlantic will be the continued rise of low-cost, low-fare airlines. Southwest, the original no-frills carrier which began life in the early 1970s, will become in 2001 the biggest airline in America, by number of passengers carried. Its network is now so extensive that it is becoming a nationwide competitor to the big six, even though it does not operate hub-and-spoke systems as they do. It is possible not just to fly between many cities direct on Southwest, using secondary airports, but also to catch an onward flight to a final destination without the annoyance of going through a crowded hub airport.

Southwest's European imitators, Ryanair and EasyJet, will expand at a hectic rate. In the past year Ryanair acquired an extra 1m passengers and EasyJet's numbers doubled. The same is happening at other cheap-fare airlines such as Buzz and Go. You can now travel from London's Luton airport to Geneva for only £80 return, instead of more than £450 on Swissair.

Expect national flag carriers such as British Airways, KLM and Alitalia to make bigger losses before cutting back their intra-European routes because they cannot compete with the new start-up airlines. Those big carriers (such as BA) which have started their own low-fare offshoots will probably float them off in 2001 as soon as they are on a flight path to profit. The big European airlines will see how they can merge with each other to gain economies of scale, and further consolidation is just around the corner in America.

Provided the United Airlines' friendly takeover-cum-rescue of US Airways gets past regulators, this will trigger two further deals (Northwest and Continental merging, while American and Delta get together) so that the big six become the big three. The conventional wisdom is to deplore this on antitrust grounds because it will reduce competition as there will be fewer players in the game. But this may not be the case: three big airlines would each have the clout to compete with each other at all big airports across the country. The emergence of three completely national networks would probably stimulate traffic and cause Southwest to move into more areas. There would be intense competition among the big three to hold on to their existing markets and keep Southwest at bay. The winners will be travellers, as fares come down across the board. Low fares are already found only where Southwest competes against the big six. □

2001

Jack Welch, head of the world's biggest company, General Electric, an icon of corporate America's renaissance, steps down in December. Under his leadership revenues have gone from $1.6 billion to $10.7 billion, and market capitalisation from $13 billion to over $500 billion. Truly an American hero.

Iain Carson: industry editor, *The Economist*

don't you just **love it** when it all comes together

www.mediasurface.com

Knowledge should not be left on a shelf.

Knowledge is for the moment. Otherwise it's history. The key to managing your knowledge is the art of making it available, any time, any place, to anyone. In business, knowledge equals content, and content management is the heart of every e-business. No content management, no e-business.

By using real-time access to virtually limitless information the benefits of content management to the business community are quite staggering. Equally impressive is the speed at which Mediasurface can deploy a content management solution that can personalise, localise, syndicate and deploy critical information throughout your organisation and beyond, delivering a rapid return on your investment.

They say knowledge is power and power is money. Don't leave it lying around.

For more information visit www.mediasurface.com or call 0800 092 4298

MEDIASURFACE™
content management is the heart of e-business

EW001A

Business and Management THE WORLD IN 2001

Home on the Net

Chris Anderson

The long-foretold broadband era is finally arriving. Consumers are discovering that getting a fast link changes more than just the speed of their surfing.

"The future", said Arthur C. Clarke, an author, "is already here. It's just unevenly distributed." Nowhere is that more true than in the home of tomorrow. The all-singing, all-dancing digital manor does exist, but it is very poorly distributed indeed: just a single example, on the leafy shores of Redmond, Washington, occupied by one Bill Gates. Yet a somewhat less wired version is spreading far more widely: by the end of 2001 nearly 10m homes, in the United States, Europe and Asia, will have broadband access to the Internet. Not as flashy as Mr Gates's digital art screens and smart shades, but more than enough to show a glimpse of the future.

The technical hitches that have held up cable modems (which use cable TV connections) and DSL connections (which use phone lines) are now fading and broadband adoption is accelerating. America has the most broadband homes, with about 6m; by 2004, half of all its wired homes will be broadband.

Most of the attention given to broadband connection has to do with its speed: between 1.5m and 10m bits per second, or as much as 200 times the fastest dial-up modems. In practice, they tend to be quite a bit slower due to bottlenecks elsewhere in the Internet, and at any rate speed actually turns out to be less important than another feature of broadband: its connections are always on, 24 hours a day, whether being used or not. Such "persistent connections" suddenly open up a whole new world based on data flowing as freely as power—always there when needed, and therefore increasingly needed. This will usher in a behavioural shift not seen since the introduction of home electrification 100 years ago.

Day one in the life of the new cable modem or DSL subscriber is not so different from the day before. Rather than dialling in to retrieve e-mail, he simply fires up his browser and things pop right up. He may set his e-mail program to check for mail automatically every few minutes, and ding when something comes in. Large video clips, a scary proposition for a modem user, are now in reach, although still miniscule. Nice, but not really life-transforming.

Over the next few months, however, the broadband bug bites. First it is Internet radio—there are more than 6,000 Net stations, catering to every conceivable taste (German industrial techno, anyone?), playing 24 hours a day online.

Then comes the instinctive urge to turn to the Web first for everything, since it is always there, always on.

> **2001**
> Mulitmedia is given a new dimension. A device capable of diffusing 200 different scents over the Internet will be available in 2001. Also look out for a portable "Sniffman" version.

Weather, traffic, news, shopping, flight schedules, even the encyclopedia—on a broadband connection are all faster than waiting around for radios, televisions or newspapers, phoning, or even dragging a hefty tome off the shelf. This soon extends to services not available elsewhere: watch film trailers online before choosing which one to see; upload digital photos to online reproduction services.

At this point, the connected PC has morphed from a work-and-sometimes-play machine to a family magnet, which may overcrowd the study. It is time to spread the wealth and wire the house. A weekend later and Ethernet cables snake into teenagers' bedrooms, to the family entertainment centre, even the kitchen (or, for more money but less wall damage, do it wirelessly). This brings broadband into family life writ large.

In the living room, a connected PlayStation 2 videogame console bridges broadband and TV, pitting family players in combat against online rivals anywhere else in the world. At other times it or a neighbouring set-top box serves as an Internet appliance, offering on-screen TV programming guides and interactive news and sport. Thanks to another link to the broadband home network, the stereo's tape deck has given way to a connected MP3 server, which downloads music and pipes it into the audio system. A wireless tuner box stands on a side table, waiting to start and change Internet radio channels on the PC upstairs, while the streams play on the downstairs stereo's big speakers.

In the kitchen, the only sign of the wired home is a curvy pastel screen on a countertop called Audrey. It serves as a family diary, news screen, phone book and messaging centre; two Palm personal digital assistants are also attached to it, ready to be snatched up as family members rush off in the morning. Someday, kitchen appliances may be connected, too—the refrigerator door is as good a place as any to order groceries.

Broadband, of course, wires up your house with the outside world. It can connect a webcam to the children's bedroom or to the security camera outside. Family members can check their house's web site (bringing new meaning to "home page") from work—monitoring the nanny, checking up on the kids, watching for anything suspicious outside, even "answering" the door with their own voice if anyone rings the bell.

Real geeks will go even further, hooking up equipment that allows them to turn on lights, appliances or lawn sprinklers via the house's web site. Although all these home automation technologies have been available for years, they begin to make sense only in a continuously connected home. A century ago electricity arrived in the home to extend the day, free housewives from drudgery, preserve food and bring entertainment—a century from now the arrival of broadband data, and the lifestyle it introduced, may be equally celebrated. □

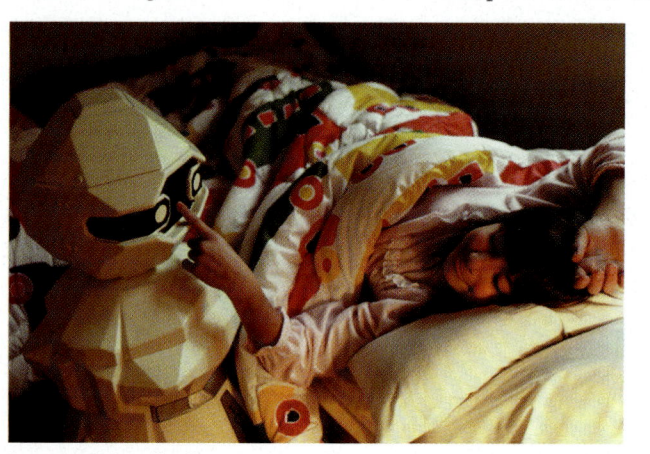

Press nose for broadband

Chris Anderson: American business editor, *The Economist*

Wireless communication.
A big vision
now available in a small card.

Tangled cables and endless wires are a thing of the past. We've created a PC card that enables you to take advantage of the huge possibilities of wireless technology today. Together with **SPANworks software,** developed by Toshiba, our **Bluetooth™ PC card** allows you to connect up to seven notebooks or other Bluetooth enabled devices, within a **100 metre range.** This means that everything from slide presentations to file transfers can be achieved instantly and effortlessly without the need for one inch of cable. What's more, this revolutionary technology is available to all Toshiba notebook PCs, such as the **Portégé 3480CT** powered by a mobile Intel® Pentium® III processor 600MHz featuring Intel® SpeedStep™ technology.* Enjoy the freedom of working where you want and how you want. Includes Windows® 98 Second Edition - the home version of the world's favourite software.

For more details visit our website at www.toshiba-europe.com/computers/tnt/bluetooth.htm

Portégé 3480CT
www.toshiba-europe.com/computers

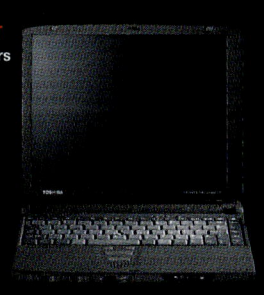

Intel, the Intel Inside logo and Pentium are registered trademarks and Intel SpeedStep is a trademark of Intel Corporation. Microsoft and Windows are either registered trademarks or trademarks of Microsoft Corporation in the United States and/or other countries. Bluetooth is a trademark owned by Telefonaktiebolaget LM Ericsson, Sweden and licensed to Toshiba Corporation. *The processor may be reduced to a lower operating speed when operating on battery power.

Choose freedom.
TOSHIBA

PERFORM THE

The ability to stay focussed in the toughest conditions, can be the difference between life and death. Maybe that's why so many racing pros choose suits made with NOMEX® brand fibres. From protective clothing to high-speed trains, to your microwave at home, NOMEX® thermal technology delivers extraordinary heat and flame management. Every day, NOMEX® brings people reassurance. Not just in protective clothing, but in automotive hose and keeping critical transformers and

WHEN HEAT'S ON

motors running for hospitals and power stations. Whenever and wherever thermal management matters, you'll find NOMEX® helping you perform when the heat's on.

www.dupont.com/nomex

NOMEX
DUPONT

GUTS & I

KEVLAR® is a registered trademark of E. I. du Pont de Nemours and Company

It's quite a

KEVLAR®

The best gear has the habit of bringing out the best performance from people. Ultra-light, soft, yet weight for weight five times stronger than steel, KEVLAR® brand fibre brings rugged performance, longer life and lighter weight to active apparel and footwear. Look for the KEVLAR® performance technology hangtag.

POWER OF PERFORMANCE

KEVLAR®
DUPONT®

combination

This advertisement has been approved by Deutsche Bank AG London, regulated by SFA for the conduct of investment business in the UK. The services described in this advertisement are provided by Deutsche Bank AG or by its subsidiaries and/or affiliates in accordance with appropriate local legislation and regulation.

Fuelling the success of our clients makes us a winning team

Deutsche Bank has again been voted the No.1 Investment Bank for Capital Raising

EUROMONEY GLOBAL FINANCING POLL
2000

In this poll of treasurers and financial officers at corporations, financial institutions, state agencies and supranational organisations, respondents were asked to nominate banks providing the best service in capital raising and liability management.

No.1 Overall Capital Raising

Capital Raising
- No.1 International Equity Offerings
- No.1 Euro-Straights
- No.1 Euro Floating Rate Notes
- No.1 Private Placements and Structured Notes
- No.1 EMTN (Arrangers & Dealers)
- No.1 ECP (Arrangers & Dealers)
- No.1 Raising Capital in Europe
- No.2 Using the Internet to Raise Capital
- No.2 Raising Capital in the Emerging Markets

Liability Management
- No.2 Overall Risk Management
- No.1 Credit Derivatives - Service
- No.1 Exotic Options - Euro
- No.1 FX Spot & Forwards - Euro
- No.1 Forward Rate Agreements - Euro
- No.1 Short-term OTC Interest Rate Swaps (Euro & Yen)
- No.1 Providing Fair Value on Instruments Previously Sold
- No.2 Credit Derivatives - Pricing & Ideas
- No.2 FX Spot & Forwards (USD & Yen)

When business needs capital, Deutsche Bank comes through.

Whether it's equities, fixed income or tools for managing risk, clients get the financing they need, in a package that grabs investors' attention.

That's why we've been voted the No. 1 Investment Bank for Capital Raising – for the second year in a row.

We've always believed that if we put our customers first, we would come out on top in global investment banking.

Global performance in raising capital – another reason why Deutsche Bank is leading to results.

GLOBAL PERFORMANCE
leading to results®

Deutsche Bank

THE WORLD IN 2001
Finance and Economics

Investment banking: Banks that bulge 142 / **Tax reform:** Tax Europa 143
Asian capital markets: Get global or get lost 146 / **Accounting:** Let's all tell the same lies 149
Growth economics: The virtue of wealth 150 / **Frank Zarb:** When investors vote 152

First the valley, then the uplands

Hamish McRae

2001
Expect a stampede of bankers from Wall Street to Frankfurt. A new law allows German corporations to sell their stakes in other companies tax-free, starting in 2002. $100 billion-worth of demergers and acquisitions are on the way.

Hamish McRae: associate editor of the *Independent*

After the jumps, humps and bumps of 2000, the financial markets in 2001 are going to be old-fashioned, sober and responsible. They will have to cope with a slower-growing world economy, but that's fine, for they have done that before. They will have to agree on pricing the new economy after the hash they made of high-tech valuations in 2000, and that is more difficult, for they are pricing hope. They will have to figure out how to cope with simultaneous deflation and inflation (think chips and oil) and hope that the central banks can figure it out too. And they will have to make up their minds about the intrinsic value of the euro before eurozone citizens have their national currencies taken away from them, starting January 2002.

Pricing a slowdown in the equity markets means peering beyond the dip in the world economy and visualising the sunlit uplands beyond: how deep is the valley, but more important, how far away is the climb on the other side? The markets spent the autumn fretting about the slowdown, gradually becoming more concerned that the downward slope might be steeper than they originally thought. Every profit downgrade by a major company anywhere in the world created a quiver. In the first months of 2001 the markets will figure out how steep that slope is likely to be and will then devote themselves to the shape and timing of the upturn.

The key questions will concern the resilience of the American economy vis-à-vis that of Europe and whether the upturn will favour the speedy or the powerful, the nimble or the strong. Be prepared for a difficult winter and spring but by autumn 2001 we should have some sight of the next speed-up in the world economy and the markets should have started to make their best guesses about the investments that will benefit most from it.

For new-economy shares it is particularly important that the markets recover their cool. In 2000 they lost it. Valuations were all over the place even when there was no significant change in a company's fortunes. As a result, bad businesses with lucky timing raised money on grossly inflated valuations while good ones were unfairly reviled. The task for 2001 is to agree on some sensible, probably old-fashioned, benchmarks—perhaps starting with, "What profit is this company likely to make over the next ten years?" By the end of the year (and maybe much earlier) the whole high-technology sector ought to be much more fairly rated. It will be more discriminating, and as a result calmer, kinder and more useful to investors and companies alike.

The deflation/inflation equation will preoccupy the bond markets—and indeed the central banks. By the au-

Finance and Economics THE WORLD IN 2001

tumn of 2001, the markets will be clear that the lift of inflation around the beginning of the year was a cyclical upward tick on a long-term secular downward trend. Bond markets will relax and central banks will accordingly relax too.

Is there any danger that either the Federal Reserve or the European Central Bank will misjudge the trend in inflation? There is always that chance but the bond markets should be robust enough to realise that even a wrong call by the central banks does not matter provided it is corrected reasonably swiftly. This is not a re-run of Japan circa 1997. Expect, by the way, structural reforms there to underpin a general lift in the Japanese economy and, providing there is some effort to tackle the ballooning budget deficit, improved financial market conditions too.

The euro's year

In the currency markets, the great issue will be the interplay between the dollar and the still-embryonic euro. The world has moved to an informal bipolar currency system and the tension between the two blocks will dominate currency markets for the foreseeable future. Expect, in all probability, 2001 to see a rebalancing take place.

This will be driven by some reassessment of the underlying value of the dollar, and real concern about the American current-account deficit. Yes, capital inflows into the United States will still support the currency. But eventually some sort of adjustment will take place. Expect a reasonable recovery of the euro throughout 2001. Do not expect, however, any dramatic return of confidence in the currency as the internal tensions of the eurozone become yet more obvious—the fizzing fringe and the sombre core. Instead, the markets will finally recognise that on a long view the euro will never be a particularly strong currency.

Europe will be a relatively slow growth zone, and the potential new entrants to the eurozone will be weak: Greece to start with, then perhaps the new Central and East European EU members, rather than the United Kingdom, Sweden or, of course, Denmark. A wild card? It is just conceivable, though not yet even a blip on the radar, that the whole venture will be aborted before the EU members lose their own currencies in January 2002. Do Germans really want to give up their marks and if not, what are they going to do about it?

Among the other currencies, expect the yen to climb somewhat against the dollar as the Japanese economy's restructuring continues. The pound will behave more like a dollar than a euro: as a rule of thumb it will behave two-thirds like a dollar and one-third like a euro, nicely reflecting the split of British public opinion against euro membership. The Channel remains wider than the Atlantic for currencies as well as so many other things.

Finally, one by-product of a cooler financial climate will be a pause in the frenzy of mergers and acquisitions. Yes, company chiefs will continue to reshuffle the packs. Yes, it will still be easier to buy a company than to run it half decently. But financial markets that ask awkward questions about value will want answers about strategy. This will translate into a more sceptical attitude towards Doing Big Deals. Given the way some of the big deals of the past five years have come unstuck, the sober shareholders of 2001 should drink to that. ☐

Not many mice left

2001
Morgan Stanley Capital International wants to readjust the weightings of Asian markets in its MSCI index to reflect their proportion of free-floating shares. Hong Kong, India and Malaysia—all with large amounts of privately held shares—will suffer outflows of foreign cash as a result.

Simon Long: writes for *economist.com*

Banks that bulge

Simon Long

For some years now, the exclusive world of investment banking has resembled an undignified game of musical chairs. Institutions with ambitions of securing a seat among the elite "bulge bracket" of global stars have been scrambling against the clock, watching the chairs stack up into ever more imposing formations. After one or two more mega-deals, this will be the year the music stops: this phase of consolidation will come to an end and the shape of the industry for the next few years will be set.

Indeed, after a period of frenetic merger activity, its broad outlines are already clear, divided into three main categories of big international investment bank. The bulge bracket proper is still there, apparently secure in its dominance. It consists of just three institutions: Morgan Stanley Dean Witter, Goldman Sachs and Merrill Lynch. It is remarkable how much investment-banking business has become concentrated into the grip of these firms and their closest rivals. To take just one measure of oligopolistic power, the top five firms underwrite three-quarters of all new share issues in America. Or, turning to Europe, Morgan Stanley and Goldman Sachs between them advise on about 60% by value of all big cross-border mergers and acquisitions. (Admittedly, that is not quite as astonishing as it sounds, because each deal will involve at least two advisers.)

The second group—of bulge-bracket contenders—consists of two giant commercial banks that have expanded into investment banking. Citigroup, formed by the merger in 1998 of Citicorp and Travelers, has been quite successful in blending the balance-sheet bulk and global reach of Citibank with the trading skills of Salomon Brothers and the investment-banking know-how of Smith Barney and, more recently, Schroders, a British merchant bank. An equally spectacular financial-services merger was the purchase, in September 2000, of J.P. Morgan by Chase Manhattan. Chase had already built up its investment-banking clout with a few niche purchases: of Hambrecht & Quist, for example, a California-based firm known for its Silicon Valley links, and Robert Fleming, a traditionally minded British firm with a strong presence in Asia. The acquisition of J.P. Morgan, one of the oldest names in American finance, makes it an investment-banking powerhouse, though it does not yet add the market-share in M&A advice or equity-underwriting that immediately challenges the bulgers.

Third are the European wannabes. In the lead is probably Deutsche Bank. Last year a J.P. Morgan report paid the German giant the compliment of suggesting it had already attained bulge-bracket status. Cynics pointed out that, at the time, Deutsche was one of the rumoured potential purchasers of J.P. Morgan. But Deutsche these days seems more inclined to grow by hiring expensive people than by buying even more exorbitantly priced institutions. It has had trouble enough digesting Morgan Grenfell, a British merchant bank acquired a decade ago, and Bankers Trust, the New York firm it bought in 1998 as its main vehicle for an assault on Wall Street. In 2000, two big Swiss firms also stepped up their efforts to gain admittance to the elite club: UBS acquired PaineWebber, a big American securities firm; and Credit Suisse added Donaldson, Lufkin & Jenrette to its ambitious investment-banking subsidiary, CSFB. Again, however, none of these European-owned confections quite musters the wide-ranging array of investment-banking skills needed to break into the very top rank.

For that reason, some further consolidation is likely. Many of the pressures that have led to so many mergers and acquisitions in the industry in recent years will persist in 2001. A rapidly globalising market puts a premium on the services of truly global financial institutions. And the electronic revolution is helping turn more and more financial products and services into commodities that can only be traded at ever-finer margins. In future, investment banks will earn their profits from fees paid for advice on everything from foreign-exchange risk-mitigation to strategic advice on mergers. That too gives big, global firms—especially those with the balance-sheet strength to back up their advice with capital—an edge over smaller rivals. So too does the mounting cost of people. Staffing makes up nearly two-thirds of investment banks' expenses. The lure of dot.com millions that was drawing talented young people away from boring old-economy banks has faded somewhat.

So why might the current wave of consolidation be approaching its zenith? The most obvious reason is the simple shortage of likely merger partners. J.P. Morgan's demise leaves only Bear Stearns and Lehman Brothers of the main Wall Street investment banks as orphans. Their scarcity value is now such that it may be a while before their prices fall to those any acquirer could justify to its shareholders. Similarly, after the creation of J.P. Morgan Chase & Co., the top three bulge-bracket firms may find the idea of adding commercial-banking muscle appealing. But there are few obvious partners for them. HSBC, a big British commercial bank, is one exception, and is often rumoured to be thinking of extending its joint venture with Merrill Lynch. Second, the recent wave of consolidation was in part a response to regulatory change: the final removal in 2000 of the remaining restrictions imposed by the Glass-Steagall act of 1933 on banks engaging in securities businesses; and the removal, from January 2001, of an accounting loophole under which the acquiring firm in a merger can avoid an immediate write-off of goodwill. Some of the merger frenzy of 2000 was a rush to sneak in under that wire.

There is a third reason, too, why activity may slow down somewhat: the business cycle. The past few years have seen an investment-banking bonanza both in the United States, led partly by the crazily volatile but rapidly expanding new-economy industries, and in Europe, where the advent of the euro has provided a further fillip to cross-border consolidation, and to both bond and equity markets. But cycles, of course, turn. ▫

Tax Europa

War is breaking out all over Europe and business will start to enjoy the fruits of it in 2001. The hostilities are over tax: income tax, corporate tax, capital gains tax, fuel tax. You name it, and somewhere in Europe someone will be slashing it. Take tax on corporate profits. Ireland set the debasing trend with a low 28% in 1999. Germany followed in the summer of 2000, promising to reduce its rate from 40% to 25% over the next five years. France will slash its rates to 33% for large firms, and to 15% for small and medium-sized firms. Italy, Portugal and even Poland are all chasing them down. And as if blowing a raspberry at all this me-too-ism, Ireland now intends to cut its rate further to 12.5% by January 1st 2003. Ireland's tax on employee stock options will also fall, from 44% to nearer 20%. The big question is who will dare to follow the Irish down?

Buoyed by resurgent growth and years of belt-tightening, European governments can now afford lower rates. Most of their budgets will be in surplus in 2001. With monetary policy for most of Western Europe now controlled by the European Central Bank, tax is one of the few weapons left for governments wanting to attract investment and foster business. And as more governments roll themselves back, those that don't will appear slack.

In 2001, Britain will still boast one of the lowest tax takes in Europe—40.4% of GDP, according to the OECD. Only Spain and Ireland will be lower. But this will not last. Even Germany, that old big-government laggard, will have a take of only 42.4% in 2001, and that has further to fall. Fears in Downing Street that the EU wants to harmonise its tax rates (and force Britain to raise its taxes) will give way in 2001 to fears that Europe will outdo Britain by, audaciously, having lower taxes. And then what is a self-respecting pro-business socialist British prime minister to do? ▫

It's raining tax cuts
Decrease in tax collected as % of GDP
1998-2001

Poland 3.4%
Finland 2.5%
Germany 1.4%
Ireland 1.0%
Italy 0.6%
France 0.5%

Source: OECD

USUAL
NEON-
AN OP

NIB CAPITAL IS AN ABP AND PGGM COMPANY

LY, THERE IS NO
SIGN SIGNALLING
PORTUNITY.

OPEN TO NEW IDEAS.

NIB CAPITAL

BANKING, ASSET MANAGEMENT AND PRIVATE EQUITY WORKING TOGETHER.

NIB CAPITAL N.V. P.O. BOX 380 2501 BH THE HAGUE THE NETHERLANDS TELEPHONE +31 70 342 54 25 FAX +31 70 365 10 71
E-MAIL THEHAGUE@NIBCAPITAL.COM WWW.NIBCAPITAL.COM

Finance and Economics **THE WORLD IN 2001**

Get global or get lost

Stephen Green

In 2001, Asia's capital markets will be healthier than they've been for years. Nearly all of them will boast second boards for high-tech stocks and will float issues the size of which the region has not witnessed since the boom of 1995-97. After an anxious 2000, things should be back to normal. There will just be one problem; normalcy will not be enough. A new era for the world's capital markets is beckoning and Asia is only just recovering from the last one. The underlying challenge for the region is to get global. And it is not sure how to do it.

Barring catastrophe—a collapse in confidence in the dollar would qualify—Asia's stockmarkets will grow, but not roar. Falling oil prices will help the region's manufacturers. All over the region, share indexes will rise, albeit gradually, as corporate earnings improve and foreign investors regain their confidence. In Japan, according to J.P. Morgan, an investment bank, earnings will rise 120% over 2000-01, while in the rest of Asia they will grow by 85%. Tokyo's stockmarket will boom, out of all proportion with the country's discreet economic recovery. The key engine to this will be the ¥106 trillion ($980 billion) in post-office savings that are maturing in 2000-01. Rising indexes should encourage Japan's conservative oldies to spend a large slice of this on shares. Elsewhere, Hong Kong will list more restructured Chinese state-owned enterprises. In Thailand, new pension schemes should push money towards equities, providing a boon to liquidity problems. The one black cloud will be Indonesia, Asia's most fragile market. Malaysia will look grey.

Japan will be home to the world's biggest government bond market. Its Ministry of Finance hopes to raise up to $450 billion in 2001. That will be on top of an estimated $3.3 trillion outstanding as of December 2000. Add $93 billion-worth of *zaito*, a new type of bond to be issued in 2001, and Japan will be left facing a scarcely believable 40% of the world's public debt. That should provide a unique opportunity to attract international investors but, unfortunately, foreigners will remain wary and buy only 5% of the available paper. The government will instead rely on Japanese banks and insurers to finance its spending. But their taste for holding relatively safe debt will make them wary of lending to business—something that is vital for any recovery to be sustainable. The banks themselves are still mired in bad debt worth around $300 billion. Only a fraction of that will be resolved in 2001.

While Japanese debt remains unpopular with foreigners, Tokyo hopes that its equity will prove more tempting. Together with Hong Kong and Australia, it has joined the Global Equity Market project. The group of ten exchanges, led by New York, plans to establish a 24-hour global platform for important shares. Some of the flesh will be put on the bones of this proposal in 2001, although serious regulatory differences and settlement problems will have to be solved. Nasdaq is also prospecting in Asia. Its Japan market will have listed over 100 companies and will introduce a new trading system by the end of 2001. It will link up with Nasdaq in America and Europe shortly afterwards. Singapore's SG stock exchange will link up with Australia's exchange in July, while its derivatives arm, SGX-DT, will be linked with the Chicago Mercantile Exchange and Paris bourse by the start of 2001. In another liberalising move, Singapore will eliminate the remaining restrictions on foreign investment at the SGX during 2001.

The Chinese way

Asia's most resolute go-slow globaliser is China. Behind the bamboo curtain of capital controls, its glitzy new second board in the southern city of Shenzhen will open. By late summer the shares of about 50 medium-sized companies will be trading there, many of them private and high-tech. Taiwan might also set up a similar board in 2001. Both will keep a close eye on the fall-out from Hong Kong's disastrous second board. Some of its companies will go bankrupt, and the rest will simply be ignored by institutional investors.

China's main boards in Shanghai and Shenzhen (until 2003, by which time all shares will be traded in Shanghai) are plagued by atrocious companies and uneven regulation. Fearless foreign investors are gearing up for joint-venture mutual-fund companies to start in 2001 and for QFII, a system that would allow them to circumvent capital controls and invest in China's main boards. Preparations for this are likely to take another three years. When QFII does come many will proclaim that Shanghai really is regaining its status as Asia's financial centre. Yet that vision, and the importance attached to it, will soon look out-dated. The Global Equity Market and Nasdaq schemes, if they work, usher in a world not defined by regions, but by a first tier of highly liquid, seamlessly connected markets listing world-class companies, and a second tier of smaller, fragmented markets.

To be a regional big-hitter is not enough: over the next ten years, it will be the exchanges that plug themselves into the global flow which will succeed. Discussion in 2001 should be focused on when and how the Shanghai and Hong Kong exchanges will merge, thereby bringing China into the global market. The real danger for Asia is that its exchanges and governments will be passive and unsure of what they want from globalisation. Note well: it is American firms which are building this new world. Without action, markets outside Hong Kong and Japan will fall into the second tier, and liquidity, the

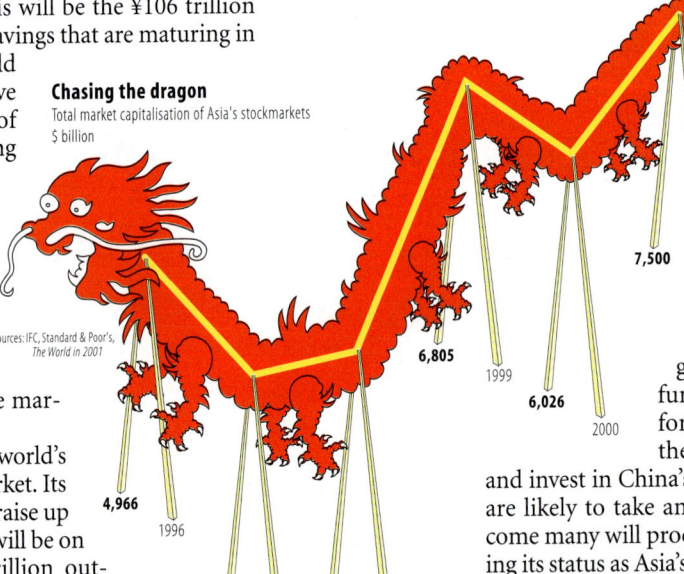

Chasing the dragon
Total market capitalisation of Asia's stockmarkets
$ billion

4,966 — 1996
3,704 — 1997
3,944 — 1998
6,805 — 1999
6,026 — 2000
7,500 — 2001

Sources: IFC, Standard & Poor's, The World in 2001

Stephen Green: Royal Institute of International Affairs

OUR E-BUSINESS SOLUTION FOR NATIONAL AUSTRALIA BANK IS PAYING DIVIDENDS.

When one of Australia's leading financial services organisations sought to transform its cheque processing system into an e-business asset for the future, it turned to Unisys with our e-@ction Payment Solution.

We worked together with the National to transform and consolidate the payment process, creating significant cost efficiencies and a real strategic advantage for the future. This advantage has put the National up to two years ahead of the competition. No less than you'd expect from a leader in e-business solutions.

If you need an e-business partner who'll deliver dividends, talk to Unisys. www.unisys.com

UNISYS

We eat, sleep and drink this stuff.

©2000 Unisys Corporation. Unisys is a registered trademark and e-@ction is a trademark of Unisys Corporation.

>> Economic growth is a strange phenomenon. You can feel it coming, but it's hard to predict exactly how and when it will manifest itself. That's why we created Euronext, a unique European trading platform formed by the Amsterdam Exchanges and Brussels Exchanges, together with ParisBourse^{SBF}SA.

Go for growth.

Euronext allows you to capitalise immediately on growth opportunities whenever and wherever they occur. >> At Euronext you will soon be able to trade with one order book, one pricing policy, one clearing system and a single list featuring many of the euro zone's blue chips. And high liquidity also means low trading costs. All this, plus our leading position in service, technology and innovation, puts Euronext firmly ahead of its competitors. >> So if you want to be prepared for the next stage of economic development in Europe, just go for Euronext. The only European exchange where you really can go for growth.

euronext
GO FOR GROWTH

www.euronext.com

best technology and the important companies from the region will drift to the first. The alternative is for markets in the region to merge. Already, some private schemes for trading the region's bonds on the Internet are in place. BondsInAsia will be launched in 2001 to compete with asiabondportal.com. Equity would be more difficult, and would require political backing, perhaps to be provided by ASEAN. The Singapore-Australia link looks promising, but it is only a start. Make no mistake: in 2001 you either get global, or get lost. □

Let's all tell the same lies

Margaret Doyle

Accountants may understand numbers, but they do not always appreciate the significance of dates. For it is 2001, and not 2000, which is set to be a year of millennial change in the profession. Across the world, standard-setters will work to ensure that a set of accounts in Japan looks as close to those in Britain and America and other countries as they can get.

For a quarter of a century, the International Accounting Standards Committee (IASC) laboured to standardise accounting principles around the world. It was largely ignored until the Asian financial crisis of 1997. Suddenly, investors found that companies were not worth what they thought they were. Accounts did not seem to mean what they were thought to have meant. In May 2000, Iosco, a group of stockmarket regulators, agreed to accept that the IASC's international standards could be used by companies to list in their member countries, though subject to national interpretation, disclosure and reconciliation.

The Iosco adoption of international standards represents a compromise by the Americans, whose SEC remains dominant in the group. The Americans will have a powerful voice in Paul Volcker, a former chairman of the Federal Reserve, who will oversee the selection of the board of the revamped IASC which is to be launched early in 2001. The SEC will retain considerable power through its stipulation that accounts of American-listed firms must be reconciled to its treasured American accounting principles, known as US GAAP. Early in 2001, if it has not already done so, the European Commission will issue its own ground-breaking proposal: that all listed companies in the Union will use the same standards by 2005.

Although international regulators are agreed that they wish to see a convergence among accounting standards worldwide, each country is attached to its own. Things will be particularly tough for American regulators. They hold that their standards and, just as important, the way in which they set them, are the most rigorous in the world. And they have the world's biggest capital markets. They could have tried simply to impose their standards on the rest of the world. Some outsiders wonder whether they will be able to accept that any alternative is superior to theirs.

Sir David Tweedie, chairman of Britain's standard-setters and chairman-designate of the standard-setting arm of the new IASC, will have plenty to keep him occupied. Battles will rage over share options, tax, pensions, merger accounting, acquisition provisions, off-balance sheet financing, leasing and financial instruments. In these areas, countries either vary dramatically in their treatment or have no standards at all.

Most controversial of all will be share options. Many American companies have enriched their staff through the granting of share options, but have failed to reflect that in their accounts. This is thanks to a defective standard that requires companies to disclose the cost, but does not insist that the cost be taken through the income statement. Not surprisingly, many companies choose to bury the charges in the notes to their accounts, rather than depress profits. Britain will produce a standard that will go beyond American practice.

America's Financial Accounting Standards Board ran into controversy in 1999 with its attempt to abolish the so-called "pooling" or "merger" method of business-combination accounting, which allows firms to combine their assets and profits. Many countries, such as Australia and New Zealand, have banned it, forcing companies to use the "purchase" method under which the excess of the price over the book value ("goodwill") has to be written off through the accounts. Britain will come under pressure to abandon merger accounting. Although it is used by perhaps as few as 1% of firms, they tend to be big companies. Britain has the toughest rules on acquisition provisions, restricting the ability of firms to smooth profits by "taking a bath" when an acquisition is made. It wants to export this rule. The British standard-setters will

Double-entry book-keeping classes, the early years

also try to persuade others to adopt their approach to pension accounting. The British are leading the way in advocating disclosure of the deficit or surplus in a company's pension fund on the face of the balance sheet.

Even trickier will be accounting for financial instruments. The British are in favour of "fair value accounting" which means marking assets, such as shares and bonds, to their market value. American regulators agree, but banks and insurance companies will resist. Because financial assets are such a large part of their asset bases, they are worried that their earnings would appear worryingly volatile if they had to mark to market. □

> **2001**
> The OECD will take action against tax havens in July, if they do not open up the books on their $6 trillion-worth of assets. Many, like the Bahamas and Cayman Islands, will sit tight.

Margaret Doyle: finance correspondent, *The Economist*

Finance and Economics THE WORLD IN 2001

The virtue of wealth

Madsen Pirie

The coming year will mark the return to respectability of economic growth. It has endured several decades of abuse and has been charged with everything from destroying individual cultures to despoiling the planet. Assorted demonstrations against international capitalism and the World Trade Organisation have all had themes in common: they were anti-progress, and specifically anti-growth. Yet economic growth is a legitimate target for humanity to pursue. It is good in and of itself, and a solution to many of mankind's abiding problems.

We were told, notably by the *Club of Rome Report* in 1972, that economic growth would lead us to use up scarce metals and minerals, depleting limited resources which "belong to future generations". In fact nearly all of these resources are more plentiful now (measured by price) than they were then.

It has also become apparent that wealthier countries are better able to protect the environment. It turned out to be the poorer countries of the socialist block that polluted most. The richer, capitalist, countries were able to afford the introduction of emission controls and water purity standards, and to enact measures to control the disposal of toxic waste. It is the poorer countries of the developing world that can least afford the often expensive techniques which accompany cleaner and safer production. Those that become rich should be able to produce their energy and their manufactured goods in less damaging ways.

The cities of the rich countries will, on the whole, be far less polluted in 2001 than they were in 1901. The shift away from coal has brought huge improvements in air quality. Rivers and water are cleaner. If cities are noisier today, they smell less. As economic growth lifts countries out of poverty, they, too, will be able to afford the luxury of cleaner air and water.

As for the destruction of "individual cultures", the poorer countries have made it clear that they prefer not to remain as theme parks of picturesque poverty for rich tourists to enjoy from their luxury hotels. Given the choice, they prefer to be wealthy, even if it means becoming like other wealthy countries. Put at its most politically incorrect: the whole world wants to be like California.

The most persistent charge against growth is that it is widening the gap between countries and even within countries. The claim is that in both cases the rich are growing richer and the poor are falling further behind. This uses relative poverty as the measure, rather than the absolute command of resources that matters for people at subsistence level. But even on this measure, the charge will not stick in 2001.

The poor set the pace

The Gini coefficients, which measure the degree of inequality in income distribution, show a sharp fall in world inequality in the past half-century. Economic growth in Asia has spectacularly closed the world wealth gap. Paul Ormerod, an economist, points out, "The economic success of East Asia has liberated millions of people from lives of unremitting drudgery and toil, and has sharply reduced world income inequality."

The upward path of economic growth has spread to China, and now India. This will destroy the argument of those who have valued India for its chaotic, overpopulated poverty, where spiritual values prevailed over profits. India will be one of the world's fastest-growing economies in 2001, which will do more for the street poor of Calcutta than a generation of aid. Most South American countries are following that same road. The prospect is for further reductions in the inequalities of world income between countries. Much of Africa is still mired in poverty, but it is becoming an exceptional, rather than a typical, case.

The idea that growth exacerbates inequalities in income distribution within countries is also wrong. The equality of the poorer countries is an equality of deprivation. Even the much-touted inequalities in the United States and United Kingdom over the past two decades are exaggerated. Wealth distribution in Britain is almost exactly the same as in France. And the inequality in America today is not different to the level France had in the mid-1970s.

There is a moral argument against growth but it, too, is proving specious. It is that growth directs us excessively towards material things such as consumer goods, at the expense of self-fulfillment and high moral or cultural goals. The counter-attack now gaining ground is that it is subsistence which causes material preoccupation. If you are not getting enough to eat, it has to preoccupy your thoughts and activities. It is wealth, generated by growth, which brings choice and culture. It enables people to choose leisure time, if they wish, to devote to charitable or voluntary work, or to self-education. It is wealth which enables people to be generous. In other words, growth and wealth bring the necessary space and opportunity for moral advancement.

Growth has been sneered at for 30 years, mostly by those who enjoy its benefits. Many problems have been laid at its door during that time. In the early years of this century it will be seen, however, as the prime tool for advancing the lot of mankind. ☐

Madsen Pirie: president of the Adam Smith Institute

SHAD THAMES SE1

From London ...

Finance and Economics THE WORLD IN 2001

A new force will be at work in the world's equity markets, predicts **Frank Zarb**, CEO of Nasdaq. It is called democracy

When investors vote

"Investors are becoming part of the political landscape, with their own causes and their own clout"

Over 30 years ago, when I started working in the securities industry, stocks were largely traded by a small group of rich guys. Reliable information was difficult to obtain, it was expensive, and the fixed commissions of brokers meant that trading itself was costly.

By 2001, all that will have changed. A new universe of investors is changing the way capital moves across borders. It is also starting to change the character and substance of political discourse as it relates to equity markets.

We owe this change to burgeoning mutual and pension funds, the increasing use of equity participation as employee compensation, and user-friendly retail brokerages. We owe it to the changing demographics that have caused more and more people to invest for retirement. Most of all, though, we owe it to technology, which has brought us our new, information-based and increasingly global economy. Advances in communications are building a new investor class. The Internet feeds the public's seemingly insatiable appetite for information, and allows it to respond to what it reads instantly.

Investors vote, so this growing class has caught the attention of governments around the world. Governments have begun to realise that prosperity is created not by their efforts to redistribute wealth through high taxation, but by capital formation and enabling investors—everyday, middle-class people—to participate in the process. This realisation has democratised capital formation.

Political decisions that affect investing have started to become front-page news. In the United States, it is unusual to see any public reaction at all to the arcane rule-changes put forward by the Financial Accounting Standards Board (FASB). But FASB's recent proposal to abolish so-called "pooling" in determining asset value during mergers and acquisitions triggered a public outcry. Citizen investors now see such rules as affecting their investments. And with America's middle class more fully invested and jobs—not to mention tax revenues—at stake, can politicians afford to be far behind?

The most politically charged and publicly conspicuous policies involve taxes. Even here partisan alignments are rearranging themselves. As more Americans accumulate wealth than ever before through 401(k)s and other investment vehicles, the estate tax is suddenly a widely debated issue, no longer relevant solely to the wealthy. Simply put, the middle class now pays capital taxes and politicians can hear their howls.

Other countries are moving in a similar direction. Japan, for example, is successfully creating a new equity culture. The introduction of Nasdaq Japan earlier in 2000 holds new promise for the middle-class investing public, although remaining protectionist policies must still be addressed.

Japan still holds back young companies with a restrictive commercial code. It requires, for instance, that the par value of a share be at least ¥50,000, or about $480, which restricts the quantity of shares issued and fuels volatility. One result is that a company cannot split its stock as the stock price appreciates, and the resulting high prices mean that the average middle-class investor is kept away.

In Europe, cross-border trading has been eased by common agreement. Obstacles still exist. There is a growing but not universal awareness that more rationally regulated, more accessible equity markets are a matter of self-interest. Free capital markets provide the foundation to start new businesses or re-invent older ones, and to create jobs.

New rules

Make no mistake about it: these political waves, the product of democratising equity markets, are not mere passing waves on the seas of public policy. Over the next five years, I am confident, we will see significant change in the rules affecting capital markets. Specifically:

● We will experience advancing harmonisation of the world's accounting standards. It is impossible to establish global securities markets without accurate and comparable disclosure of financial information. Investors (read: voters) demand it.

● There will be a rationalisation of regulatory rules around the globe. Insider trading, front running and fraudulent advertising, to choose three abuses, will be treated similarly across borders. Regulatory diligence in monitoring these practices will become uniform: it is not today. The good news here for investors is that, in general, the integrity bar will be raised, and its level standardised across all markets.

● Governments will rewrite tax codes to address capital investments in a different way. Voters are no longer indifferent to such issues. Political leaders grasp this change and see that facilitating capital investment improves their economies.

This broad movement will not be stopped. There may be setbacks, but the momentum is clearly for change. When we opened Nasdaq Europe in London, I thanked the British Chancellor of the Exchequer for his assistance in dealing with regulatory questions. To his credit, he answered that it was his job to improve the British economy and create jobs, rather than protect institutions. The transformation has thus begun.

Perhaps we have the making of a new, and positive, economic spiral: freer capital markets create and help companies grow; these companies then spawn new jobs and enlarge tax revenues. Companies may also become profitable investment opportunities for citizen investors—investors who vote, and encourage the political class to enlarge and secure the freedom of the capital markets. Wealth is produced at each turn of this spiral and everyone benefits. That sounds like something worth nurturing. □

www.kpnqwest.com

... to Prague, in a flash.

Not so very long ago, business data communication across Europe seemed to take an age. Low bandwidth connections via networks that were originally designed in the 19th century. Now there's a completely new network, designed and built specifically to meet the needs of today's businesses. A network that operates at the speed of light itself to deliver the bandwidth you need to compete in the 21st century. KPNQwest's EuroRings™ fibre-optic network spans Europe and connects to the world, providing a secure, high-bandwidth platform for e-business, IP connections, intranets, extranets or any other corporate data communications requirement. What are you waiting for?

KPNQwest. Business communications @ the speed of light.

kpn Qwest

INVESTOR:
When it comes to stock market recommendations, just about all banks head in the same direction.

DG BANK:
Well, we drive off the beaten track too.

INVESTOR:
So what's growing there?

The juiciest high potential Small and Mid Caps! Companies known today to only a few, in sectors we know inside out: Internet, IT, Telecommunications, Media. So to get our latest analysis call us on ++49 69 74 47-64 34 or visit our website for details www.dgbank.de, Deutsche Genossenschaftsbank AG

Head Office: DG BANK Deutsche Genossenschaftsbank AG, D-60265 Frankfurt am Main, Germany. Offices in: Amsterdam, Atlanta, Bangkok, Beijing, Budapest, Cayman Islands, Hong Kong, Jakarta, Johannesburg, London, Luxemburg, Madrid, Mexico City, Milan, Moscow, Mumbai (Bombay), New York, Paris, Prague, São Paulo, Seoul, Shanghai, Taipei (planned), Tokyo, Warsaw, Zurich.

DG BANK

Photo: M. Ehrhart

THE WORLD IN 2001
Science

Dying languages: Speaking in fewer tongues 156
Genetics: Send in the clones 157
Supercomputers: Faster than fast 158
Medicine and the developing world: Pill paupers 158
Bill Gates: Now for an intelligent Internet 161
2001: A space odyssey updated 162

The mathematics of mayhem

Alun Anderson

If you want to know what might happen to society, look at the mathematics of networks. One of the big surprises for Europeans in 2000 was the extraordinarily rapid spread of protests over the high price of fuel. Strangely, no organisation appeared to have planned them. Like-minded people from different occupations simply came together spontaneously to form new groups that organised themselves as protests developed. There was just one constant—almost every protestor appeared to be wielding a mobile phone.

Travel to the other side of the world and you will find that Japanese teenage girls are forming groups around the powers of their "I-mode" Internet phones. There is nothing political here: groups of friends, for example, send out waves of "goodnight" e-mails to everyone else just before going to bed.

What has science got to do with such disparate phenomena? Science certainly won't predict whether there will be fuel protests in 2001 or what particular fads teenagers will follow. But the study of communication networks does suggest that there might be a mathematical imperative behind the rapid appearance of new social groupings as communication webs develop. The new mobile high-speed communication and wireless Internet technologies that will begin to appear in 2001 will further accelerate the creation of fluid new groups. Some might be political. Others might be highly practical, facilitating business or information exchange. Others might be hopelessly silly. Most will be wholly benevolent. But transient group formation is going to boom and organisations that rely on dealing with traditional hierarchies are going to be ever more confounded.

To understand the mathematical imperative take a look at the different communication networks that have appeared historically. The simplest are the "one-to-many" broadcast systems familiar from television. In such systems, the overall value of the network rises in a simple relationship to the size of the audience. The bigger the audience, the more you can charge for advertisements and the more valuable your network. To put it mathematically, when you have a "one-to-many" system, the value rises with N, the size of the audience. This relationship is known as Sarnoff's Law, after a pioneer of radio and television broadcasting.

Now turn to the telephone network, a "many-to-many" system, where everyone can get in touch with everyone else. Here the mathematics are quite different. With N people connected, every individual has the opportunity to communicate with $N-1$ other people (you exclude yourself). So the total number of possible connections for N individuals = $N^{(N-1)}$ or N^2-N. This relationship is known as Metcalfe's Law, after Bob Metcalfe, the inventor of computer networking. The value of a telephone network, which will be related to the number of possible transactions, N^2-N, rises dramatically as N grows larger. Of course, not every person will actually contact every other person on the network, but the value of a "many-to-many" network increases with the number of users much faster than a broadcast system. That has been borne out historically with the growth of the

2001
Commercial satellites will take perfect pictures of your back yard from 425 miles up. Anything above a metre across will be identifiable. Global sales of the photos taken will be worth $2 billion by 2005. Watch out.

Alun Anderson:
editor, *New Scientist*

telecommunications industry.

What about the Internet? At first it looks like just another telephone system, with e-mail replacing speech, and its value following Metcalfe's Law. But the Internet—and particularly the mobile Internet which will hit us in force in 2001—adds something extra. Internet users have the opportunity to form groups, in a way they cannot easily do on the telephone. Any Internet user can easily join discussion groups, auction groups, community web sites, chat rooms and so on. And now Internet users can build their own group meeting places and web sites.

Now the mathematical laws become really interesting. As David Reed, former chief scientist at Lotus Development Corporation, has recently shown, if you have N people they can in theory form 2^N-N-1 different groups. You can check this formula by considering a tiny N, of let's say just three individuals, A, B and C. They can form three different groups of two people: AB, AC, CB and one group of three people ABC, making a total of four groups as predicted by the formula.

A group of three is nothing to get excited about, of course. What's really remarkable about the mathematics of Reed's Law is that as N increases, the number of potential groups and the value of the network rises at an astounding rate. Of course, only a tiny fraction of potential groups will ever form. But that potential is so stupendous that a lot of the value of the web will be realised by facilitating its extraordinary power to form spontaneous groups.

Politics must change

The trend is already there to see. Early days of the Internet were dominated by a small number of centralised services (Sarnoff's Law), then e-mail exchange (Metcalfe's Law) and now the formation of groups (Reed's Law). This process will accelerate in new ways in 2001 and beyond. In 2001 third-generation high-speed mobile Internet phones will go on sale in Japan. Soon afterwards, we'll see the ready availability of mobile phones that allow people to read and transmit their precise location, wherever they are. In your pocket, you'll be able to carry a device that has a web connection faster than the one you have in your office, that can work from anywhere, and knows exactly where it is. And simpler tools will be available to build web sites tailored for mobile phone access.

These developments will allow the formation of ever more fleeting groups in time and space. For businesses, there are lots of obvious opportunities for new services: a store could make an instantaneous special offer to any of its customers currently located within a few minutes walk. Or just as easily, a message can go out to all members of a pressure group close to a building where a spontaneous protest is required.

From a scientific point of view, we can't predict what people will do. But we can reasonably predict that businesses will maximise the value of the web by exploiting its extraordinary capacity to form multiple groups, however fleeting. How people will group and re-group themselves in a post-2001 world where everybody can be connected everywhere and any person can become a participant or a hub for a self-organising group, we can only begin to imagine. But it won't be the hierarchical world that politicians have long been used to controlling. □

Speaking in fewer tongues

Steve Connor

One day in 2001, somewhere in the world, an old man or woman will die and with them will go their language. It might be in one of the secluded highland valleys of Papua New Guinea, one of the richest linguistic regions on earth, or it could be among the isolated tribes living in the Andes of South America. It might even be in California, where about 50 native languages are under threat—the Northern Pomo language became extinct there in 1995.

The vulnerability of many languages is self-evident. Only 250 or so languages are spoken by more than a million people, and something like 90% have fewer than 100,000 speakers. In all, it is thought that there are about 6,000 languages. Linguists liken the fragility of this diversity to the Galapagos islands, where the rich but delicate tapestry of life provided the insight that inspired Charles Darwin.

The rate at which the human species is losing the diversity of the very feature that makes us unique is unprecedented. Linguists estimate that by the end of the 21st century over half of the world's languages will have been lost. Probably as many as 20 will disappear in 2001.

To date, about 1,000 languages are fully described, with their syntax, grammar and vocabulary well documented. This means that the majority of tongues remain largely a mystery. Many of them will be lost without yielding up the linguistic secrets they may hold. Linguists are understandably concerned that such a valuable part of human culture should vanish without trace.

As minority languages die out, the popularity of three languages continues to grow: Mandarin, Spanish and English. Sheer demographic expansion has ensured that more people than ever before will be born in a household where Chinese or Spanish is the mother tongue. But English, the universal language of commerce, has emerged as the second and sometimes the first language of choice of people who have little or no historic links with England.

Although this trend has been widely commented on, it is its future projection that will produce remarkable consequences. Many languages will not die out in the next generation but merely become redundant curiosi-

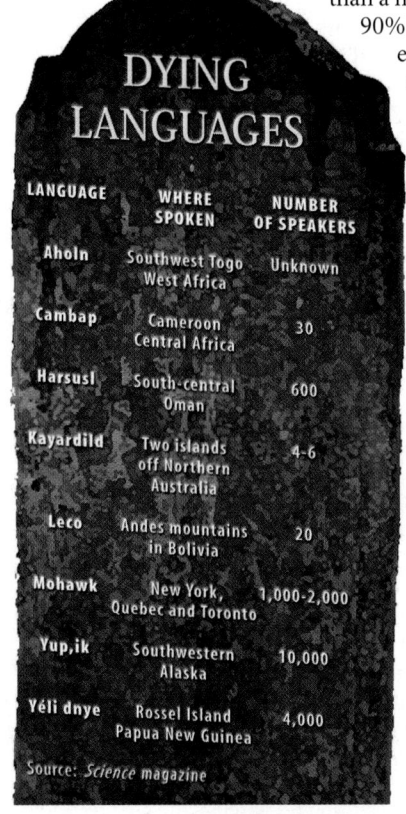

DYING LANGUAGES

LANGUAGE	WHERE SPOKEN	NUMBER OF SPEAKERS
Aholn	Southwest Togo West Africa	Unknown
Cambap	Cameroon Central Africa	30
Harsusi	South-central Oman	600
Kayardild	Two islands off Northern Australia	4-6
Leco	Andes mountains in Bolivia	20
Mohawk	New York, Quebec and Toronto	1,000-2,000
Yup,ik	Southwestern Alaska	10,000
Yéli dnye	Rossel Island Papua New Guinea	4,000

Source: *Science* magazine

Steve Connor: science editor, the *Independent*

ties. They will become like Scottish Gaelic: codified, respected and largely useless. As people with these languages seek to bustle in the wider world their native tongues will cease to be used. Everywhere, from businesses to universities to diplomatic corps, the learning of foreign "local" languages will be on the wane. This is not merely a long-term trend: the cumulative effect will be quickly felt.

In Papua New Guinea, which many linguists study precisely because its languages are so diverse, many young people now communicate between themselves in *tok psin*, which literally means "talk pidgin" English. It is precisely because children are growing up and talking between themselves in a "foreign" language that makes the tongue of their grandparents so vulnerable. This is how the Northern Pomo language died out with the demise of its last, aged speaker.

Arguments over the genetic basis of language and grammar have raged since it was first suggested by Noam Chomsky in the 1950s, and more recently by Stephen Pinker in his book "The Language Instinct". It is only by studying a wide range of languages that it becomes possible to decide whether there are indeed universal rules of grammar among all peoples, which would indicate that it is under the control of genes rather than culture. For instance, many linguists had until recently assumed that there were only three ways of arranging the sequence of subject (s), object (o) and verb (v) in a sentence. It could be "svo", like English; "sov", like Japanese; or "vso", like Irish Gaelic.

However, it now appears that the "ovs" sequence also occurs in about 1% of languages. One of these is the highly endangered Hixkaryana language, spoken by about 300 people living along a tributary of the Amazon river in Brazil. If linguists had waited another 20 years, languages with this construction would have died out and they would have continued to think that this form of sentence arrangement was impossible.

It seems that the more effort linguists put in to understanding rare languages, the more likely it is they will find evidence to argue against universal rules of grammar. A long study of the Kayardild, an aboriginal language spoken on Bentinck Island off north Australia, has, for example, revealed many grammatical anomalies. Whereas most languages change only the verb to indicate past or future tense, Kayardild marks the tense on other words as well, including nouns. Thus, they might say: "The boy spear-ed the fish-ed." (Or more accurately: "Spear-ed fish-ed the boy.") Such findings emphasise the intriguing complexities of the rarer languages.

During the course of 2001, anthropologists, scientists and linguists will attempt to raise the awareness of the cultural heritage we are losing. The Linguistic Society of America, for example, has established a special Committee on Endangered Languages and their Preservation, and a European Union organisation called Eurolang will help to preserve the many endangered languages of the continent, from the ancient Sard of Sardinia to the Sami tongues of the Lapps. This will form part of a wider programme to mark 2001 as the European Year of Languages, even though some EU countries have been known to discourage the promotion of minority languages within their borders for political reasons. □

Send in the clones

Shereen El Feki

Everything has been modified but the moo

Given the storm in Europe over genetically modified foods, one might expect cloning to receive a frosty reception as it inches out of the laboratory and into public life in 2001. If souped-up soyabeans are enough to send British newspapers into a frenzy, then surely "unnatural" creatures such as Dolly, the world's first cloned sheep, and her menagerie of successors are prime candidates for a popular backlash?

Apparently not, or at least not yet. Three years after Dolly's birth, the reproductive cloning of farmyard animals, such as cattle and pigs, is no longer an academic curiosity, but a viable commercial activity. Cloning involves transferring the nucleus of an adult cell into an egg, bypassing the normal sperm-meets-egg fertilisation step by providing it with all the genetic material needed to get on with the business of becoming a fully fledged being. As such, cloning offers a new way of generating genetically modified animals and a faster, potentially more reliable means of reproducing them en masse.

How the public will respond to this technology largely depends on its application. Agricultural uses of cloning, for improving animal health or meat quality, may well encounter opposition from a public uneasy with high-tech engineering of the food supply. But medical applications might find a warmer response. A handful of companies in America, Europe and Australia are busy producing cloned livestock with a view to using their genetically tinkered tissues in the clinic. Pharming, a Dutch biotechnology firm, for example, is harvesting an essential human blood-clotting protein from the milk of cloned, genetically modified cattle, which is a cheaper and potentially safer production method than conventional techniques. The company hopes that the obvious benefits of such medicines for needy patients will outweigh objections to the use of cloned animals. But the debate over animal reproductive cloning will intensify in

2001
Noah, the cloned Gaur Ox, opens the floodgates. Bringing animals back from extinction using genetic cloning will be the scientific fad of 2001. Watch out for the Bucardo, a Spanish mountain goat, and the Tasmanian Devil, a voracious marsupial, returning from the dead.

Shereen El Feki: health-care correspondent, *The Economist*

Science THE WORLD IN 2001

Faster than fast

IBM's planned new supercomputer, Blue Gene, represents the first major revolution in computer architecture since the 1980s. The radical cellular SMASH (simple, many and self-healing) concept makes it not only more compact, but 500 times faster than the most powerful computers used today. Uniquely, Blue Gene will also be self-healing—able automatically to isolate and remedy a fault in any one of its 1m processors. These will deliver "petaflop" scale performance, making IBM's brainchild capable of more than a million billion operations per second. Simulation testing of the concept has already begun and a mini Blue Gene will be built and tested in 2001. By 2004 the machine will be ready.

For what could such a powerful computer be used? After successfully sequencing the human genome in 2000, the next big step for scientists endeavouring to solve the puzzle of life is understanding its protein-folding structure. A protein folds into a highly complex three-dimensional shape that determines its function. Even a slight variation can turn a desirable protein into a disease. An understanding of how proteins fold will give doctors better insight into diseases and how to cure them. There is, however, a problem: it is believed that there are as many ways a protein can fold as there are atoms in the universe.

It is for solving such grand science challenges that IBM will invest $100m in building the world's fastest computer. It does not expect to sell Blue Gene commercially. But IBM believes it is pioneering the computer of the future. Expect baby Blue Genes in the years ahead. □

2001 as the first, clinically useful, products of this process will start human testing.

Human reproductive cloning is, for the moment, a remote prospect. Most countries with the scientific wherewithal to do such work have legislative bans in place; in any case, there remain formidable technical hurdles to the process. However, the controversy is likely to ignite in both Europe and America in the coming year as one particular type of human nuclear transfer, known as "therapeutic cloning", takes off. Therapeutic cloning is envisaged as a means of creating ready supplies of human tissue for transplantation, correcting defects such as Parkinson's disease or diabetes. It would involve moving the nucleus of a cell from a needy patient into a human egg, courtesy of a female donor.

This new creation would have the capacity to develop into a human embryo and into a live baby if the law permitted. Instead, researchers see such embryos as a steady source of stem cells. Unlike normal cells, stem cells can reproduce indefinitely and can be pushed into producing all sorts of tissue replacements which genetically resemble those of a patient, thus avoiding the problems of graft rejection. At present, researchers are still working out the fine details of therapeutic cloning with animals. Roslin Biomed, a Scottish firm, is busy studying cloned embryos from sheep, better to understand the biochemical processes that go on as such cells develop. Once they have worked out this "reprogramming" process, they would like to do the same directly in adult cells, eventually avoiding the cloning step altogether.

For the moment, therapeutic cloning is prohibited in Britain, but it may be allowed in 2001 if Parliament votes to accept the recommendations of a government commission that such work be added to the current roster of approved embryo experiments. Public opinion will be put to the test across Europe as France, Denmark and others reconsider their own bans on therapeutic cloning.

In the United States, research on embryonic stem cells has been privately financed until now by firms such as Geron (which owns Roslin Biomed), because of restrictions in federal funding; that should change in 2001 because of a recent decision to provide government money for embryonic stem-cell research but not, as yet, human therapeutic cloning. Further debate is in store as cloning comes closer to life. □

Pill paupers

Shereen El Feki

Prepare for a new war on drugs in 2001. Not the one where men with guns in jungles try to stop the spread of narcotics from poor to rich countries. This is the one where men with pens in boardrooms struggle to speed the flow of pharmaceuticals from rich to poor.

When it comes to disease, the West has always been quick to spread its inheritance. For centuries, tuberculosis, smallpox, syphilis and measles made inroads into much of the poor world, courtesy of European colonialists. In recent years, however, Europe and America have been less ready to share their pharmaceutical solutions to these and other ills.

Modern medicine has proved successful at devising drugs to treat a variety of infections, such as HIV and tuberculosis, which plague both rich and poor (see chart). But the high cost of developing such medicines—up to $500m in some cases—and the need for drug companies to recoup their investment means they are sold at prices in rich markets which exceed the grasp of poor countries. How can Kenya, for example, afford a drug such as fluconazole, to treat AIDS-related infections, when a single pill costs $10 at wholesale prices, almost a fifth of the country's entire annual health spending per person?

This vexing question is prompting an unprecedented level of co-operation between the World Health Organisation (WHO), the World Bank, private charities, the drug industry and national governments. There is little time to waste. In 2001, there will be another 8m active cases of tuberculosis, 5m new HIV infections and a daunting 300m malaria cases to manage, most of them in sub-Saharan Africa and South-East Asia. The sheer scale of such human suffering ought to be moving enough, but it is the

The rich die differently
Deaths per 100,000 population

- Low- and middle-income countries
- High-income countries

	Low/mid	High
Tuberculosis	29.7	2.0
Diarrhoeal diseases	44.4	0.8
HIV/AIDS	45.2	3.5
Cancer	104.7	222.5
Cardiovascular disease	263.1	395.7

Source: WHO

158

LINDE. Ideas that create markets.

Mobility has a future. A future assured by the energy source hydrogen which, in combustion, forms nothing but pure water. In the global growth market now developing, we already enjoy pivotal positions. Because we've been advancing hydrogen technology and its innovative applications for years. Today we master all hydrogen production and collection processes. A know-how lead with which we are further expanding our world market leadership in this sector.

For further information: +49 611 770 317

www.linde.com

Emission-free mobility. Powered by Linde.

Linde

We know how.

Engineering and Contracting
Material Handling
Refrigeration
Industrial Gases

Before you invest in your next big IT solution, consider one thing. How quickly can you turn it around?

It's becoming harder and harder to predict what's round the next corner. Because the new e-business economy is evolving so fast. To succeed, your organisation needs to be as flexible and agile as you are. Perpetual re-invention has become a fundamental business imperative.

The same is true of your IT systems. Microsoft provides the platform to help your organisation maximise its overall corporate agility. No other IT platform has the range of proven business applications, combined with a choice of thousands of industry partners to deliver a best-of-breed solution at Internet-speed.

Give yourself the freedom to respond quickly and easily to whatever the future may bring. Above all, don't end up in a blind alley.

www.microsoft.com/uk/business

Microsoft
Where do you want to go today?®

Microsoft, 'Where do you want to go today?' and the Microsoft logo are trademarks of the Microsoft Corporation in the US and/or other countries.

Science

Tomorrow's Internet will look a lot like today's, asserts **Bill Gates**, chairman of Microsoft. But it will be a whole lot smarter

Now for an intelligent Internet

"Tomorrow's web page won't be a passive picture but your personal, interactive database"

In 2001 more than 400m people worldwide will surf the web's 4 billion pages and spend half a trillion dollars on goods and services in the process. Yet for all its wonders, the technology will be roughly where the automobile was when Henry Ford launched his Model T. Both the Internet and the PCs we use to access it represent a big advance on the age of the mainframe—computing's horse and buggy era—but the bigger advances in digital technology are still to come.

In many respects, today's Internet actually mirrors the old mainframe model, with the browser playing the role of "dumb terminal". All the information you want is located in centralised databases, and served up a page at a time (from a single web site at a time) to individual users. Web pages are simply a "picture" of the data you need, not the underlying data itself. You can look but you can't touch—editing, annotating or otherwise customising the data is hard to do. If you want to pull together data from multiple web sites, you often end up scribbling it down on a notepad. That is far from the "intercreative space" envisioned by Tim Berners-Lee, whose pioneering work led to the creation of the web.

To transform itself into more than a medium that simply presents static information, the next generation Internet needs to solve these problems. Instead of being made up of isolated islands where the user often provides the only integration, it must enable constellations of computers, intelligent devices and web-based services to collaborate seamlessly. It must offer individuals complete control over how, when and what information is delivered to them, and allow them to protect their privacy and security by controlling who has access to their personal information.

At the core of that transformation is Extensible Markup Language, or XML. An open industry standard defined by the World Wide Web Consortium (with extensive input from Microsoft and other high-tech companies), XML offers a way to separate a web page's underlying data from the presentational view of that data. It works in a similar way to HyperText Markup Language (HTML), which uses "tags" to define *how* data is displayed on today's web pages. XML uses tags to provide a common way of defining precisely what the underlying data actually *is*.

The effect of this technological lingua franca on the future of the Internet will be far-reaching. XML "unlocks" data so that it can be organised, programmed, edited and exchanged with other sites, applications and devices. In effect, it turns every web page into a programmable mini-database (so you can actually analyse those stock price statistics you find on the web without having to cut-and-paste them into a spreadsheet first). XML enables different web sites to share all kinds of data without having to use the same computer language or software application. Individual web sites can collaborate to provide a variety of web-based services that can interact intelligently with each other. And information can more easily move from one device to another.

The next generation Internet will be a computing and communications platform in the same way that the PC is. Programs "written to" the Internet (just as they are written to the PC platform) will run across multiple web sites, drawing on information and services from each of them, and combining and delivering them in customised form to any device you like. The distinction between the Internet and your PC or other devices will break down—advanced software (like that of Microsoft's .NET initiative) will automatically determine whether the information you need is available locally or remotely, then bring it together to best serve your needs.

Many pictures, one canvas

As the barriers between online information, services and devices break down, how you interact with them will also be revolutionised. Today, you use separate software applications for every computing task you want to perform, whether it is browsing the web, writing and editing, e-mail and instant messaging, accessing your calendar and contacts. The next generation Internet will enable a more integrated approach. You will use a single, unified interface that moves transparently between the Internet and the PC or device you are using, allowing you to browse, write, edit, schedule, communicate or analyse data. I see it as a "universal canvas" for the Internet Age. You will also interact with your computer in many more ways. Today, the amount of e-mail I receive that has handwriting or voice annotation is negligible. In future, the majority of messages will come in some form other than typed text.

Today, you always know whether you are on the Internet or on your PC's hard drive. Tomorrow, you will not care and may not even know. Your business and personal information will be safely stored on the Internet, automatically synchronised and instantly available to you—no matter where you are. Everything that can think will link—transparently and automatically.

So if you are travelling and need medical attention, your personal physician service will be able to locate the best local doctor, make an appointment that fits into your schedule, share the appropriate medical records and arrange payment. All you will need to do is give your permission. Think of it as a "personal web," intelligently acting on your and your family's behalf. Think of it as the ultimate business tool, boosting your firm's productivity and taking a big step closer to friction-free capitalism.

Just as the system of musical notation made the orchestration of instruments possible, the power of XML and advanced software is making the orchestration of online and offline data and services a reality. □

Science THE WORLD IN 2001

2001: a space odyssey updated

Joshua Winn *Cambridge, Massachusetts*

In 1968, Arthur C. Clarke and Stanley Kubrick thrilled cinema audiences with the "Space Odyssey" awaiting them in 2001. Nobody knew then that much more progress would actually be made in the special-effects technology of movie-making than in rocket propulsion.

The Apollo programme, the successful gambit by the United States to land men on the moon, was certainly a triumph, but did not lead to anything grander. A few robots have explored a few planets, and there is an unfurnished studio apartment (the International Space Station) floating 220 miles above the earth, but colonies on the moon and voyages to Jupiter are as much science fiction as ever. Why is this so? Was Apollo really a cold-war aberration, a morale-boosting, reality-based adventure show for the American public?

Yes. And it achieved its purpose brilliantly. However, in a democracy, in the absence of military emergency, it is hard to justify spending huge sums on exercises meant only to raise the human spirit. It sounds self-indulgent, when there are serious problems involving pensions, education, health care and poverty. Most space advocates try to get around this by insisting Apollo was really all about science or refer to "spin-offs" such as Teflon (although building rockets is an inefficient way to improve non-stick saucepans). The public sees through such arguments.

If democratic governments want to subsidise something space-related, the way forward will be the one enterprise in which space has a proven comparative advantage: learning about the universe. The Hubble Space Telescope is the crown jewel of astronomy. Whole disciplines, such as ultraviolet and x-ray astronomy, are impossible from the ground because the atmosphere is opaque to those radiations.

Astronomy reflects the human endeavour at which Apollo succeeded: eliciting confidence and optimism, and putting earthly things in perspective. It is hard to feel too angry at your neighbour when you realise we are all stuck on the same spinning ball in a puny corner of an impossibly large and ever expanding universe. And it is easy to be proud of humanity for figuring out how old the universe is, and for adventurously stepping off the spinning ball. Clarke and Kubrick's cinematic vision realised this better than today's political leaders. □

Joshua Winn: doctoral student in astronomy

A star is born

2001
The 25m-square-kilometre hole in the ozone layer has stopped getting bigger. But it wobbles. Southern cities, notably in Australia, Argentina and South Africa, will suffer higher levels of radiation.

---

economic implications of this onslaught which are galvanising the West's response. Studies show, for example, that malaria is draining away as much as 2% of sub-Saharan Africa's GDP annually.

Drugs are only part of the answer to this problem: better health care infrastructure in developing countries and better access to other medical interventions, such as bednets to stop the spread of malaria or condoms to reduce HIV transmission, is also needed. But pharmaceuticals are the most contentious item. Why? Because developing countries are starting to abide by international treaties on drug patents. However, they know that if they bent those rules they could produce generic copies of drugs that could bring cheap relief to their populations. South Africa has been the most vocal challenger of these rules, but other dissenters in the poor world will come to the fore in 2001.

One way of getting drugs to the poor is simply to give them away. It would be much better to create real markets in poor countries that offer drug companies a commercial incentive to consider their needs. Already five large international pharmaceutical companies, including SmithKline Beecham, Roche and Merck, have agreed to sell their expensive anti-HIV drugs at considerable discounts to poor countries struggling with the epidemic; what is needed is enough money to ensure their purchase. One project paving the way is the Global Alliance for Vaccines and Immunization, which has arranged $850m in funding from wealthy donor governments such as Norway, and private philanthropists such as the Gates Foundation, to help poor countries buy costly vaccines against infections such as *Haemophilus influenzae*, which causes childhood meningitis.

Creating markets in low-income countries might help to encourage drug companies not just to make existing medicines more available, but to develop completely new drugs and vaccines for diseases which afflict mainly poor, tropical countries and for which they can expect little return in the rich world. At the moment, there has been precious little interest in conditions such as leishmaniasis, a parisitic disease, which disables millions of people. According to research by Médecins Sans Frontières, a medical aid agency, of the 1,223 new compounds launched on the market between 1975 and 1997, less than 1% were designed for tropical ailments.

There are many innovative schemes to entice drug companies in Europe and America into this business, among them tax credits on their research and development expenses, and patent extensions on their most profitable drugs in the rich markets in exchange for developing useful products for the poor. But these are still on the drawing board, and are likely to stay there until firms can be convinced that there is a market for their existing drugs, let alone their future ones. □